T4-BBU-667

Watching
Channel One

0287477

SUNY Series,
Education and Culture:
Critical Factors in the Formation of Character
and Community in American Life
Eugene F. Provenzo, Jr., and Paul Farber, editors

Watching Channel One

The Convergence of Students, Technology, and Private Business

Edited by
Ann De Vaney

STATE UNIVERSITY OF NEW YORK PRESS

Published by
State University of New York Press, Albany

© 1994 State University of New York

All rights reserved

Printed in the United States of America

No part of this book may be used or reproduced
in any manner whatsoever without written permission
except in the case brief quotations embodied in
critical articles and reviews.

For information, address State University of New York
Press, State University Plaza, Albany, N.Y. 12246

Production by E. Moore
Marketing by

Library of Congress Cataloging-in-Publication Data

Watching Channel One : the convergence of students, technology, and
    private business / Ann De Vaney, editor.
        p.   cm. — (SUNY series, education and culture)
    Includes bibliographical references and index.
    ISBN 0-7914-1947-9. — ISBN 0-7914-1948-7 (pbk.)
    1. Television in education—United States—Evaluation.
    2. Educational technology—United States.   3. Educational
    innovations—United States.   I. De Vaney, Ann, 1938–   .   II. Title:
    Watching Channel 1.   III. Series.
    LB1044.7.C44   1994
    371.3'358—dc20   93-28980
                                                                                CIP

10 9 8 7 6 5 4 3 2 1

*With respect and love for the thousands of elementary
and secondary students we have taught.*

Contents

Acknowledgments   ix

Introduction   1
   Ann De Vaney

1. Investigating Channel One: A Case Study Report   21
   Rhonda S. Robinson

2. The Effects of The Channel One Broadcast on Students'
   Knowledge of Current Events   42
   Nancy Nelson Knupfer and
   Peter Hayes

3. Channel One: Reactions of Students, Teachers, and Parents   61
   Nancy Nelson Knupfer

4. Is This the News?   87
   John C. Belland

5. Advertising and Channel One: Controversial Partnership
   of Business and Education   102
   Ann Marie Barry

6. Reading the Ads: The Bacchanalian Adolescence   137
   Ann De Vaney

7. Form, Style, and Lesson: An Analysis of Commercially
   Produced School News Programs   153
   Barbara Erdman

0287477

8. Whittling Away at Democracy: The Social Context of
   Channel One   167
   Michael W. Apple

9. Drawing the Line: Questions of Ethics, Power, and
   Symbols in State Policy and the Whittle Concept   189
   Robert Muffoletto

10. Two Rhetorics of Cynicism in Debates over Channel One:
    Two Riders in a Barren Landscape   208
    Henry St. Maurice

Contributors   235

Index   239

Acknowledgments

The idea for this book was conceived in conversation a few years ago, after a stirring presentation by Anne Marie Barry on children and *Channel One*. The authors owe a debt of gratitude to her for introducing us to the topic at one of our professional meetings.

I would like to thank Chapman College in Orange, California for a visiting professor appointment during a summer in which I was preparing early parts of this manuscript. Professor Barbara Tye, chair of the Department of Education, as well as faculty and staff members made me welcome and provided research and writing facilities. I would also like to thank Dr. Alan Hoffer, Chair of the Department of Education, University of California, Irvine and his faculty for supporting my sabbatical year, during which the final preparation of this manuscript took place.

Likewise, I am grateful to those who helped prepare the manuscript for this book, particularly Tonja Meyers, Suzanne DeVaney and Joann Foss.

Introduction

BACKGROUND TO CHANNEL ONE

When war in the Persian Gulf started, Jason was a senior and an average student at a large high school in the Southwest. His best friends, Ron and Mike, attended school in another part of the city. Because Ron and Mike were eighteen, they were able to and did enlist in the army after the start of the war. They had only two weeks of school left in late February 1990 before they had to report for military training, so they invited Jason to spend the day with them at school. Jason's mother, Sarah, had to drive him across town that day to be with Ron and Mike.

On the return ride, Jason said, "Hey Ma, they had Channel One in that school, and I watched it today."

Jason knew that Sarah, an instructional technology professor, was studying the effects of Channel One. "What was it like," she asked.

"Oh, I don't know," he replied.

"Come on, Jason," she prodded. "What do you remember?"

He hesitated and tried to recall. "Mom," he said finally, "did you know that Snickers has a new peanut-butter bar?"

"Jason." She was exasperated. "What else do you remember?"

He took his time and thought. He said tentatively, "There was an ad for Nikes."

"Is that all you remember?" Sarah was disappointed.

"Yup," he said defensively and then was quiet.

Jason's best friends were in danger of being shipped to the Persian Gulf. His mother was studying Channel One and spoke of it frequently at the dinner table. Whatever learning theory one selects to describe Jason's preparation to view and recall Channel One, he was ready. He was rehearsed and cued. He had advanced organizers and a "mind set" to view, not only the news program itself, but segments on the War in the Gulf which were prominent that Wednesday. Yet, he could not recall seeing any news.

Channel One is a twelve-minute video news program which by mid 1992 was beamed daily to 11,900 high-school classrooms in the United States. Produced by Whittle Communications, the program attempts to combat a perceived teenage ignorance and apathy about current events. The contract between schools and Whittle Communications offers a free satellite dish and cable wiring for the building, plus videotape recorders and televisions in exchange for the promise that students will view the twelve-minute news program every day. (Schools who break the contract within the first three years must pay for all the electronic gifts.)

The controversy surrounding the program stems primarily from the fact that two minutes of advertising are embedded in each twelve-minute program. Whittle Communications charges advertisers $150,000 for a thirty-second spot on Channel One. The New York Times estimates potential revenue from these ads to be approximately $100 million a year. The venture has been so successful that Chris Whittle is raising his rates to $200,000 for a thirty-second spot on the news program (Becker 1992). Some legislators argue that student time in tax-supported buildings is being sold to advertisers who will profit handsomely from addressing a captive audience. Questions have arisen about the legality of selling student time in exchange for free television equipment. Consequently, New York and Rhode Island have banned the program from public schools, while California reduces state support for those schools that adopt the program. While it is important to question sanctioned ads in public classrooms and to ask what students learn from viewing Channel One, this book will consider broader issues in an attempt to describe this cultural event. Some key concerns are the incursion of a private-sector entrepreneur in public school curriculum; the implications of private-sector wiring of public school buildings; the production and reception of Channel One commercial and noncommercial messages; and the attitudes of all the Channel One participants, including students, teachers, administrators, school boards, and parents.

It would be foolhardy for educators to underestimate the importance of this enterprise because it provides a window on the world of Chris Whittle, owner and president of Whittle Communications. The form and structure of his video news magazine, the terms of his Channel One contracts with schools, and the manner in which his staff interacts with school administrators divulge his intentions for U.S. education. Further intentions are revealed in his plans for the opening of proprietary schools. Because these plans are closely linked to buildings wired for Channel One (Whittle speaks of an existing eight million electronic seat system), I will turn for a moment to the Edison Project.

THE EDISON PROJECT

The Edison Project is Whittle's plan to create hundreds of private schools for profit which rely on a technology infrastructure. In 1992, Chris Whittle hired a seven-person team to design new and better schools that could earn a profit.

The group includes Chester E. Finn, Jr., professor of education and public policy at Vanderbilt University, who was a top aide to education Secretary, William J. Bennett in the Reagan Administration; John E. Chubb, a senior fellow with the governmental studies program at Brookings Institute, and an advocate of parental choice in determining where to send children to school; Benno Schmidt, former president of Yale University; and Sylvia Peters, principal of Alexandre Dumas Elementary School in Chicago, the only team member directly connected with schooling for children.

Other team members have had no professional experience in education. They include Lee Eisenberg, former editor-in-chief of *Esquire* magazine, which Chris Whittle used to own; Nancy Hechinger, manager of Hands-On Media, a company that produces computerized reference material; Daniel Bierderman, president of the Grand Central and 34th Street Partnerships, organizations that assist property owners and tenants in Manhattan; and Dominique Browning, a former assistant managing editor of education, the family, television, and psychology for *Newsweek* magazine.

At a February news conference announcing the Edison Project team, Ms. Browning

> . . . adopted a tone of amused wonderment [and said] "I think some of us feel as though we've thrown ourselves out of the window or into a black hole, . . . some of us don't know anything about anything and we need to catch up." (New York *Times*, 141:48, 890, Friday, February 28, 1992; Sec. A, 14)

When the former Esquire editor asked Chris Whittle why he, Eisenberg, had been chosen for the Edison Project team, Whittle replied, "Think of this as eight to ten hours of programming to a young audience . . . Think of generating ideas that inform and entertain in several media" (Becker 1992, 173).

(The necessary expertise of two team members from the world of magazines would not surprise the classroom teacher who views Channel One each day.)

INSTRUCTIONAL TELEVISION IN THE 1950s

This is not the first time the private sector has mobilized to rescue an educational system defined as failing. Dissatisfaction with U.S. schools was rampant in the mid–1950s. Even before the capstone event of the Soviet Sputnik launch, the public was asked *Why Johnny Can't Read* (Flesch 1955) and was told that schools were *American Wastelands*, (Bestor 1953). Hirsch (1987) and Bloom (1987) were the 1980s counterparts of Arthur Bestor, and a similar movement for education reform was launched in the 1980s, partially on the basis of their critiques. The 1950s and 1980s reform movements have some interesting similarities—not the least of which is a reliance on technology.

Video technology was introduced to the classroom in the late 1950s in response to the postwar crowding of classrooms, dissatisfaction with the U.S. public school system, and the launching of the Soviet missile. The Ford Foundation—and private-sector representatives who sat on Ford foundation boards—dispensed money for the development of instructional television programs, thus deciding on subjects to be addressed and formats for delivery. Instructional video software was sponsored and approved by private sector businessmen while educators were bypassed. (It should be pointed out, however, that these men did not stand to profit by development of curriculum. They simply thought it was their civic duty to improve public education.) Ford Foundation agencies supplied 90 percent of the television-program dollars spent on every elementary and secondary student in the United States between 1953 and 1963 (DeVaney 1990). The 1950s video hardware—much of which eventually collected dust on library shelves—was purchased through National Defense Education Act grants. This expensive effort ($100 million from Ford in 1950s currency) failed to achieve its goals, but was the start of instructional television in the schools.

That private sector businessmen—then or now—should turn to technology—especially television—is paradoxical. It may be said that reliance on TV to educate is an articulation of the American love affair with technology, but commercial television is cast as a major culprit in the critiques mounted against public schools. Periodically—and especially when school budgets are constrained—studies are cited in which the number of hours in which students view television is correlated with their grade-point averages. Whether the ploy is deliberate or not, it usually stirs enough indignation at the electronic monster to deflect attention away from educational budget cuts (Felter 1982).

WHITTLE AND TECHNOLOGY

Unlike their counterparts in the 1950s, private sector educational innovators of the 1990s do not rely solely on television, but also on electronic learning stations. Chris Whittle envisions, not only Channel One but additional technology at the heart of Edison Project proprietary schools.

Technology will play a heavy role. Each student will probably have his own learning "partner" both at school and at home, consisting of a monitor, a computer, a printer and a VCR, a fax machine, a paintboard, a stereo and a telephone. Through this setup, there will be unlimited access to an electronic library of books, films, lectures, speeches and thousands of learning games. Mr. Whittle sees this library as "America's new textbook industry." (Chira 1992, A12)

Technological innovations—such as film, television, and mainframe computers—have, over the years, been touted as the panacea to many educational ills but have failed to fulfill their promise. The personal computer was introduced in classrooms and homes through a top-down, bottom-up process which makes its presence more stable and enduring than other innovations. This perceived stability has tempted both educators and noneducators to embrace desktop computers as an answer to many educational concerns. Because a decade of classroom computer use has uncovered its shortcomings, proponents with an undying belief in technology are not abandoning PCs, but they are suggesting the connection of additional hardware—such as video and telephone—to the desktop computer. The new panacea will be a multimedia learning station, and Whittle plans to plug the student into such a station, both in school and at home. There would be less need for teachers or parents to interfere in the learning process, a fact that Whittle has noted.

> Let's not be locked into the standard student-teacher ratios . . .
> The rigidity—twenty-to-one, thirty-to-one, with the teacher in
> front—is part of the problem. With technology in place, the
> idea of "teacher" will be expanded. Yes, we may have fewer
> paid teachers . . . (Becker 1992, 174)

A large body of literature about computers and television supports the notion that students learn better with human partners such as classmates, teachers, and parents who participate in the electronic lesson. But this research does not serve the political nor market goals of the Edison Project. At the heart of Whittle's educational policy is the publication, *Politics, Markets and America's Schools,* (1990) which John Chubb, an Edison Project member, and Terry Moe wrote. It has been cited as the blueprint for believers in parental choice, and as a justification of the voucher system. Another Edison Project team member, Chester Finn, translated Chubb and Moe's dissatisfaction with the current U.S. educational system into President Bush's voucher plan. This plan formed the basis for the "New American Schools," a proposal by former Education Secretary Lamar Alexander to present parents with the freedom of choice through vouchers. He and others believe that successful private schools will force changes in public schools. Former Secretary Alexander, who is a former business colleague of Chris Whittle, has not publically commented on the Edison Project, but the similarity between the Edison Project design and "New American Schools" is marked.

Whittle's strength in the past has been in identifying and selling specifically targeted markets to single advertisers. (See chapter 5.) The Edison Project would sell students in proprietary schools to communications corporations who might own the network configurations and could conceivably produce educational software; to electronics corporations who might produce the educational hardware; to publishers who would produce educational software; to service corporations, such as McDonald's that would operate cafeterias; and to advertisers of products which teens consume. Whittle envisions his educational enterprise as big business and claims,

> There is going to be a Silicon Valley of education and Knoxville
> [Whittle headquarters] could well be where it's based. . . . With
> Channel One we've effectively built an eight-million-seat sys-

tem—and we may well double its size. That pipeline becomes a freeway to providers of educational software. I see a link between that pipeline and those providers. And Edison might be one of the big software providers. (Becker 1992, 174)

Understanding the profitability of such a venture, partners have already joined Whittle in the enterprise. They are the Time-Warner communications conglomerate, Phillips Electronics N.V., and Associated Newspapers of Britain.

Issues of diversity are not mentioned in reported Edison Project plans, and methods for teaching a multicultural student body are not discussed in "New American Schools." When Chris Whittle was asked by news reporters about access to his schools for profit, he indicated that all students, regardless of race, who had the ability to pay would be accepted (Chira 1992). He hopes to be able to offer 20 percent of the students full scholarships. His intent is to charge approximately $5,500, tuition which is the average cost per student in today's public schools. However, he would actually have to operate the schools at a $3,500-cost-per-pupil figure to accommodate building costs and scholarships. In his design, scholarships have been tied to the accomplishment of a fiscally ambitious—and perhaps impractical—plan. Charges of elitism—which have been levelled against former Secretary Alexander's voucher plan—can certainly be levelled against the Edison Program plan. Although these proprietary schools are in the future, part of the electronic "freeway" for their implementation has been established and built with Channel One.

CHANNEL ONE

All the studies included here have been generated by the need to examine what the authors consider to be a groundbreaking innovation in public schools. These studies have been jointly designed and coordinated to address a common set of concerns, and they have theoretical and methodological coherence. They answer many questions about Channel One that simple comprehension and retention measures alone cannot answer. (These measures, however, have not been neglected. See chapter 2.)

The groundbreaking aspects of the innovation which generate a common set of concerns include the following:

1. This is the first time a precisely targeted captive audience—such as high school students—have been sold to television advertisers

with the sanction and permission of the schools. (Channel One is not similar to an ad on the wall of a school gym which students may elect to view.)

2. This is the first time that a private-sector entrepreneur who develops instructional television has exercised such control over the design, delivery, and reception practices of his product. The Whittle contract is restrictive. For example, students must view 90 percent of Channel One programs per year. They may not do any other work while the program is being shown and cannot be excused from the room to study elsewhere. School personnel have no input to the program, nor any choice of delivery time. If any aspect of the contract is broken, Whittle Communications will cease delivery of the program and charge the school for the electronic wiring and hardware which it supplied free. No instructional nor educational television innovation to date has exercised such control over classroom practices.

3. This is the first time that a private sector entrepreneur has electronically wired 11,900 high schools in the United States. These high schools are prepared to receive additional Whittle channels that are being tested.

In addition to similar concerns about this innovation, the authors of this book share common ideas about television which shaped the manner in which their studies were conducted. Some common assumptions about the medium of television—whether commercial or educational—are important to an understanding of the significance of Channel One.

THE STUDY OF TELEVISION

Commercial television is a major transmitter of culture today. Practices of production, transmission, and reception shape our lives in a substantial way. Patterns of speech, dress, fashion, family rituals, group behaviors, and other social roles are simultaneously reflected and exaggerated on the TV screen. Broadcast and cablecast television help shape children's actions, beliefs and empirical knowledge. Educators often neglect to assign enough influence to television. Whether at home or in the school, television is a powerful teacher who competes daily with classroom teachers from preschool through college.

Traditional educational studies of television have endeavored to ascertain what children learn by applying behavioral or cognitive theories of learning. Some researchers even considered the medium to be neutral in shaping information. Many current researchers understand that learning is a social as well as a psychological construct.

Humans learn because of their membership in groups which provide access to the construction and production of communications. Long ago, the signs and symbols of these communications were negotiated in and by practice, and are renegotiated daily by their users. Thus, analysis of communicative systems becomes central to researchers attempting to access the social construction of knowledge.

Analysis of language is the obvious avenue of address to social knowledge, but the human environment consists of many additional communicative systems, not the least of which is television. Just as linguists and literary critics analyze texts, so can the communicative system of television be analyzed.

A television program such as Channel One has all the elements of a text and may be considered to be a social text that has been constructed with intent by a producer. It may also be considered to be encoded in socially constructed signs and symbols that are interpreted by members of a community who have access to those signs and symbols. As other texts do, Channel One draws its visual and verbal language from larger, more amorphous texts or discourses. While the authors of this book ask important questions—such as what and how many facts are retained by students watching Channel One (chapter 2), these questions concern only one narrow aspect of a cognitive discourse and do not address the context of Channel One. (The authors do realize that this narrow aspect influences political funding decisions.) The transmission and reception of Channel One is an event which incorporates signs, symbols, codes, and the rhetoric of discourses from broadcast and cablecast TV; from the marketplace; and from instructional television. The advent of Channel One breaks through the curricular rhetoric of U.S. high-school classrooms and includes decisions of administrators, school boards, and parents. Not only does it alter the student's classroom experience, but electronic wiring alters the function of the school building. Whether the alterations improve education or not, the event is major in its proportions and deserves close scrutiny. As scholars, the authors of this book address the event of Channel One.

In these chapters, larger texts than television are identified. For example, high-school teachers and administrators participate in marketplace discourses as well as educational discourses. They may discuss and agree with former Vice President Quayle's pronouncement about Murphy Brown, depending upon the discourse of which they are subjects. Also, they may support the notion of private-sector incursion in public schools depending upon which educational discourse they have adopted as their own. Discourses or systems of thought are textual, because they have been also constructed by producers, contain encoded messages, and are interpreted by receivers. The discourses identified in this book are not discrete. They overlap, and one person may have membership in several groups which produce different discourses. However, the discourses themselves may be verified by the manner in which they incorporate their own assumptions and values, by the language that they call their own, and by the prestige that they ascribe to certain concepts and, ultimately, to certain knowledge. Channel One is a small text which has been thrown like a pebble into a pond in which it activates and participates in widening circles of discourses. It is the television text, as well as these widening discourses, which these chapters address. This approach, however, breaks with traditional methods of researching television in the classroom.

INSTRUCTIONAL TELEVISION RESEARCH

Since the late 1950s, educators considering the purchase of video hardware and software have been plagued by a basic question of "What and how much do students learn while viewing television in the classroom?" Early instructional television research, like other instructional technology studies, pitted television against live lecture with the hope of discovering how much students learned when exposed to the medium (Williams, Paul, and Ogilvie 1957; Pflieger and Kelly 1961; Schramm and Chu, 1967; and Sykes 1964). These studies—informed early on by behaviorism and later by cognitivism—assumed that the medium was neutral. Not only was that assumption false, but the research design and statistics employed in these studies were rigorous. True and quasi-experimental designs and the application of T tests or ANOVAs called for a comparison of slightly different—not widely different—treatments such as television and live lectures. Unfortunately, most of that early research must be jettisoned. (It is interesting to note that some of these same designs are being employed today in educational computer studies. This is because political agendas, not appropriate research agendas, often determine research designs. Agencies which offer computer research grants demand that the grantee supply numbers which verify the efficiency and effectiveness of this instructional technology.)

In the early 1970s, there were isolated researchers who noted the unique nature of television, in and out of the classroom. They attempted to describe the impact of TV structure on viewers. Anderson (1972) explored the visual rhetoric of instructional TV, and Morrow (1975) attempted to map a grammar of media. *Sesame Street* studies (Lesser 1974) added information about the effects of pacing, linearity, and sequencing upon viewing. Baggaley and Duck (1975) explored the structure of commercial television. The largest contribution to research on the structure of educational television and learning was made by Salomon (1979, 1981, 1982, 1984) with his early investigation of aptitude treatment interaction and his later exploration of television as a symbol system. However, it is the nature of instructional technology researchers—as with some other educational researchers—to conduct studies in isolation. Also, the findings already mentioned, have never formed any cumulative body of knowledge about instructional television nor have the designers of educational television consulted this body of research.

The assumptions of psychological learning theories and their concomitant research designs unduly strain any investigation of a cultural artifact such as television. Any analysis of individual brain function does not have the power to account for the assemblage and origin of various communicative codes found in any television program. Such theories do not have the power to address the manner in which students participate in a community to master and read these codes.

TELEVISION AND CULTURAL CRITICS

Several cultural critics, however, have explored forms of commercial television and established the tenor for inquiry about that medium which pervades our personal lives and institutions of schooling. (Ellis 1982, Fiske 1988, Fiske and Hartley 1978, Gitlin 1980, Hall 1980, Heath and Skirrow 1977, Tuchman 1978, Williams 1975). Although these authors produce diverse analyses, they perceive television as a cultural form around which unique aesthetic practice, institutional organization, and social roles coalesce. They see the practice of television embodying powerful change and inherent contradictions. Their work forms a body of knowledge to which scholars in media studies refer, and some continuity can be said to exist in this arena. It is this body of knowledge which informs the common beliefs about television that the authors of this book share.

ETV AND ITV

There is a distinction between instructional television (ITV) and educational television (ETV). The former originally consisted of telecourses designed for credit, and the later consisted of informational and aesthetic programs for general viewing. Recently, the distinction has become blurred for several reasons.

The financially beleaguered Public Broadcasting System, which is the largest producer of educational television, has been bolstered by Annenberg Foundation money since the mid 1980s. Annenberg Foundation board members provided the fiscal and political impetus to deliver junior-college telecourses for credit to homes across the country. With Annenberg grants, PBS entered the instructional television market, but additional distinctions are fading.

The production and delivery of ETV and ITV originally generated separate video grammars, with ETV borrowing most of its visual codes from commercial television, and ITV incorporating visual codes from classroom lectures, World War II demonstration films, and documentary films. However, with the continued success of *Sesame Street* and the popularity of MTV, instructional television grammar is changing drastically.

Fast-paced, mixed-format codes—some of which are unique to television—are borrowed frequently by ITV producers. However, neither visual grammar, whether it is classroom or commercial grammar, has produced outstanding curricular materials. Indeed, an ongoing tension between designers of ETV and ITV has spawned a sometimes acrimonious debate about production styles. ETV producers, many of whom started in commercial television, often rejected designs of ITV producers who were usually educators. The elements of instruction, that is, advanced organizer, repetition, and summary, were often too boring for ETV producers. They argued that boring ITV programs would not maintain the attention of students. ITV producers, on the other hand, argued that the fast pace and superficial treatment of commercial television would hinder viewer learning. Such arguments were largely responsible for the failure of many well-funded joint efforts in instructional television.

Attempts to deliver credit courses to adults at home have been particularly plagued by this debate, including that of the Open University of America, the University of Mid-America, and many Annenberg projects. Actually, both visual grammars are constrained; ITV by its excessive use of the talking head and omniscient voice-over narrator, and ETV by its blind incorporation of the shifting visual styles of commercial television. The current trend on both sides is to imitate commercial television. (See the Children's Television Workshop production of *Square One TV.*)

Chris Whittle bypassed this debate, when he hired his own producers from commercial television. The Channel One format is borrowed intact from MTV and includes visual or "sight bites" as well as "sound bites" of the news. Young DJs, similar to those on MTV, introduce and segue the bites. Gavriel Salomon (1984) found that children were predisposed to be entertained when watching television at home, and that this predisposition had to be confronted before a video program was screened in the classroom. In other words, students must be carefully prepared to attend to televised instruction in a manner that will heighten recall. Such is the drawback of trying to teach with television. If a program incorporates the codes of MTV, it most likely encourages a predisposition for entertainment in the classroom.

CHANNEL ONE STUDIES AND ANALYSES

Most of the chapters in this book report studies which were designed, coordinated, and conducted by the authors to describe the cultural event of Channel One. The authors are primarily educational technology professors and were selected for their common research interest and varied methodological approaches. To achieve a rich and articulated description of this event, all studies were designed to explore separate issues, but also to complement each other.

The event of Channel One is articulated on many planes. As I have indicated earlier, it is the first time that thousands of public schools have been wired by an entrepreneur in the private sector. It is also the first time that so restrictive a contract has been written for students viewing television in classrooms, and it is the first time that television ads have been aired daily to millions of students. Discourses of public schooling, pedagogy, the marketplace, media communications, law, and other factors construct the Channel One event and the knowledge which it generates. When exploring this cultural event, the authors apply a range of methods such as narratology, structural, and poststructural techniques for reading the news program, rhetorical analysis, political and ideological approaches, and quasi-experimental design.

Because all communications are some form of narration, Robinson opens this book with a vivid description of daily life in a Midwest suburban junior high school. She makes the sights, sounds, and smells of this building available to the reader as she considers what, if any, important contribution Channel One makes to this school. Students speak frankly if tersely, about their reaction to the current events program. Teachers are more detailed in their responses. All staff members are worried, not about Channel One, but about finances during this recession and, additionally, about control over the curriculum. The principal notes that the "real driving force behind the school is the three B's—buses, bread, and basketball."

While educational scholars sometimes write about structural and post-structural theories, they seldom apply methods suggested by these theories to discourses, and rarely do they apply these methods to specific media texts. This book breaks ground in this area by providing specific models in chapters 4, 6, and 7 for the analysis of educational television programs. Structural techniques are borrowed from the formal film model developed by the cinema scholar, David Bordwell (chapter 7). His exploration of aesthetic style and production techniques are used by Barbara Erdman to examine the emergence of a new educational genre, the school news television program. Although informed by the dictates of structure, Erdman's work incorporates a consideration of popular culture and the environment of the classroom in which lessons are produced. As with the more sophisticated semiotic models, her analysis explores the paradigmatic origin of the structures encountered in the school news program. She conducts a formal analysis of both Channel One and CNN's *Newsroom*, another current-events program produced for public schools. The form, style, and lesson of each program selected for analysis are described. The stylistic slickness and attractive format of this new genre are weighed against the content of the lesson offered.

While structural theories of meaning construction offer a unique opportunity to explore the codes, design, production techniques, and other formal aspects of television, they do not address the reader nor the viewer. Poststructural theories reinstate the reader in the communicative troika of author, text, and reader. In fact, they valorize readers and locate the construction of meaning in the reading process, rather than in the text itself. Some reader theories, such as reception theory, provide the opportunity to explore the relationships between and among reader, text, and the author or producer. Poststructural theories have been more widely discussed by educational scholars and more frequently applied by language arts researchers than were structural theories in the field of education. Nonetheless, they are seldom applied to the analysis of educational media.

While reader theories form a fully articulated paradigm which includes psychological, phenomenological, and social models, those forms popular in the United States are the social models, especially that of deconstruction. The challenge to all authority which is inherent in deconstructive thought has captured the imagination of U.S. literary scholars both on the left and the right. This amethodilogical theory appeals to those who wish to challenge the status quo in radical or reactionary, progressive or regressive ways. With the exception of language-arts scholars, most educational researchers use post-structural theories only for discourse analysis, not for textual analysis.

Chapter 6 in this book applies an adapted reader theory to explore the manner in which Channel One advertisements construct their audience or subjects. Cues within the visual and audio channels of the ads are examined to answer the question of "Just whom do these ads think their viewers are?"

Advertising is also the topic of chapter 5 which traces the inception of Channel One in public-school classrooms, and describes the nature of pilot programs and early testing of the current events program. As an advertising professor, Barry's primary focus is a consideration of the ethics of advertising in the classroom. This factual chapter provides vital background information on Chris Whittle and other Whittle Communication enterprises. An early version of this chapter provided the impetus for several studies in this collection.

If structural and poststructural theories disclose the constructed nature of that which is considered to be true, one might believe—as does Ellen Rooney (1989) in *Seductive Reasoning* and Steven Mailloux (1989) in *Rhetorical Power*—that all construction of meaning and, consequently, all knowledge, is rhetorical in nature.

Chapter 4 returns to rhetoric as a device for the analysis of media. To investigate what students view, Belland conducts a visual and verbal discourse analyses of a week of Channel One programming.

While most readers are familiar with discourse analyses of written and spoken words, Belland's work emphasizes the rhetorical nature of visual communications. In addition to content, he considers framing, transitions, pacing, duration of sequences, and other elements which create the televised message. The construction of these elements are traced to discourses from the domain of public-school pedagogy, journalism, commercial television, the marketplace, and pop culture. His analysis also explores the ethics of this event.

A separate and more traditional incorporation of rhetorical analysis can be seen in chapter 10. Here St. Maurice delineates the rhetoric of the debate surrounding Channel One and the rhetoric of the pedagogy evinced in the program itself. Although he cites John Dewey's call for the protection of the U.S. curriculum from the "money motif," St. Maurice speaks practically about schooling in the 1990s. Because Channel One offers synthetic ways of seeing the natural world and the other, he believes that an opportunity exists for teachers to employ critical analysis in the classroom. Teachers have a chance to uncover "artificial modes of experience" which are offered on electronic media. By doing so, they continue a time-honored pedagogical tradition in U.S. public schools—namely, critical rationality.

As I have noted, the dominant educational reform discourse in the United States has been constructed by a few authors, and politicians such as Hirsch, Bloom, Chubb and Moe, Finn, Alexander, and others. Informing the work of most of these reformers is the seminal book *Free to Choose; A Personal Statement* by the Nobel Laureate economist, Milton Friedman (1980) and his wife, Rose. Although Friedman's work and the writings of these reformers have officially and inextricably entwined the marketplace, privitization, vouchers, and public schools, a separate reform discourse runs as a subtext to this dominant one. One of the proponents of democratic, not capitalistic, public education examines the politics and ideology of Channel One in chapter 8. Apple explores the program as part of Whittle's broader efforts to help reform the "failing" U.S. public educational system. His analysis is situated within the debate over the control of school structure as well as school knowledge. The adoption of Channel One is, for him, part of a larger conservative move in this country to re-capture the curriculum for the purpose of transmitting ideas of a "common culture," which would ultimately work against the goals of equity and diversity. Channel One participates in this transmission.

Politics and ideology are also the topics of chapter 9 which follows the event of Channel One as it worked its way through the educational systems in California and North Carolina. Muffoletto attempts to describe the political patterns which emerged in these two specific deployments of the news program. The ethics, economics and symbolic function of the event are delineated within an institutional and historical context.

A cognitive paradigm is invoked for the case reported in chapter 2 in which Knupfer and Hayes offer findings from a large (n = 2,267) quasi-experimental study in which they determined the ability of students to recall news items and advertisements. They also assess the effectiveness of Channel One to teach overall knowledge of current events. In addition to ascertaining what place, if any, this news program had in the cognitive life of students, their anecdotal recollections are an important part of this book. Their presence in fifteen schools over a period of several weeks gave them access to information about how Whittle Communications staff interacted with administrators and provided wiring and hardware.

Knupfer also reports survey results in chapter 3 which provides information about how students, teachers, and parents in three school districts reacted to the adoption and daily broadcast of Channel One. Important habits about the consumption of news are also described.

Stories have been told here about the cultural event of Channel One from a multivoiced platform of various, but coherent, education theories. These stories have been articulated through numerous and divergent research methods to provide the reader with a rich description of a significant juncture of public-and private-sector interests in the U.S. educational enterprise. The authors of this collection invite you, the reader, to evaluate this event.

REFERENCES

Anderson, C. M. 1972. In search of a visual rhetoric for instructional television. *AVCR* 19. 43–63.

Baggaley, J., and S. Duck. 1975. Experiments in ET: Effects of adding background. Research notes. *Educational Broadcasting International.* 7:208–209.

Becker, J. 1992. Chris and Benno's excellent adventure. *Vanity Fair,* August. 142–147, 172–176.

Bestor, A. 1953. *Educational Wastelands: The Retreat from Learning in Our Public Schools.* Urbana: University of Illinois Press. (Reissued 1985).

Bloom, A. D. 1987. *The Closing of the American Mind.* New York: Simon & Schuster.

Chubb, J. and Moe, T. (1990). *Politics, markets, and America's schools.* Washington, D.C., Brookings Institute.

Chira, S. 1992. Yale president quitting for private teaching venture. New York *Times,* May 26, A1, A12.

DeVaney, A. 1990. Instructional television without educators. In *The Ideology of Images in Educational Media,* eds. E. Ellsworth and M. Whatley. New York: Teachers College Press.

Ellis, J. 1982. *Visible Fictions.* London: Routledge & Kegan Paul.

Felter, M. 1982. Television viewing and school achievement. California Assessment Program. Sacramento: California State Department of Education.

Fiske, J. 1988. *Television Culture.* London: Routledge.

Fiske, J., and J. Hartley. 1978 *Reading Television.* London: Methuen.

Flesch, R. 1955. *Why Johnny Can't Read,* New York: Harper.

Friedman, M. and Friedman, R. 1980. *Free to Choose.* New York; Harcourt, Brace, Jovanovich.

Gitlin, T. 1980. *The Whole World Is Watching.* Berkeley: University of California Press.

Hall, S. 1980. Encoding/decoding. In *Culture, Media, Language,* eds. S. Hall, D. Hobson, A. Lowe, and P. Willis. London: Hutchinson & Company. 128–138.

Heath, S., and G. Skirrow. 1977. Television: A world in action. *Screen* 18:2. 7–59.

Hirsch, E. D. 1987. *Cultural Literacy: What Every American Needs to Know.* Boston: Houghton Mifflin.

Lesser, Gerald S. 1974. *Children and Television* New York: Random House.

Mailloux, S. 1989 *Rhetorical Power.* Ithaca, N.Y.; Cornell Univ. Press.

Morrow, J. 1975. Toward a Grammar of Media. *Media* and Methods, October, 78–80.

Pflieger, E. F., and F. C. Kelly. 1961. *The National Program in the Use of Television in the Public Schools.* New York: The Ford Foundation and the Fund for Advancement of Education.

Rooney, E. 1989 *Seductive Reasoning.* Ithaca, N.Y.; Cornell Univ. Press.

Salomon, G. 1979. *Interaction of Media Cognition and Learning.* San Francisco: Jossey-Bass.

———. 1981. *Communication and Education: Social and Psychological Interactions.* Beverly Hills, Calif.: Sage.

———. 1982. Television literacy and television vs. literacy. *Journal of Visual and Verbal Languaging* 2:2. 7–16.

———. 1984. Predisposition about learning from print and television. *Journal of Communication* 34:2. 119–135.

Schramm, W. and Chu, G. 1967 *Learning from Television; what the research says.* Washington, D.C.; National Association of Educational Broadcasters.

Sykes, R. E. 1964. The effectiveness of closed circuit television observation and of direct observation of children's art classes for implementing elementary teacher's training in art education. *Dissertation Abstracts,* 25. 2387.

Tuchman, G. 1978. *Making News.* New York: The Free Press.

Williams, D.C., J. Paul, and J. C. Ogilvie. 1957. Mass media, learning and retention. *Canadian Journal of Psychology* 11. 157–163.

Williams, R. 1975. *Television: Technology and Cultural Form.* New York: Schocken Books.

RHONDA S. ROBINSON

1

Investigating Channel One:
A Case Study Report

In a world where cheerleading practice is Thursday night
  and the Hawks play on Friday,
Where the halls are filled with T-shirted, blue-jeaned adolescents
  and the lockers are painted in "hot" colors,
Where the office has an electronic billboard greeting visitors
  and today is Mexican Fiesta in the cafeteria . . .
In such a world, what impact could any technological innovation really have?
What role could any one addition play,
  in the school day or the classroom world?
In such an involved and noisy society,
  would any one new technology even be noticed?

—R. Robinson

These are the questions that intrigued me as a I started to observe one school's use of the news broadcast from Whittle Communications, Channel One. I'd like to share that world with you, to
provide a rich and detailed description of what a school day, a class
period, a lunchroom mealtime, a study hall really are like for these
students. I'd like you to meet some of the teachers, the principal, the
Learning Center coordinator, the counselor, the other players in this
complex society. I'd also like you to hear the comments of the students themselves—adolescents who are busy, growing and learning,
with or without technological intervention.

The school is a twenty-year-old "new" building on the edge of
a housing development, just outside of a previously small country
town recently absorbed into the megopolis that is Chicagoland. The
school is in a middle-class neighborhood, but kids come from all

economic brackets and types of homes. They are bused to this one of two junior highs in the district, which has a new high school building even further on the outskirts of town. All three schools have been using Channel One since the 1990 school year began and the equipment was installed. As is typical in such situations, the equipment was not installed in time for the opening of school, nor for teachers to get used to the technology or the idea of using it before the semester began.

What is any school all about? What happens on any given day, during any class period, at any specific moment? Have those involved with school improvement projects or innovations really looked at what is happening in schools? Are they aware of the sights and sounds which surround students in schools today?

Whittle Communications has offered a technological bail-out to schools in the form of free media equipment in trade for a mere twelve minutes of student time. Many schools have accepted this offer, mostly for the equipment. However, has an innovation actually occurred? How does one describe a school using Channel One?

Case-study methods were used to approach an answer to this question. Case-study methods include interviews, observations, and document reviews in order to provide a detailed picture of a setting under investigation. This case study used those methods over a seven-month period to discover a picture, from one point of view, of what one such school is all about. Twenty teacher interviews, group interviews with ten classes of students, several individual student interviews, and repeated interviews with the principal, superintendent, district technical coordinator, and the building-level Learning Center director were conducted. More than ten days of observation were used, as were surveys of teachers' attitudes and reviews of the contractual agreements with Whittle.

RESEARCH "BIAS"

I was once a junior high school teacher myself, from 1971–1976. I taught English and language arts in the second largest school district in Illinois, at a junior high with more than 1,200 kids. The experience is now a fond memory, although it was a very difficult job at the time. I loved junior high teaching—the kids, the freedom to teach important topics and use methods in which I believed. I left thinking that I was only seeking a year or two of graduate study—but I never went back to teaching there. I have visited junior high schools fairly often since then, using them as sites for several research projects on children and television. However, there is a big difference between being a teacher and being a visitor. In this study, I was still a visitor, but I tried to put myself back into the environment as much as possible—watching, listening, and talking to students and teachers as if I belonged there. The longer I was in the building, the more I felt that I did belong. Although I was a guest, I was not intrusive, nor was I always really noticed in the halls or the lunchroom.

What goes on in a junior high school? What is schooling all about for these kids and teachers? What matters to them? What makes a difference? What changes occur when a new technology enters their building and their day? This study sought to describe the answers to those questions as seen through one set of eyes. It was obvious to me that I am not a junior high school teacher any longer, that I probably never will be again. However, having been there, having tried to succeed at some of the same tasks, and having faced some of the same frustrations and joys, I felt that I could enter the building and describe what I saw from perhaps a closer perspective than that of some other university researchers.

MONDAY: ENTERING THE SCHOOL

Loud noises. Clanging lockers, music, laughter, shouts, giggles, wails, dropping books, shuffling feet. Bell. A hush . . . a new almost-silence. The ebb and flow of sounds in a school hallway, a pattern repeating itself ten times each day, noise advancing and retreating, doors opening and shutting—along with mouths and minds, no doubt.

Loud noises. Hot colors, fast-paced movement, crowds. Not chaos at all, just activity. Enter the office and find an oasis of quiet. Surrounded by glass walls, windows on to the cafeteria, and pleasant posters . . . and the quiet that only an official place can provide. Kids don't come in here unless they are sick, have lost or broken something, have to make a phone call, or have been called by the principal or the counselor. Kids come in, but only one or two at a time. Lunch money is borrowed, books are retrieved, stuck lockers are reported, and upsets dealt with here. The principal of the building is often in sight. The nurse or a school secretary is sitting in view behind a desk, and kids have ready access to assistance if it is needed. These are still young kids grades—six through eight, and ages twelve through 14—and they often need help with something crucial to their immediate activity.

Announcements are read from the office. The school schedule is available here, and kids report here to pick up notes, books, assignment sheets. It is a pleasantly busy, involved place, with several adults keeping attendance, health, counseling, and behavior records while they engage in the many necessary activities of an active junior high.

The school is fifteen years old, a fairly new building for the area. It has a student population of 550 kids, with 35 teachers on staff. The school day has nine periods, including lunch and directed reading study (DRS) during which Channel One is played. Each teacher has six periods of classroom instruction, with most having three different preparations. They also have lunch, DRS, and a preparation period. The school is grades six through eight, with the sixth graders being kept somewhat separate from the others as far as classrooms are concerned. The curriculum includes math, prealgebra, science, reading improvement, speech/drama, language arts (divided into two periods, one of composition and the other of literature), Spanish, music, band, choir, shop, home economics, art, world history, American history including current events, physical education combined with health, and sixth grade curriculum. The staff includes a principal, a school secretary, a nurse, a learning-disabilities resource person, the Learning Center coordinator, two counselors, a Learning Center aide, a reading aide, a gifted coordinator, a part-time science coordinator, and a clerical aide.

The building has recently entered a more site-based management era, and has an active School Improvement committee (SIC) which selects areas for improvement and makes recommendations to the principal for changes. He is adamant that it be *their* committee, and has enacted several changes based upon their recommendations. When I first approached the faculty about becoming a part of the school for this project, it was during one of the SIC meetings. The principal stressed that I was not to take much time, as it "is their meeting, not mine."

BEGINNING THE STUDY: THE SETTING

The faculty showed little interest in my researching Channel One in their building. One male teacher did want to know who was paying me to conduct the study. When I told him that I was doing the research on my own time, unfunded, he was incredulous. He was unaware that professors did such research. In his experience, studies were conducted by groups or grants, not individuals. Throughout my semester there, the faculty was a bit wary of me, asked few questions of me, and were mainly busy doing their jobs. At our initial meeting, the faculty had an agenda for school reform, and, throughout the semester, they had to deal with issues of financial exigency and cutbacks. While I was there, several teachers were pink-slipped. So the question of Channel One really did take a back seat to other more pressing issues.

The financial difficulties in the district only worsened over the semester, and the school board initiated some cuts for the next school year including cutting several competitive sports and the untenured faculty. "Cutting sports could save as much as $60,000, with uniforms and insurance and so on," the principal explained. Of course, for faculty members who were coaching after school sports, a pay cut was part of the savings. "Some will lose $6,000 because of the cuts he reported." So, morale in the building was at a low point. The principal reported that it was the worst he'd seen in more than twenty years. People were worried about their security, concerned about the quality of programs, and complaining about the lack of community support.

"The community is a conservative one. Parents don't think school needs to be any different than it was when they went to school," the principal told me. The community was also divided on support. While this building had an active parent group, the referendum for increased school funding failed.

A picture of this building, then, would include the following details: an active faculty and parent group, a very dedicated and hardworking faculty, enthusiastic or disinterested students, and a financial situation not unlike many others in the country. The average teacher had more than ten years of experience. The principal and Learning Center coordinator each had more than twenty years. The faculty had little, if any, warning about Channel One, and no training on its use—other than the admonition that, by contract, students had to be able to hear and see it each day. Regardless of the local control issue and the School Improvement Committee, no teachers had been consulted about the Channel One contract or its inception. No teacher had been a part of the decision for this building's use of the system; they were not even consulted about the location or height of the monitors. They merely came back into the building after summer break to discover the system in place and just about ready to use.

Teachers commented, "If they had asked us, I would have told them a much better place to put the TV."

"We were not told at all. I feel this was just crammed down my throat."

"Channel One was not crammed down our throats at all. We were told about it last spring, and I thought it was a great opportunity to try something new. We were going to benefit from the equipment, and the program was going to help kids with current events and geography."

Thus, the teacher opinion was as diverse as the colors in the building.

WATCHING CHANNEL ONE: A TYPICAL DAY

Before we entered the room, the hallway noise level was deafening. This group is returning from lunch; they've been on break from class-level "quiet." They are full of questions, full of conversation, and busy continuing their break until the last moment. We enter just before the bell. "Are you our sub?" "Where's our teacher?" "Want to sit here?"

The room is visually, as well as auditorially, busy. Posters and slogans hang everywhere. Many are student or teacher made, using simple computer programs, such as those in Printshop programs. The desks are like small tables—two or three together—plus two rows of six desks each. There are thirty desks crowded into the room, with fifteen students in the DRS period assigned to them. Also in the room is a listening carrel with music tapes, and a gerbil in a glass cage. Seven mobiles—again mostly teacher-made—hang from the ceiling and turn slowly.

Lots of colored-chalk writing appears on the chalkboard, most of it pertinent to standing assignments and instruction. There is a work area in the middle of the room with an overhead projector and colored markers. The screen is down, ready for use.

I sit down at Kara's desk. She is absent today and has been for a few days. On her desk are weekly assignments sheets and an assignment sheet from this teacher for the previous day. Also on the desk are notes from other kids, written on red hearts. They are wishing her well and sending her their best for her return. This is a caring group, as evidenced by their thoughtfulness.

The teacher asks for quiet and for eye contact. She responds to their questions about me by introducing me and letting them know that I may want to interview them after the broadcast. She lets me tell them I'm interested in their opinions and am really just here to see Channel One with them.

At 12:15, the broadcast begins. The students and the teacher are very quiet, and most are working at their desks on schoolwork they brought in with them. Five seem to be watching intently. Unlike usual, the commercials come on in the first two minutes—one for a breath mint, and one for a popular TV show being broadcast that day. All heads look up for that particular ad. The show must be a favorite in this room. No one looked up during the mints ad.

A three minute story on the Holocaust followed. After the introduction section, an interview with a survivor is played. Many heads go up for the interview. Five or six students are still watching regularly; others just look up and down as they work.

Most are doing math homework; nine kids are working diligently from their math texts. One boy is reading the novel *Fellowship of the Ring*.

At 12:22, ads for Starburst and Slice come on. Both have interesting music, and many heads go up to see the screen. The final stories of the day are on the National Science Foundation, a piece on computers, and a piece on thinking and physics. Fewer students watch than when the ads came on. Kids get a bit restless toward the end. Some have finished their assignments, and are free to watch the ending.

After the broadcast, students return to homework or note writing or just doodling on paper. The teacher works with two kids on their math homework, and the room is quiet. The program is not discussed nor summarized. Students agreed to be interviewed, and we talked quietly until the period ended.

ADDITIONAL COMMENTS TO A TYPICAL DAY

This was a typical Channel One viewing. Most of the classes I observed were quiet, and had about one-third of the kids watching at any one time. The rooms were all visually busy with the kids energetic and opinionated when asked to share their thoughts. Some variations existed, of course.

For example, in some of the rooms, quiet was not enforced so much. It happened that the difference, as I noted, was also the difference between male and female teachers, with male tea.hers' classes tending to be much noisier overall. It was also male teachers who let the kids shout out the answers to the pop quiz or sing along with the commercials. The male teachers were more often watching with the kids and interacting a bit with the broadcast. Some even en-

couraged the class participation—the shouting out and the singing—
letting the kids be more verbal as they watched. Other differences in
other viewing situations include the fact that some few teachers have
a remote control to turn up the volume or to change the channel on
the set once the broadcast is over.

Kids shouted out things in all the rooms, anyway. More than
twice, I heard "Oh no! Here it comes. I'd rather do my work" just as
the show started. Often kids groaned when a particularly hated ad
came on. Groups or individuals had ads that they had really gotten
tired of and made that opinion clear. The kids really liked the pop
quiz segment, and they really hated the drop-out public service announcements that featured, as one kid said, "really depressing kids.
It makes you go home and wonder why you are happy." Kids this age
do not relate well to scenes of inner-city kids and minority kids' problems. These are twelve-to-fourteen-year-old white rural and suburban kids, and these ads are just not made for them.

Other differences are created by the classes of kids themselves.
Some groups are less interested in homework and consequently
more interested in Channel One. Several groups told me that watching TV is better than having to study, and that they wished the program lasted the whole DRS period so they had no time during which
they were expected to work. Other groups mentioned that they often
don't watch, saying that they have too much to do and would rather
spend the time doing homework or catching up with their friends.
"Channel One is educational, but it's boring" one boy told me. Even
during the Gulf War, some of the students were not interested in seeing the news.

The war was a real opportunity for Whittle Communications. If
any event could convince schools that they need to be cabled for
news coverage and wired for classroom monitors, it is a national
emergency like that war. Several teachers and students liked the war
coverage and thought it was helpful to have it on each day. They also
liked the fact that, because of the cable and satellite equipment in the
building, they had access to CNN all day, each day. I found this
ironic, but the equipment is used as it is intended to be—that is, to
extend information sources for the school in whatever ways possible.

The typical viewing situation was also altered by teachers' attitudes and actions. Many of the teaches had voiced concern that the
twelve minutes for Channel One would be taken out of their school
time. In fact, the school day was lengthened by twelve minutes to accommodate the program. Still, many teachers worried that showing

television during what was to be a study hall would be too disruptive. They also resented that it might make more work for them, or prevent them from doing the grading and planning that they usually accomplished during this quiet time. Many of the teachers discovered during the first few months that the program was fairly innocuous, that they could still work and help students while it was being broadcast, and that they were not losing any instructional time. This helped them become much more accepting of the idea. Few teachers were openly supportive of the system, but even fewer were still openly critical. As with many other additions to their days, they had gotten used to the program and accommodated themselves to the change.

EFFECTS OF INNOVATION ON THE STUDENTS

One of the questions driving most innovation research has to do with the overall effect and the impact that the innovation might have on the setting, the students, and the teachers.

To summarize the effects on the students, their comments will help introduce the range of their opinions. For the most part, the thoughts are positive, focusing on the alternative to studying. The music and sports, as well as the commercials, come up as favorite features. Others opinions emerged as well.

"Yeah, we want to have this again next year. Only more sports and more music and less commercials."

"It's cool. We like it. It's better than having to study."

"It shows us some ideas for careers, you know, it would be cool to be the people doing the features and interviewing kids and stuff."

"It's boring, and I don't watch it."

"I never talk about it with my friends or my parents. No, teachers don't bring it up much either."

"No, we don't go out and buy candy bars because of the ad on Channel One. We'd buy them anyway! But Channel One does give me ideas about the world and stuff."

"The war stuff was really good. I watched it because my cousin was in it."

"I wish there were more sports."

"I like the pop quiz the best. The ads for stay in school and stuff are dumb."

"This can help you in world history and math."

"My parents say we're lucky to have it."

"We like it because it passes the time. It should be longer. It should last the whole period, not just part. Or we could have news every period, but just for five minutes."

"We like the commercials, especially the ones for Certs, Fritos, Snickers, Pepsi [MC Hammer], Starburst, and peanut butter M&Ms."

"I don't like watching the news at home, and this is more interesting. I don't think there's anything wrong with our watching the commercials."

"Channel One is a good time-filler when you have no studying to do. I like the features about other schools the best."

"The ads are aimed more at us too, I think, but some of them are the same that you'd see at home."

"I like it because the hosts are teens and the music is OK, and the pace is not too fast. It's not too complex for us. I get more about current events from watching this. The ads don't bother me at all."

Overwhelmingly, students interviewed alone or in groups really liked having Channel One in their building. They like the music, the sports, the commercials, the teen hosts, and the pop quiz. Very few mentioned that they liked the news particularly. Even so, they did mention that they like this news better than the news at home, which most of them do not watch.

However, Channel One did not seem to have much of an effect beyond their preferring it over having to quietly study. Few, if any, mentioned that they used the information in classes or discussions at home. Many said that they read the paper for the sports and that the news is just not that important to them. The effect that watching seemed to be having was to say to kids that watching this TV was more important than studying, and that, if they watched this—commercials and all—they had seen and heard enough news for the day and did not need to spend more time on current events.

The commercials are linked to their love of music. Most of the interviews mention the music segments and the commercials, with the music as students' favorites. The students could name the products advertised much more often than they could name countries or areas mentioned in the news portions. They never reported having trouble understanding the news, but they had trouble recalling what they had just seen and heard.

EFFECTS OF INNOVATION ON THE TEACHERS

The student' opinions were somewhat echoed by their teachers when they expressed their thoughts on the effect that the Channel One broadcast was having on their students. Teacher comments were gathered while we observed the broadcast as well as in private interviews which were tape recorded. The range of opinions was fairly broad, with some teachers quite accepting and others having their own very critical thoughts.

"I remember reading about Channel One in the newspaper," said one teacher in a rather lengthy opinion. "I talked to the principal, and I read about this in *U.S. News and World Report* and I thought, 'My God! Here's the onward march of the one-eyed monster. Television invades the classroom . . . the nightmare of all school teachers. . .' And I thought, 'Well, our school is destitute. They're going to give us all of this equipment, like giving beads to the natives.' So, I guess you could say that I had some rather negative thoughts and some trepidations and reservations. My earliest thoughts were a little bit of queasiness.

"But now, six months later, it hasn't been as bad as I thought it would be. It seems to have become established institutionally, like part of the woodwork. For the first few days, my students watched it quite attentively, and then, I've seen that my students can do their homework and watch television at the same time. So it's kind of slipped into a thing of, well, the television is on, but they're doing their homework . . . talking to their neighbor, just like at home.

"So, I prefer to say that I have gone from being against it to being neutral on it because I see that advertising is here but it is largely innocuous. If you stop to look at it, the Channel One broadcasts are very benign and innocuous . . . they are so mundane. They avoid any controversy. They present news in such an almost tepid manner. I'm an old print journalism guy, and I, of course, have my bias for the written news. But the kids seem to have accepted this and have treated it like part of the woodwork."

Other teachers were as accepting, and most agreed with this teacher that the passage of time had quelled their initial fears or reservations about the project.

"I had read about Channel One, and thought it was real interesting. I was more positive. I think that the availability of information is important. I even watch CNN during my prep. period. I like to keep up. Channel One hasn't been a big hassle, but when the kids aren't really interested, then it can be hard. Mostly, they really do watch. My attitude has stayed positive throughout. I never viewed it as an imposition [like other teachers] nor did I think it was crammed down our throats."

"Now that we're used to it, it's a positive influence. I don't think kids see or read the news or get current events otherwise. It also gives them teen surveys, like dating, money, earning money, and so on. The dating issue was good; there was a moral and ethical message. It's very well done, personable, outgoing, and it relates well to kids. I felt the idea [of Channel One] should have been introduced to us earlier. It seemed shoved down our throats. But to other teachers now, I would say, give Channel One a chance. Most initial reactions are negative, but if you can control the viewing and get kids to listen, they really can absorb and understand."

"I was less favorable when I first heard about this. I wasn't too happy about the TV, but it was because it was during my DRS period and that was work time for me. I thought it would be taking away form my work time. Now, when I do take time to watch, I think it is good, better than regular news and certainly very watchable. I enjoy it. I had to train my kids to really be quiet in this period. I keep my group quiet and insist that they not chat after the show is over. I'm more enthusiastic now that I see that it does not keep us from working."

"I saw this as a technology innovation, not as the news or for content. Our teachers here are pretty technologically literate, concerned in trying to keep up. I know that, when it was introduced, some teachers thought it would be time-consuming, that it would distract from study and review time, and that it caused us to add extra time to our school day. But the school-day length is really set by the high school and scheduling concerns, not by TV. I think Whittle did a good job covering the war [Desert Storm]. Any newsworthy topic, the kids carry throughout the day. They do like it."

This last teacher's comments reveal not just initial impressions but what emerged as positive influences of Channel One.

Positive Uses

Several teacher's comments did highlight the positive results of having Channel One in the building. These included the increased awareness of social events and geography, a heightened interest in the news, some aspects of the content, and some use of the system equipment for other projects.

One social studies/language arts teacher felt sure that the program was helping his students.

"I think TV does help; a picture is worth a thousand words. The kids have their imaginations and their senses enhanced by watching. It does serve as an example, and helps with descriptive ability for some kids. I do worry that, depending on the attitude, Whittle could mold kids for better or for worse. I did have that fear at first, with this coming from the South, that we might see some attitudes or ideas that I don't hold or prefer for the kids."

One of the sixth-grade teachers told me, "We have used the TV system for other things, and language arts [classes] used it. There are lots of ways to use it in the classroom, work it into curriculum. I can foresee good uses to extend the use of the TV into the school." Sixth-grade classes had not used the system too much beyond the two or three all-school uses.

The school's Spanish and language arts teacher told me, "I do use a VCR, and I use the Learning Center to play tapes for me through the system. I have the kids perform skits and record them to play back, plus we tape Christmas activities which we do in Spanish like a pinata. I could use the cable stations now that we have them, and I like to bring in travel tapes, but I still use a cart and monitor so I can control the viewing."

The Learning Center aide reported, "I have seen an increase in interest in the news, and we have noticed an increased use of the news-related magazines and the newspapers in our Learning Center. I think the kids seem much better informed or more aware than they might have been last year."

I was told by the science coordinator that "we've used our camcorder to record the kids with science projects Even the language-deficient kids were narrating their own. There is lots to be gained from planning, speaking in front of the camera, and so on. I think the Channel One equipment has raised our interest in using more T.V. in the classroom."

Another teacher said, "I find that my group really likes the pop-quiz segment. The social studies teachers did a unit on the Middle East which came during the war, so that it was coordinated really well with TV each day."

Other teachers commented on particular aspects in their experiences with Channel One. "We used the system to promote candidates for the Student Council Elections. We've also shown movies like *Anne Frank* and *To Kill a Mockingbird*, and shown them to all the grades at once using the system. The Holocaust segment that Whittle did was helpful because of our unit on *Anne Frank*."

"We've used the system to show a video to everyone at once—in fact we've done that twice, with a fire video and with an earthquake safety video. There may have been a few other things as well."

"It comes in handy since I teach current events. I'll use anything, from the *New York Times* right down to the grocery store tabloids. So, having Channel One has made an impact, a difference. It hasn't made a big difference, let's put it that way. It hasn't made a profound impact."

Concerns

While all these comments present some positive opinions, it must be noted that the same few examples of extended use of the equipment kept coming up. Even the current-events teacher reported no real impact from the news broadcast, preferring to say that he was now "neutral" on their use of Channel One. There were curricular concerns expressed, as well as control, implementation, or decision-making concerns.

"It's hard to incorporate into my curriculum because some of the kids just have not seen it. The band kids don't hear it often," one of the sixth-grade teachers said.

"Since I teach Spanish, it really doesn't come up in class. The kids never talk to me about it. It never comes up with parents, either. One important improvement I would recommend would be to introduce this earlier to the teachers, to ease us into it as teachers. We really had no input on the decision, nor on how or when the stuff would be used."

Several other teaches told me that they were not given much warning nor help with the use of Channel One in their classrooms.

"I'm not criticizing, but I haven't been told what to do except to leave the lights on. I have been asked to use in [information from the broadcast] and *not* to use it. I haven't been asked to pull together with other people."

More substantive concerns came up often, especially those related to the budget problems the district was having due to several years without a successful referendum vote for increased funding.

"We have such budget problems. Control [by teachers] is so low. We don't schedule, don't get asked . . . and it may be control that drives motivation. With morale so low, what help is Channel One?"

The Learning Center coordinator reports that the School Board has cut many programs—including junior-high-level sports and all temporary positions—and has shortened the school day for the next year. "People are mad at the School Board, the School Board is mad at the superintendent, and it's a mess."

It may be these control and budget issues that are at the heart of the matter with the use of Channel One. Teachers are not that happy about their lack of control or the severe money problems in the district. These come out in little ways as attitudes more than as behaviors. The teachers are convinced that they are a tight-knit, professional, extremely positive, and dedicated group. The important qualities to them seemed to be their ability to work together and to act as professionals.

"Our building is professional. We get along better than any other building as colleagues. We work together."

"I've been in five or six buildings. This school has serious professional teachers with lots of interest in working. It's too bad we're getting zapped with all these changes . . . class size is going way up."

"The faculty is very loyal to one another. We expect teachers to respect others' efforts. We've worked on eliminating complaining and talking behind backs."

"The faculty is a tremendous organization. They have a sort of 'Well, let's give it a try' approach. So, even though when this was introduced there was some apprehension, we're willing to give it our best shot. We went into this with an open eye . . . even if, down deep, we had some qualms . . . up front, people were willing to give it a try."

"We don't want to be hammered to do certain things with it [the system]. We don't want more added on to our load. But we have an attitude of excellence; we want the best from each other and our students."

The pride that teachers had in themselves and in their work was evident in the building and classrooms, in the teachers' lounge, and in the kids themselves. The school fairly hummed with activity, and with kids who were anxious to do their best. Each day that I observed, I found something new and encouraging. Some days, it was the displays of handmade quilt squares hung in the hallways. Some days, it was the politeness of a boy in the cafeteria line. The conversations in the teachers' lunchroom almost always centered around kids and what to do to help problem students. Every day, someone would interrupt someone's lunch to ask if "So-and-so had improved in math" or if it was true that one student or another had turned in their homework or had permission to work with another teacher or student for extra help. The teachers were always bringing each other up-to-date on problems of kids—home troubles, family problems, skill-development difficulties, even kids' romances were the topics of conversation. A slogan found on a classroom wall captures this attitude:

People want to know how much you care before they care how much you know . . .

It was extremely interesting to note that the teachers' lunchroom was largely segregated. The women ate in the lunchroom, as did one or two men and, occasionally, the principal. The men ate elsewhere—in a room next to the boiler—so they could smoke, talk sports, and get away from work talk. "The women didn't like our jokes so they kicked us out," I was told with a laugh. The women denied this, and said that the men just left so they could watch TV or discuss the sports program instead of talking about kids. However, conversations between these groups still occurred, and students were handled in quick plans between bites.

As in most schools, treats were common and teachers organized to keep each other rewarded. Each payday, someone provided doughnuts. Often, the home economics classes provided some delicacy for tasting. The cooks pitched in with delectable cinnamon rolls available before school and at lunch, if you hurried. When the School Improvement committee met, many healthy and some sweet snacks were provided for the hungry after-hours workers. Overall, the attitude that teachers care for each other and respect each other was absolutely born out by all I observed.

However, their perceived lack of control and lack of time for innovation were observable, too. These teachers had three preparations, seven classes, and lots of planning and grading to do. Several mentioned their feelings of anger and lack of control over the budget and over their own plans. While they were proud of being "professional," they had very little choice over what and when they taught, the length of classes or school day, the books or materials they used, and, of course, no control over when Channel One came on or even how loud it played.

The metaphor for all this was that only two or three teachers had remote control devices to control their out-of-reach monitors. Most had literally no control over their sound, picture, or channel. Those that did have a remote device were friends of the Learning Center coordinator or were perceived to be real innovators with technology (or both) who could actually benefit from using such a remote device.

One example of the lack of control which teachers had was a short tirade I overheard between the principal and the Learning Center coordinator. The principal had been described by the coordinator as a man who was "conservative but willing to listen to persuasive arguments to try new things. He stays away from controversy, but the school is flexible and innovative and willing to try anything new if a teacher can show how it might work." However, on this particular day, the principal had discovered what getting satellite delivery and cable delivery into the building might really mean. The tirade included a request to shut off the cable access to the monitors in the classrooms, so that teachers could not ever tune in to what was being shown on any network or cable station. His concern? That a teacher being paid $200 a day might just show TV to kids . . . or that a substitute might get talked into the baseball broadcast with a "but we always get to watch on Fridays" ploy . . . or that kids would go home to conservative families and report that they saw Madonna, VH1, or NBA in class that day. This group of professional, dedicated teachers was not to be trusted with cable television, no matter what. The matter was later resolved, but the principal remained concerned that the television would be misused. He did not see the irony in his position.

The main issues that have been discussed have related to the teachers' lack of control and to the lack of effective use of the news broadcast within the curriculum. Another issue has to do with faculty development. As has been cited, teachers did not get much help in learning how they could use Channel One in their classes. None of the teachers reported using the materials which Whittle Communications sends to the school to help teachers plan ahead. One teacher told me, "I have looked at them. They come in my mailbox, and I look at them very carefully, and they don't seem to do me any help. There's nothing there for me that either I don't know, or I'm not doing already, or I can't key on when it [the show] gets there. Although I do look at them, they tip me off to what's coming. It helps me about as much as any TV guide would."

The Learning Center coordinator reported that the staff development tapes had gone out only two or three times. Teachers are just not interested or do not have time. The tapes themselves are not all new and exciting. They are often just rereleased educational tapes being provided to the teachers. Those that I looked at had very little new to offer teachers, and were not about how to use the news broadcasts to better effect.

When asked if they would like to use the Channel One broadcasts differently, some teachers explained that they supposed that the news could be made more integral, or that study of television visual elements, advertising, feature writing, or electronic journalism could be incorporated into their classes. "But we would have to work that up. It is not part of the current curriculum, nor do we have text materials to do that. We could, I suppose, but we would really have to start from scratch for such a unit," one language-arts teacher admitted. With low morale, lack of control, shortened days next year, and other budget problems, innovative new units seemed unlikely to her. So, again, the issue of staff development arises.

When I mentioned that there were several such developed units on media study or television/literacy, that language-arts teacher was surprised but interested. The time and the help had just not been provided for this staff to realize the potential of the daily broadcasts. They had spent much of the first year just getting used to the added daily responsibility and the change in schedule.

Another related issue had to do with the role of the media specialist in this building and his relationship to the success of the project. He was extremely instrumental in promoting to the staff the use of the broadcast, as well as other uses of the equipment. His philosophy was obvious from his Learning Center, which was extremely large, well-equipped, and included a comfortable reading area, a networked computer laboratory, and a special program in reading/study skills for kids needing special help. With one aide, this specialist taught computer skills, research paper development, current events research, and a regular group-study skills and math enhancement class. Students came to the center to find current events for their civics class, research their assignments, use the word processing programs, do their homework, or just check the scores of the local teams. The rules were strict and well-enforced. The center was always quiet but humming with activity and lots of questions. Teachers and students obviously used it as a place to solve learning problems.

The coordinator was a promoter of the Whittle project. He felt that the equipment would really help the school, and that the wiring would be very useful. "The equipment has really helped. Conflicts for the monitors have really been eliminated." Several times in reporting on uses they had made of the system or of video equipment in general, he would say that they had done it this year, but that "I'll do more with it next year; I'll make it better next time we do it." He was learning with this first year what was possible, what the kids could do, what the equipment could do, and how he could better utilize the package. "There are lots of possibilities for us with Channel One. We could be using it to teach about advertising, television production. I hope to do that more next year. I'm not sure when, with the school day being shorter, periods shorter. I had to do some 'selling' to get the principal and teachers in favor of Channel One. It was a financial decision; we got monitors, we got wiring. We'll use the monitors next year more, with the VCR. It has saved us, but the usefulness had to be demonstrated. Teachers needed to see how this could work . . . how it could save us."

This coordinator has every intention of making the Channel One project a success in his building. He will take the time—and has—to help individual teachers, to make recommendations to content-area faculty groups, to suggest uses to grade levels, and so on. Obviously, the project is an innovation which takes some effort to make successful. It cannot just be beamed into the building and improve schooling. It takes teachers and media specialists to work with ideas related to their own curriculum areas and their own needs to make the broadcasts anything but twelve minutes of TV in the school day.

The real message seems to be this: That the mere receipt of equipment and the daily broadcast of any news program is not much help to this school. The teachers must be convinced and encouraged. The kids must be guided to recall any news. The building, faculty, and students must also commit themselves to make special efforts to do something useful with the addition of all that "free" equipment and the loss of the twelve minutes per day. If none of this takes place, then the kids, as reported, are merely getting the impression that television is very important, and that twelve minutes of news and commercials just about covers their need to know. The teachers would also be getting the message that anything that Whittle Communications can put out for that twelve minutes is better than anything they could be doing with that same time.

Are these the messages that Whittle intended? Chris Whittle has said that "If Channel One is allowed to succeed, education will never be the same" (Whittle 1990). However, what will he consider to be success? Enough schools contracting with him to sell lots of advertising and be profitable? Also, now, with his new school system on the horizon, what will he consider to be success, and does this school faculty and students stand to gain anything from such a development? The fear among educators has been that the Channel One project will become one more example of the "television as curriculum" so well-explained by Postman (1979).

If a curriculum can be defined as an information system that "is used to influence, teach, train, or cultivate the minds and characters of our children," (Notar 1989, 67), then this television news and commercial project has a definite curriculum, in twelve minutes every day, and for thousands of American children. Part of this curriculum is certainly that they should view life "in terms of commodities" (Notar 1989, 67). The fact that the students in this school really enjoyed the entertaining aspects of the broadcast, including the commercials, should not go unexamined. That they see and hear these messages elsewhere is not disputed, but that the school showing them gives the commodities more import cannot be argued either. (Note: See pg. 58) Information is in quick-cut sound bites, and does not need further explanation or discussion. At least, this is the message given kids in this school. This message comes by the fact that classes never discuss the broadcast, teachers don't use the materials to add units of study, and the only requirement is that the kids can see and hear the broadcast every day.

The portrait of this school and its use of the innovative news broadcast by Whittle Communications has included a picture of busy and committed teachers, eager students, and lots of business-as-usual throughout the building, regardless of the use of the system. There have been no remarkable additions to the curriculum, no extensive uses of the equipment, and no really strong feelings about it from the teachers. It just has not made much difference to them, nor to the kids.

Most students receive the news and features each day without any instructional guidance or further discussion. Anything else is extra or added on by the Learning Center coordinator and individual teachers, outside of their other assigned duties. The equipment and the cable, the attention paid to the school, the promise and potential—all these come to nothing without extra effort and thought which is not funded by Whittle and not encouraged by the financial position of this school district.

We are left with a picture of the school, close to the end of the year. Students rush about as usual, and teachers look tired. Final projects are being finished, summer vacations are planned, and uncertainty about next year is voiced by many. To this outsider's eyes, the real issues in the school—whether they are financial or student-life related—have not been touched by the use of Channel One.

The principal explained to me that the real driving force behind schools is the "three Bs—busses, bread, and basketball . . . athletics, transportation, and lunch are the big three." This type of sloganism may not mean too much, but there is a kernel of truth in it. Schools operate at the pleasure of their school boards, and they must be responsive to the conservatism of the community or the limitations of financial problems. Innovations, such as the Whittle offer, are accepted for the equipment offer, not because they fit into the curricular goals of a school district such as this one.

And television doesn't even start with a B.

REFERENCES

Notar, Ellen. 1989. Children and TV commercials: Wave after wave of exploitation. *Childhood Education*, Winter. 66–67.

Postman, Neil. 1979. The first curriculum: Comparing school and television. *Phi Delta Kappan*, November. 163–168.

Whittle, Chris. 1990. Personal notes from presentation at the 1990 Association for Educational Communications and Technology Conference. February, Anaheim, California.

NANCY NELSON KNUPFER
PETER HAYES

2

The Effects of the Channel One Broadcast on Students' Knowledge of Current Events

As new technology is developed and placed into classrooms, its purpose is to improve instruction. Yet, all too often, no firm evidence is collected to show improvements in the learning environment, nor in the relationship of those improvements to the costs involved. Costs can be real dollar amounts, or they can be more subtle. Some subtle, but potentially significant, costs might include the effect of the technology on the curriculum content, the lesson structure, the structure of the school day, or the autonomy of a teacher's style. Researchers can measure some of the costs qualitatively while others are best measured quantitatively.

It is important to measure the value of the Channel One broadcast both qualitatively and quantitatively. While much of this book discusses the qualitative aspect of broadcasting Channel One to the schools, this chapter focuses on the quantitative data that can be used to measure the broadcast's effectiveness in teaching students about current events.

The study reported in this chapter was conducted in two parts. Part one measured the overall effectiveness of the Channel One broadcast as it affected students' general learning of current events over the course of an entire school year. Part two measured students' retention and understanding of news information as well as advertising from specific Channel One broadcasts. This chapter first reviews some background information about students' knowledge and learning of current events, then it reports on the effectiveness of the Channel One broadcast as a teaching tool.

BACKGROUND

In April 1983, the National Commission on Excellence in Education released a report titled "A Nation at Risk: The Imperative for Educational Reform." That document and many related research reports have declared that the United States' educational system is seriously deteriorating, and that the nation's very future is at risk (Passow 1989). A large number of educators, school administrators, college professors, journalists, and social commentators agree that young people in the United States are deficient in their knowledge of mathematics, science, geography, history, literature, democratic principles, and current events (Bennett 1986, Hirsch 1987, Ravitch and Finn 1987). Further, a national study revealed that the majority of college journalism students fail to maintain adequate knowledge of important news events and geography (Atkins 1985). Hirsch claims that achievements in all academic areas may be hindered when the students lack a common body of information, reference points, meaningful examples, and familiar symbols.

The importance of student knowledge of news and current events is well documented in the educational literature (Atkins 1985, Ravitch 1985, Yager 1988). Many educators recommend keying instruction to current events in order to provide realism and meaning for lesson content (Yager 1988). Others recommend that schools improve instruction by implementing new technologies (Cohen 1988, Nickerson 1988) and forming partnerships with the business community (Gardner 1989).

Partnerships between schools and businesses could provide financial relief during lean economic times and offer opportunities that students would not have otherwise. Such partnerships might very well use the practical, realistic perspective of the business community to guide the curriculum to meaningful endeavors, such as those that would prepare students with marketable work skills. These partnerships present opportunities for using technology within schools in a way that would otherwise be impossible to accomplish. Unfortunately, business partnerships can potentially put school curricula at risk in terms of outside control.

For example, Channel One broadcasts include content that is determined by Channel One staff, not according to any specific curricular objectives within the schools. Further, contractual agreements require school personnel to use the broadcast for a specified number of days, with a certain percentage of students, over a duration of a fixed number of years. Although many administrators report that certain criteria for viewing were mandated, others were able to negotiate contractual variations, none of which seemed to be based upon curricular objectives within the district.

Even though Channel One has received more attention than most educational television programs, the literature concerning the program defers from issues surrounding its educational value and social impact on schooling. Instead, the literature is dominated by the controversy of including commercial advertisements within the daily broadcasts of news and general information (Berry and March 1989, Cheatham 1989a and 1989b, Gallagher 1989, Olsen 1990, Rudinow 1990). The National Teachers' Association has gone on record as moving beyond the issue of advertisements to raising objections to the curricular control imposed by the Channel One contracts. The difference between Channel One and other educational television rests in the imposed criteria for viewing the programs and this criteria raises questions about owner Chris Whittle's real motives in distributing Channel One programs.

Educational television is not new. It has been utilized for public school instruction for many years (Chu and Schramm 1979, Condry 1987, Cuban 1986). What is new, however, is the proliferation of new educational program offerings made available to national cable networks by using satellite technology. For example, satellite technology allows national cable network organizations the opportunity to broadcast educational news programs specifically targeted for use in today's classrooms. At the forefront of satellite broadcasting for education are Disney's Discovery Channel, Turner's *CNN Newsroom* and Whittle's Channel One.

Channel One officials report that, by 1993, more than ten thousand public and private schools in the United States, with more than eight million students, will have contracted for its services. Yet, despite this potential for broad impact on the educational system, few studies have investigated the effectiveness of the Channel One broadcast to teach the news and current events. It appears that many administrators, school board members, parents, and teachers have decided to use Channel One as an instructional tool, yet their decisions are based upon a very limited amount of research-based evidence. Instead, they are making decisions without the benefit of knowing whether or not the endeavor is educationally sound.

Many educators believe that this decade will bring a merger of video-based programs with related computer technologies to create a revolutionary new medium that will be widely used in our schools (Milone 1989, Nickerson 1988). Perhaps that is the case. If so, educators must pay attention to the content and the method of implementation of such programs so that the students can receive the full benefits of the technology. Recent research suggests a need to place different emphasis on implementation strategies so that schools go beyond traditional use of educational television and put more emphasis on applying today's advanced technologies for current events instruction across curriculum areas (Cohen 1988, Condry 1987, Nickerson 1988).

The advent of new instructional television programs, such as Channel One, raises new questions and problems for school administrators, legislators, teachers, students, parents, and network officials. For example, what do we know about the effectiveness of such programs? Do they positively impact student learning as they claim? How do we fund such technologies? Who controls for quality and excellence? These questions suggest a need for comparative research to help provide some answers. The study reported here seeks to address those questions and provide some of the needed answers concerning the effectiveness of Channel One as a tool for teaching about current events.

RESEARCH QUESTIONS

Specific questions for this study are:

1. Is Channel One effective in increasing students' knowledge about current events? Will current events scores for students participating in the broadcast be significantly different from scores obtained by students not participating in the program?
2. Is there any significant difference in the effectiveness of Channel One between junior-high and high-school students?
3. Is there any significant difference in the effectiveness of Channel One between at-risk students and students who are not at risk?
4. Is there any significant difference in the effectiveness of Channel One between males and females?
5. Is there a significant difference in the effectiveness of Channel One concerning world news versus national news items?

6. Do students understand and remember the Channel One news?
7. Do students remember the Channel One advertisements?

Independent research is needed to answer these and other important questions about the impact of the Channel One broadcast on learning prior to placing too great of an importance on its role as an effective instructional tool. This study presents such an investigation.

METHODOLOGY

This study measured the effects of the Channel One broadcast along two related lines. First, the study investigated the effectiveness of Channel One to teach overall, broad knowledge of currents events over the course of a school year. Second, the study measured student's short-term recall of the news and advertisements from specific programs.

Subjects

Subjects for the study were junior and senior high-school students in three school districts in a large metropolitan area of the United States. The first part of the study—measuring overall current events knowledge—included 1,081 students in two of the three districts. The third district had agreed to be used but could not be included because of delays in receiving the program due to slow equipment installation. Those delays might have skewed the overall current-events data.

The second part of the study—recall of specific news and advertising—was able to use the students in the third district as well. Accordingly, five classrooms of subjects from each of fifteen schools were selected to participate in the second part of the study. Students in this part of the study received two styles of pop quizzes—one immediately following the broadcast, and one that was delayed by nearly twenty-four hours. In total, 2,267 students received an immediate pop quiz, and 2,154 students received a delayed pop quiz.

Materials

Materials for the study included two types of instruments. First, standardized current-events test instruments were used to measure general and overall knowledge. The second type of test instrument was developed by the researcher and teachers to quiz the students about lesson-specific information. The two parts of the study—and more information about the test instruments—are explained here.

Part one: overall current events. Part one of the study included a series of standardized current-events tests produced by *U.S. News and World Report.* Although available on a monthly basis, these tests had not been previously used in any of the junior or senior high schools involved in this study. These tests were designed specifically for use with high-school students and were concerned with improving the students' general knowledge of current events. Because some of the tests were longer than others, they were modified slightly by the researchers so that each one was worth twenty-five points. Modifications involved simply removing certain questions so that the point value remained equal for all of the tests. Each test then consisted of five matching, five true/false, five multiple choice, five fill-in-the-blank, and five correction types of questions, with each worth one point. The correction-type questions contained an underlined phrase. If a phrase was correct, the students marked "correct" by the question. However, if a phrase was wrong, the students had to correct the phrase by writing in the correct wording.

Part two: specific news and advertisements. The second part of the study utilized quizzes constructed by the researcher and selected teachers. Each quiz contained several open-ended questions about a specific news broadcast. These questions required students to recall information about news events and advertisements contained in the specified broadcast. News portions of each quiz were worth fifteen points as follows: five facts, five explanations, and five syntheses or implications. In addition to news-related information, the quizzes asked students to name and tell about three advertisements that had been shown during a particular broadcast.

Methods and Analysis

Part one. This part of the study was measured with a posttest-only control group design with repeated measures. According to the research design, a treatment group received the Channel One broadcast throughout the school year, and a control group did not receive the broadcast. The Channel One broadcast was viewed by all students in the treatment group every day and was never viewed by the students in the control group. Posttests about general current events knowledge were administered periodically. The research design controls for history, maturation, and regression.

Six high schools and eight junior high schools from two large school districts were selected to participate in this part of the study. Two high schools and two junior high schools—one from each district—served as the control schools which did not receive the Channel One broadcast. The two school districts contained similar populations of students. Note that the decision to use Channel One was made on a school-by-school basis, so that some schools within each district did not participate in Channel One.

The decision to participate in the study was made by the teachers and the principal at each school to assure continued cooperation once the study was begun. Remaining schools within these two districts were not included in the study because of either installation or operational delays with Channel One that could have affected the results of the testing.

With some restrictions, three classes of students were randomly selected from each participating school. To help prevent loss of students from the study during the semester switchover, the sample was restricted to include only those classes that were scheduled to meet over the course of the full school year or had the likelihood of attracting the same students, such as a course scheduled as part one and part two. In addition, students could not be enrolled concurrently in any history or social studies type of course as that would likely give them more practice with the material than students not enrolled in such focus classes. Once the sample was narrowed to appropriate classes, the school principal randomly selected the participatory classes from within each school.

A search was conducted for an appropriate standardized test series to use for the study. Several publishers produce standardized current events tests, so a selection had to be made about the best choice. None of the schools in the study were using standardized tests produced by *U.S. News and World Report* magazine, and that publication was also not connected to Whittle Communications. The tests were a bit longer than desired so each was modified to include the same number of questions. Identical tests were administered to the treatment and control groups on five occasions, with each test being unique to the occasion.

Because of installation procedures and delays in receiving the Channel One broadcast, the testing began in October of the school year. Additional tests were administered in November, February, March, and April. No tests were administered during December and January because of a lengthy semester break occurring during those months.

Teachers were given a testing folder once a month and instructed to issue the current events test during the time usually allotted for Channel One viewing. No answer key was provided. Students completed the tests independently without consulting anyone else. Tests were completed in approximately ten minutes, placed in a folder, and returned to a central site for the researcher to pick up for scoring.

A total sample of 1,081 students from junior and senior high school began this study. As expected, several students were eliminated from the study because of schedule changes at the semester break along with normal patterns of migration within the school year.

Data collection included raw scores for five current events tests, student grade level, cumulative grade-point average, gender, and the identity of the school and class where the testing occurred. Based upon low cumulative grade point averages, a select group of at-risk students was identified within the original sample population. Tests were scored and MANOVA was used to analyze the resulting data for significant differences between the treatment and control groups. The level of significance was set at .05.

Part two. The second part of this study involved pop quizzes to measure the students' retention of current events and the advertising contained within specific programs. Pop quizzes were given in two ways: immediate and delayed.

Immediate pop quizzes were administered directly following the Channel One viewing, while delayed pop quizzes were administered approximately twenty-four hours later, but prior to viewing the next broadcast. To make the immediate pop quizzes possible, the researcher and at least one teacher viewed a broadcast prior to the beginning of the school day, then constructed and duplicated the tests immediately. The delayed pop quiz was identical, but was not administered until the next day.

Because all three school districts participated in the pop quizzes, a larger number of students was involved. In sum, 2,267 students received an immediate pop quiz, and 2,154 students received a delayed pop quiz. This number represented five classrooms of students, from the fifteen participating schools, who were randomly selected by their principals to receive the immediate and delayed pop quizzes.

All students who were present in a given class at the time of quizzing received the pop quiz. As with the current events tests, the pop quizzes were given to the teachers in a folder, distributed, collected, and then scored by the researcher for consistency.

The same classes were given the immediate and delayed pop quizzes on a rotating basis, so that one school was quizzed per trial. For example, if school A received an immediate pop quiz, then school B would receive the delayed quiz. Next time, school B received the immediate quiz, and school C received the delayed quiz. This rotation continued until all sample classrooms had received an immediate pop quiz and a delayed pop quiz. Each student received one immediate quiz and one delayed quiz. Any variation in sample numbers was because of absences.

There was no control group measured against the sample. The quizzes simply investigated whether students remembered and understood the broadcast material, and if there were any difference in memory displayed between specific groups of students. Summary statistics were recorded first for the entire group of immediate pop quizzes, and then for the entire group of delayed pop quizzes. The statistics calculated memory of the news items separately from memory of the advertisements. T-tests were conducted among particular student groups to check for significant differences in quiz performance, with the level of significance set at .05.

RESULTS

Results will be reported separately for reach of the two parts of this study, with part one followed by part two. After the quantitative results are presented, conclusions will be discussed based upon the combined evidence presented by the quantitative, qualitative, and anecdotal information gathered throughout the course of the study.

Part One: Overall Current Events

As expected, a limited number of students were eliminated from the sample as schedule changes were made at the semester break. By year's end, 880 students with complete data from all five tests remained in the study. Another 566 were treatment-group students, and 314 were control-group students. Table 2.1 shows the breakdown of the student sample by grade level, and table 2.2 specifies a breakdown of the sample by gender.

The data in tables 2.3 display mean scores and standard deviations on the five cumulative current-events tests for both treatment and control group subjects within the total sample. The two groups

TABLE 2.1. Student Sample by Grade Level

Grade Level	n	Percent
Seventh	160	18.2
Eighth	178	20.2
Ninth	65	7.4
Tenth	266	30.2
Eleventh	139	15.8
Twelfth	72	8.2
Total Sample	880	100.0

TABLE 2.2. Student Sample by Gender

Grade Level	n	Percent
Male	438	49.7
Female	442	50.2
Total Sample	880	99.9

TABLE 2.3. Mean Scores for Cumulative Tests

Group	n	Mean	Standard Deviation
Treatment	566	52.82	13.84
Control	314	52.43	12.18
Total Sample	880	52.74	13.26

obtained almost identical mean scores. Scores ranged from 15 to 87 of a possible 125 points. Mean scores and standard deviations for the five individual tests are shown in table 2.4.

Mean scores for the five individual tests for the senior-high-school students and then for the junior-high-school students, are shown in tables 2.5 and 2.6, respectively. Comparisons between these two tables reveal performance patterns, but further analysis shows that those patterns cannot be attributed to the influence of Channel One.

MANOVA on these data revealed no significant difference in current-events test scores between students who received Channel One and those who did not receive the broadcast. Further, there was no significant difference in current events scores between at-risk students and those who were not at risk, nor between males and females. In general, senior-high-school students had higher test scores

TABLE 2.4. Mean Scores for Individual Tests

Group	n	Mean	Standard Deviation
TEST 1			
Treatment	566	9.27	3.85
Control	314	9.49	3.63
Total Sample	880	9.45	3.78
TEST 2			
Treatment	566	11.33	3.41
Control	314	11.18	3.38
Total Sample	880	11.28	3.41
TEST 3			
Treatment	566	10.90	3.38
Control	314	10.86	3.22
Total Sample	880	10.89	3.32
TEST 4			
Treatment	566	11.58	3.31
Control	314	11.47	3.26
Total Sample	880	11.55	3.29
TEST 5			
Treatment	566	12.25	3.40
Control	314	12.14	3.39
Total Sample	880	12.21	3.40

than did the junior-high students, but this overall advantage in knowledge existed in both the treatment and control groups and was not related to whether or not they viewed Channel One.

Part Two: Pop Quizzes

Mean scores and standard deviations for the pop quizzes are listed in table 2.7. The total possible score for the news items is fifteen, and the total possible score for the advertisements is three. At first glance, it appears that students remembered roughly half of the news items, but further analysis concerning the level of news understanding is revealing.

Each question about the news was constructed in thirds. The first part of each news question required students to simply recall the topics of the news stories. The second part asked them to explain something about the news stories, thus requiring them to demonstrate understanding. The final third of each news question required the students to explain the relevance or implications of the story. Most of the students were able to name the story topics. Fewer stu-

TABLE 2.5. Senior High School Mean Scores for Individual Tests

Group	n	Mean	Standard Deviation
TEST 1			
Treatment	296	11.17	3.38
Control	191	10.96	3.25
Total Sample	487	11.09	3.33
TEST 2			
Treatment	296	12.64	3.05
Control	191	11.74	3.18
Total Sample	487	12.29	3.10
TEST 3			
Treatment	296	12.74	2.83
Control	191	12.33	2.74
Total Sample	487	12.60	2.80
TEST 4			
Treatment	296	13.05	3.11
Control	191	12.63	2.86
Total Sample	487	12.89	3.01
TEST 5			
Treatment	296	13.64	2.90
Control	191	13.15	2.79
Total Sample	487	13.45	2.87

dents were able to explain what the stories were about, and only one student of the entire sample was able to explain the importance or implications of the news stories viewed.

Students remembered the advertisements. They were asked to recall three advertisements and tell about them. A point was given if the student could recall something about the advertisement that referred to its content. No points were given if the student simply referred to the name of a product or service. It is possible that students remembered the advertisements because these pieces are deliberately designed to get attention and be persuasive during a short period of time. Then again, it is possible that students remembered the advertisements because they saw them repeated so many times. In one school, the infamous M & Ms commercial brought chants of "Billy Bob," while the students hummed along with the tune. The students laughed and made fun of that particular advertisement. How could anyone *not* possibly remember it after the classroom antics involved?

One day, a high-school senior visited school with a friend. The guest student did not receive Channel One at his school, but had heard about it and was very enthusiastic about getting a chance to

TABLE 2.6 Junior High School Mean Scores for Individual Tests

Group	n	Mean	Standard Deviation
TEST 1			
Treatment	270	7.18	3.21
Control	123	7.20	2.95
Total Sample	393	7.18	3.26
TEST 2			
Treatment	270	9.89	3.23
Control	123	10.30	3.60
Total Sample	393	10.02	3.35
TEST 3			
Treatment	270	9.10	2.87
Control	123	9.50	3.05
Total Sample	393	9.24	2.93
TEST 4			
Treatment	270	10.00	2.76
Control	123	9.67	3.02
Total Sample	393	9.90	2.84
TEST 5			
Treatment	270	10.73	3.26
Control	123	10.59	3.65
Total Sample	393	10.60	3.38

see the broadcast for the first time. Some background information is that his good friend had just enlisted in the military service and was due to go into active duty upon graduation from high school a few months later. The news report of the day contained information about the war in the Middle East, and his friend was nervous about his future.

After viewing Channel One, the guest student was casually asked what he thought about it. His reply was, indeed, interesting. Even though he viewed the broadcast during a time of Desert Storm news, he replied excitedly, "I didn't know that they made peanut butter Snickers!" and proceeded to tell all about the "really neat commercial" for the candy bars. This scenario hardly suggests that the advertisements are trivial pieces that will be ignored.

Observations

During the course of the study, the researcher popped in on numerous classrooms to observe the students and teachers using Channel One. Many observations of classroom procedures and infor-

TABLE 2.7. Mean Scores for Pop Quizzes

Group	n	Mean	Standard Deviation
JUNIOR HIGH			
Immediate	998		
News		7.88	2.30
Advertisements		2.90	.29
Delayed	942		
News		7.07	2.41
Advertisements		2.85	.40
SENIOR HIGH			
Immediate	1,269		
News		9.55	2.25
Advertisements		2.90	.29
Delayed	1,212		
News		8.58	2.42
Advertisements		2.90	.29
TOTAL SAMPLE			
Immediate	2,267		
News		8.82	2.42
Advertisements		2.90	.29
Delayed	2,154		
News		7.92	2.53
Advertisements		2.88	.34

mal questioning revealed that teachers usually did not introduce the Channel One program, nor did they follow through with any discussion of the program after its viewing. This left students to understand, interpret, and situate the news on their own with no meaningful grounding of the lesson. It is no wonder that they were unable to explain and interpret the importance of the featured news items.

During the broadcast, students paid attention in varying degrees. Some students attended the entire broadcast, while others attended part of it. Still others seemed to ignore the entire thing, opting to read, work on other paperwork, write notes, and so on. Because most students were not called upon to discuss the broadcast, their only motivation for viewing was intrinsic.

What part did the teachers play in implementing the broadcast? The large majority of teachers did not view the program but did paperwork or prepared lessons while the broadcast aired. A few teachers actively attended to the Channel One broadcast and took a few minutes to discuss parts of it after the broadcast ended. Some teachers referred to shortage of time and the need to get on with the lesson, but reminded the students that a discussion would probably occur at a later time during a social studies class. This, of course, had no chance of happening for those students who were not enrolled in such a course.

The structure of the school day or curriculum responsibilities may have had an impact on the teachers' ability to follow through with a discussion of the broadcast. Some schools showed Channel One toward the beginning of a class period while others showed it toward the end of the class time. Still others showed the broadcast during homeroom period.

Those teachers with viewing time slots toward the beginning of a specified class period seemed to be anxious to get started on the regular class material, so they rarely discussed the broadcast. Those with viewing time toward the end of a class period tended to allow students to continue working on written assignments during the broadcast and used the last few minutes of class to wrap up the session by reminding students of assignments instead of discussing the broadcast. Teachers who had the broadcast scheduled during homeroom period seemed to be less pressured by the demands of the regular curriculum and did engage in more follow-up discussion.

Also, junior-high teachers, in general, seemed to be a bit more concerned than the high-school teachers about discussing the broadcast, and seemed to make a better effort to do so. Conversations with those junior-high teachers indicated that they believed the material needed discussion, but they were hard pressed to deliberately set time aside for that.

Although the schools taped the broadcast and had it available for teacher preview before school, none of the observed teachers had previewed the broadcast prior to showing it to the class. Further, the vast majority of the teachers did not know that there were classroom support materials for Channel One available to them. Nearly all of the teachers who did know about the support materials said that they had never looked at them because they did not have time for any additional preparations.

Students and teachers alike seemed to take great interest in some of the activities that emerged as a result of using Channel One. For example, several schools began using the system for school announcements made by the students. There was a bit of trouble with live student broadcasts at one high school, so the announcements then went to a videotaped format which was then broadcast. This certainly took more time than the old way of broadcasting announcements over the school's audio speaker system, but the students enjoyed seeing their peers on the monitor and seemed to pay better attention to the announcements when offered in this manner.

Another school began broadcasting its own news program. At first, the news segments were produced entirely on the school grounds. Then the students began covering some local community events. This news show, in a junior high, was a big hit with students, teachers, and administrators. The students did the research, wrote the stories, videotaped the events, gave their news show a name, and wore specially designed T-shirts with the program logo during production of the show. Although everyone involved seemed to enjoy this activity very much, only a select group of students had the opportunity to be actively involved. So the school planned a news-show production class for the next year to provide more students with the opportunity to participate.

The one who carried the heaviest burden during this activity was the media center director. This person had to make sure that the camera was transported safely to and from events, and had to oversee student activities in various phases of news production. In addition, this was the only school that kept an archive of Channel One broadcasts. The media center director was responsible for taping Channel One broadcasts, cataloging them, and communicating with teachers about programming. Toward the end of the school year, the media center director was very interested in the activity that had emerged, but was also very overworked and tired. The principal was, therefore, asked to hire additional media center staff to assist with additional duties.

One of the high schools planned a video production course as a result of the students' interest in the Channel One broadcast. The goal was to allow students to earn credit toward English requirements while getting their ideas onto videotape. Teachers claimed that students could learn English by writing and editing scripts, plus they would be learning valuable job skills that would be necessary for employment in the information age. The catch, then, became the issue of how to raise the money for a top-notch television studio and editing suite, complete with necessary remodeling and equipment.

Obviously some of these ideas went beyond the original intent of school personnel when they decided to try Channel One. The interest in these emergent activities seemed to be quite high and, therefore, the cost in time was considered to be a worthwhile investment. Teachers continued to claim that Channel One came to them free of charge—even though the monetary cost involved in purchasing video cameras and editing equipment, plus the need for additional salary for added personnel, was substantial in some cases.

CONCLUSION

The Channel One program, as implemented, does not appear to be effective in increasing students' knowledge about current events. Although senior-high-school students obtained better scores for current events knowledge than did junior-high students, this was true for both the treatment and control groups. Thus, the higher scores seemed to be unrelated to the viewing of Channel One.

Although some teachers expressed hope that the Channel One broadcast would serve as a stimulus or motivator for at-risk students, there is no evidence that students in that category paid better attention to the broadcast or remembered it any better than did students who were not at risk. Nor did the broadcast have different effects according to gender. Likewise, there were no knowledge differences demonstrated between items classified as national or world news topics.

It appears that Channel One is not necessarily effective in fulfilling its claims of teaching current events knowledge. Although students could recall the news story topics immediately for a pop quiz, they had difficulty explaining what the stories were about and had even more difficulty producing a statement about the importance of events. Students did seem to remember the advertisements, yet most teachers failed to discuss either the news or the ads with the students and, thus, missed an opportunity to teach interpretation of current events or critical, informed consumerism.

Because there was no significant difference between the treatment and control groups, Channel One does not appear to be an aid nor a hindrance to learning, but simply ineffective in terms of its claims. The question to raise now centers on what else is sacrificed during the time that Channel One takes away from other curricular activities? Or, asked in the opposite way, what substantial benefits, obvious or subtle, does Channel One offer to the students?

The method of implementing Channel One might be improved if teachers would preview the program and provide some sort of introduction and follow-up to the twelve-minute sequence. To do so would provide an opportunity to prepare the learner for the broadcast and emphasize the meaning and relevance of the news. As this was not being done in most cases, and the value of the broadcast is unfounded in terms of its claims to increase knowledge of current events, one might look to other reasons to continue viewing the program.

For example, one might ask what hidden agenda and alternative benefits are likely to emerge from the broadcast activity? Could there, for instance, be student benefits in the area of increased visual literacy, interest in producing a news program, or skill-building that emerges as a result of planning and producing a local, in-school news program of their own?

What are the detrimental factors that balance against these potential benefits? Is the quality of the program educationally sound, or is it a show with good production values but little educational substance? What hidden social messages emerge? What real, financial costs are involved? And how does the job of the media center director change? Whatever the many possible costs and benefits, Channel One has potential for teaching, but not necessarily in the anticipated current-events realm of the curriculum—and certainly not in the way that it currently is being implemented.

More research is needed over time to properly address the value of Channel One as an educational tool. This research must address Whittle's claim of increasing current-events knowledge, but it also must address the emergent and more subtle issues surrounding use of the broadcast. In addition, teachers and students need to respond with their opinions after they have more experience with Channel One.

REFERENCES

Atkins, P. A. 1985. The general knowledge void. *Journalism Educator* Spring: 40. 11–14.

Berry, B., and J. March. 1989. Is $50,000 worth two minutes a day of commercials? *NEA Today* May/June: 35.

Bennett, W. 1986. *What works: Research about Teaching and Learning*. Washington, D.C.: U.S. Department of Education.

Cheatham, B. M. 1989a. Channel One forges ahead despite complaints about ads. *School Library Journal* July. 9–10.

———. 1989b. Critics of pilot T.V. program oppose ads. *School Library Journal* March. 91–92.

Chu, G., and W. Schramm. 1979. *Learning from Television: What the Research Says*, 4th edition. Washington, D.C.: National Association of Educational Broadcasters.

Cohen, D. 1988. Educational technology and school organization. In *Technology in Education: Looking Toward 2020*, R. Nickerson and P. Zihiates. eds., Hillsdale, N.J.: Erlbaum.

Condry, J. C. 1987. TV as educator. *Action in Teacher Education* June 9. 15–25.

Cuban, L. 1986. *Teachers and Machine: The Classroom Use of Technology since 1920*. New York: Teachers College.

Gallagher, J. 1989. Wooing a captive audience: A controversial plan to beam news—and ads—into classrooms. Time February 20. 88

Gardner, J. 1989. Balancing specialized and comprehensive knowledge: The growing educational challenge. In *Schooling for Tomorrow: Directing Reforms to Issues that Count*, eds. T. Sergiovanni and J. Moore. Boston, Mass.: Allyn & Bacon.

Hirsch, E. D. 1987. *Cultural Literacy*. Boston: Houghton-Mifflin.

Milone, M. 1989. Channel One, administrator's eye. *Classroom Computer Learning* October. 8–9.

NEA Today Bulletin. 1989. *Debate: Channel One*. May/June, 7. 89

Nickerson, R. 1988. Technology in education; Possible influences on context, purpose, content and methods. In *Technology in Education: Looking Toward 2020*, eds. R. Nickerson and P. Zidhiates. Hillsdale, N.J.: Erlbaum.

Olsen, J. 1990. Do not use as directed: Cooperative materials in the schools. *Educational Leadership* December/January. 79–80.

Passow, A. 1989. Present and future directions in school reform. In *Schooling for Tomorrow: Directing Reforms to Issues that Count*, eds. T. Sergiovanni and J. Moore. Boston, Mass.: Allyn & Bacon.

Ravitch, D. 1985. *The Schools We Deserve*. New York: Basic Books.

Ravitch, D., and R. Finn. 1987. *What Do Our 17-year-olds Know?* Boston, Mass.: Houghton-Mifflin.

Rudinow, J. 1990. Channel One whittles away at education. *Educational Leadership* December/January. 74–77.

Yager, R. E. 1988. Keying instruction to current events bring life to the classroom. *American School Board Journal* December, 175. 37–45.

3

Channel One: Reactions of Students, Teachers, and Parents

In the flurry of activity surrounding contractual agreements and installation of equipment to support the Channel One news broadcast, many people have neglected to ask critical questions concerning the implementation of this innovative educational program. The program is designed to be used as a complete, twelve-minute broadcast, but the literature on educational media contains ample evidence showing that teachers frequently use only specified parts of media products rather than entire sequences as they are packaged (Cambre 1987). Furthermore, past experience demonstrates that rushing to place technology in schools without adequate planning can lead to failure of an innovation (Cuban, 1986; Fullan and Pomfret, 1977; Goodlad, 1975; Knupfer, 1988; Rogers, 1983). As with any other educational tool, the success of Channel One will not rest solely within the product itself but will depend upon how it is received by the key people who use it and the way in which it is implemented.

It follows, then, that some key questions must be addressed, such as:

• Does Channel One offer a product that is worthwhile?
• Is it answering a need in the curriculum?
• How do the schools implement the twelve-minute news show?

• What are teachers doing to reinforce the news teaching and to teach critical viewing of advertisements?

In order to determine the answers to these questions, it is important to investigate how the decision to implement Channel One was made; how the program is being utilized within schools; and what the parents, teachers, and students think of it. The purpose of this study was to examine those three areas: initial decision making; implementation strategies; and the reactions of students, teachers, and parents to the broadcast both initially and after their experience with the program.

Following statewide telephone interviews with school superintendents, a survey of a sampling of students, teachers, and parents in three school districts gathered information about their reactions to Channel One as well their habits concerning news consumerism.

These groups were surveyed twice—once at the beginning of their experience with Channel One, and again at the end of the school year to see if their opinions about the broadcast or their news-related activities changed after experience with the program. Spot checks were done in the form of interviews and classroom observations to see how the broadcast was being implemented and if it had any effect on students' interest in the news.

RESEARCH QUESTIONS

1. Were decisions to adopt Channel One based on curriculum support?
2. Were decisions to adopt Channel One based on opportunism?
3. Who made the decision to adopt Channel One?
4. What factors most influenced the decision to adopt Channel One?
5. How has the broadcast time been accommodated within the schedule of the school day?
6. How are teachers implementing the content of Channel One?
7. What are the opinions of teachers, students, and parents upon initial introduction to Channel One and after experience with the program?
8. Do senior high school students react any differently to Channel One than do junior high students?
9. Is there a relationship between Channel One viewing and news consumerism among students and teachers?

TABLE 3.1. Demographics

	Teachers	Students	Parents
Round One			
Junior High	275	1,105	58
High School	306	1,322	82
TOTAL	581	2,427	140
Round Two			
Junior High	272	1,118	316
Senior High	301	1,339	336
TOTAL	573	2,457	652

METHODOLOGY

Subjects

All superintendents in a southwestern state were interviewed. Once the recipient school districts were identified, a sample of three districts was selected to receive a written survey. In each of the selected districts, the decision to use Channel One was made on a school-by-school basis, so not all schools within any given district received the broadcast. For this study, every school that received Channel One within the three chosen districts was surveyed. This included eight high schools and seven junior high schools.

In total, the subjects for this study included 113 superintendents, 581 teachers, 2,457 students, and 652 parents from the junior and senior high schools within the three chosen school districts. The subjects were selected randomly within each school. Forty teachers and six classrooms of students at each school received written survey instruments. Numerous classroom observations were conducted, and several spontaneous, informal interviews were conducted as the situation allowed.

Materials and Method

One survey instrument was developed for telephone interviews with school-district superintendents. This method was chosen to expedite data collection and ensure the most complete set of information. The telephone survey contained open-ended questions that called for short responses.

In addition, three sets of written survey instruments were developed for use respectively with teachers, students, and parents.

Each written instrument contained questions that were measured on a five-point, Likert-type scale as well as open-ended questions intended to draw out more information.

Teachers, students, and parents were surveyed twice—once, after two weeks of experience with the Channel One broadcast; and again, at the end of the school year. Each set of survey instruments for the parents and students remained identical between the initial and end-of-year experience. However, teachers received written surveys that contained slight differences between the initial and end-of-year forms. A few questions were modified to reflect a shift from inexperience to experience with Channel One. Specifically, the end-of-year survey asked teachers to describe their experience with certain aspects of Channel One and queried them as to whether the advertisements had caused any problems or concerns.

Cooperation of the administration was secured to provide for smooth distribution and collection of survey instruments. It was hoped that this strategy would help to provide the best return rate.

Surveys were distributed to school principals who, in turn, requested cooperation of teachers in gathering the data. Student surveys were distributed to entire classes of students and were collected immediately upon completion. In addition to completing a written survey instrument, student subjects were asked to take a survey instrument home for their parents to complete. Return rates were 100 percent for students, about 95 percent for teachers, and about 25 percent for parents in both rounds.

Numerous surprise visits were made to classrooms in order to observe the implementation of Channel One. Two or three classrooms were observed every week and field notes were maintained. As situations allowed, spontaneous interviews were conducted with the students. Interviews also were conducted with several teachers, support staff, and administrators throughout the course of the school year.

Analysis

Quantitative data analysis was conducted with summary statistics. These allowed accurate comparisons to be made between groups and visually diagrammed for presentation. Information collected by observation and interview was analyzed qualitatively.

RESULTS

Early in the decision-making process, Channel One personnel contacted and offered the broadcast to 78 percent of the public-school superintendents within the state. In one case, the decision to adopt Channel One was made solely by a superintendent. Forty-six percent of superintendents made the decision with their school boards, 35 percent involved individual school principals along with the board, and 19 percent remained undecided. In cases of principal involvement, those key decision makers varied greatly in allowing teachers a voice in making the decision.

Thirty-nine percent of superintendents cited educational value, curriculum enhancement, or a solution to geographic isolation as a key factor that influenced the decision to try Channel One. However, 57 percent cited the opportunity to get equipment during times of little money as the most influential factor in contracting for the broadcast.

Initial Complications

Complications always seem to plague a certain percentage of otherwise good intentions, especially when large numbers of people are involved. About one-forth of the superintendents claimed that complications arose from contractual obligations or disagreements, installation problems, or lack of commitment of from Channel One employees in getting the school ready to receive the broadcast. Forty-three percent claimed that complications arose from teacher or community reaction to the commercial advertisements, using the students as a captive audience, or other negative publicity in the local community.

Within the three districts that were closely studied, installation problems seemed to be largely the result of poor planning on the part of Chris Whittle's staff. For example, local contractors were sent across country to make installations, while local installations were made by contract teams sent in from long distances away. This caused a breakdown in communication and, what appeared to be, a lack of commitment from installation teams. For school district personnel, trying to get things straightened out consumed enormous amounts of time and energy.

Schools were also wired improperly. Specific rooms were designated by principals, but instructions were often ignored, and other rooms were wired instead. Further problems resulted because installation teams did not bother to investigate local construction codes and social climates.

For example, building codes required that all cables be buried, but Whittle's crew were instructed to string the cables aboveground. Loose cabling was hung down the sides of buildings without being encased in conduits, thus creating a challenge for vandals who repeatedly attacked the wires. Satellite dishes were placed on flat schoolhouse roofs without being secured. Although students were not supposed to go onto roofs, teenagers commonly roller skated on roofs of single-story school buildings and tended to move satellite dishes. A misaligned dish would then cause the broadcast to come in as static image and noise until someone climbed up on the roof to realign it. This problem continued throughout the entire first year of the broadcast. It was resolved at some schools, but not at others.

Each of the three school districts had agreed on an installation schedule for individual schools and had planned class schedules around the expectation of having Channel One operational. In all three of the districts, individual school schedules were ignored, and contractors installed equipment according to their own plans.

Television monitors were hung so high that teachers complained of not being able to reach the on/off switches or volume controls. In one case, a special-needs classroom lacked a sufficient number of students needed to qualify for a monitor from Whittle Communications. When pressed by the teacher, the principal negotiated to have a monitor installed, only to find that the installation team would not honor the agreement. The teacher threatened a discrimination lawsuit within the school district for unfair allocation of educational opportunity. This led to an uproar of bad feelings among faculty members.

Each district received a few telephone calls from irate parents who complained about specific content matter of the broadcasts. The parents' complaints focused on the mature subject matter or sexual innuendo associated with specific items. For example, one parent complained about an advertisement for a movie that was clearly not meant for junior-high-school-aged students, while another parent complained about a sequence on dating. In all cases, parents were told that school-district personnel would communicate the complaints to Whittle Communications.

Implementing the Broadcast

The twelve minutes of time needed for Channel One was handled in various ways, but all schools tried to implement the program in a way that did not subtract time from existing subjects. One district added twelve minutes to the school day for each school that used Channel One. The other two districts provided the twelve minutes through a combination of shortening passing time between classes, shortening lunch period, or using homeroom time for the Channel One broadcast.

In some way, each school planning to receive the broadcast rearranged their schedule to accommodate the twelve-minute time slot. Imagine the irritation that developed as certain school installations were delayed, and teachers had to find ways to use the twelve minutes. This would have been a minor problem if teachers had received clear messages about what to expect so that they could plan accordingly. Instead, some schools repeatedly received word of last minute delays, which caused frustrations to the point that some teachers tried to reverse the agreement and bar Channel One from entering their school.

Numerous observations throughout the school year revealed that, in general, teachers had little investment and did not seem concerned about making a serious effort to implement the broadcast in a meaningful way. Those teachers who were involved in the decision to adopt Channel One seemed to be making a better effort than were those who were not consulted prior to implementation. In some schools, the staff believed that the real value of Channel One was not in learning about the news, but instead was related to an outgrowth of activities attributed to the Channel One broadcast.

For example, several schools used the system for school announcements. One school started its own within-school news program, and another one extended that idea beyond the school to support community events.

Four of the schools planned to offer courses in video newsroom production that would carry English credit. This sounded like a good idea initially, but it quickly became complicated as parties involved began to sort out the logistics of such course offerings. The most obvious implication was the need for large sums of money to build and furnish studios and editing bays. When balanced against the initial impression that Channel One provided something for little cost, it soon became obvious that the outgrowth of activities would come at a very high cost and, thus, be available only to wealthier school districts.

For one reason or another, additional duties associated with Channel One seemed to fall most heavily upon the media-center director at each school and media coordinator within the district. Staff who served in that capacity expressed genuine enthusiasm for helping with extra activities, but also emphasized the need for additional assistance because they could not imagine keeping up with the hectic pace of increased demands beyond the current school year.

A close look at classroom activities revealed that teachers generally turned the broadcast on and off without benefit of introductory preparation or follow-up discussions. Although many teachers claimed to engage students in active discussion, observations revealed that the broadcast was very rarely discussed. Instead, one of two things usually occurred. Either teachers pressed on with regular activities of the day, or students were allowed a few minutes of free time prior to passing through the hallway to their next class. Indeed, when asked what usually happened immediately following broadcasts, the written student survey revealed that nearly all of the students (96 percent initially, 98 percent toward year's end) either moved on to the lesson at hand or switched classes.

Observations of teachers' activities during broadcasts revealed that teachers rarely paid attention to the entire twelve-minute sequence. Typically, teachers attended to work at their desks and appeared to notice only a few minutes of the broadcast. Two media-center directors claimed that teachers liked Channel One because it was "flashy" and it provided a "babysitting service" which gave them a few extra minutes to catch up on routine paperwork.

Opinions of Teachers, Students, and Parents

Because the success of any educational innovation hinges upon its acceptance by key individuals involved with its implementation, opinions of teachers, students, and parents are critical in early stages of the broadcast. This section reports the reactions of those key individuals upon initial experience with Channel One and, then again, toward the end of the school year. The subject matter is categorized into questions concerning Channel One's ability to teach and treat topics in a stimulating manner, general opinions about advertisements, patterns of news consumerism, and thoughts about whether Channel One should be continued.

Numerical values are based on a five-point Likert-type scale, with one indicating strong disagreement and five indicating strong agreement. Scores reported in the graphs include the percentage of those subjects who agreed or strongly agreed with a particular statement.

Figures 3.1, 3.2, 3.3, and 3.4 include data about Channel One's perceived ability to teach. The first three tables indicate the opinions of teachers, students, and parents, while figure 3.4 breaks down students' opinions by junior- and senior-high-school levels.

It is evident from the graphics that, initially, about 70 percent of teachers and 50 percent of students agreed that Channel One is easier to understand than other television news broadcasts. Each of those

FIGURE 3.1 Easier to Understand Than Other TV News

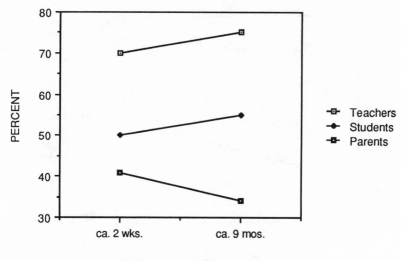

DEGREE OF EXPERIENCE

FIGURE 3.2 Teaches Current Events Very Well

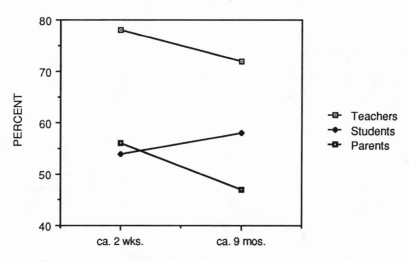

DEGREE OF EXPERIENCE

percentages increased by approximately 5 percent after experience with the program (see figure 3.1). Parents had a lower initial opinion than did teachers and students, and the parents' opinion about the broadcast dropped during the course of the school year.

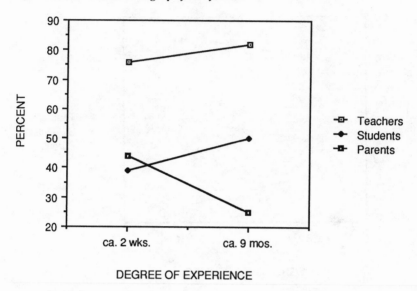

FIGURE 3.3 Teaches Geography Very Well

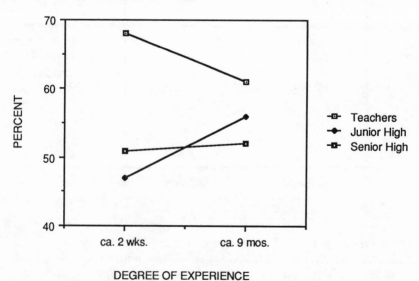

FIGURE 3.4 Students Learn Much

Some of Whittle Communications' strongest claims about the value of Channel One viewing revolve around its ability to teach current events, cultural literacy, and geography. The percentage of teachers and parents who agreed or strongly agreed that Channel One teaches current events very well dropped after experience, while the percentage of students' agreement increased (see figure 3.2).

The percentage of teachers and students who agreed that Channel One teaches geography very well ran a parallel increase during the school year, while parents showed an opposite pattern (see figure 3.3). For these questions, teachers were obviously more positive than either students or parents.

Figure 3.4 shows an overall teacher opinion along with student opinions that are broken down by junior- or senior-high-school level. The statement here is that students learn a lot from Channel One. Approximately 68 percent of teachers agreed with that statement initially. However, that rating fell to 61 percent after more experience with the program. The pattern of agreement among junior-high students jumped about 10 percentage points during the year, while senior-high students maintained their percentage of agreement around the 50 percentile rank.

In sum, teachers were most optimistic while parents were least optimistic about Channel One's value. Further, while parental optimism decreased during the school year, teachers' optimism fluctuated, and students' optimism became more positive within the junior high but remained about the same within the senior high. Students never reached the level of enthusiasm expressed by the teachers.

When polled about the complexity of broadcasts as a teaching tool, around 10 percent of teachers agreed that students seemed bored, or that Channel One is too simple (see figures 3.5 and 3.6).

A higher percentage of senior-high than junior-high students agreed with these statements. When asked a nearly opposite question about whether Channel One is too complex to be covered within such a short broadcast time, approximately 10 percent of teachers agreed, while a higher percentage of students agreed (see figure 3.7). Initially, more junior-high than senior-high students believed that broadcasts were too complex for the time slot. However, those figures nearly evened out by the end of the year.

There is quite a difference between student and adult agreement concerning Channel One's ability to stimulate thinking about the news. Initially, the percentage of students who agreed was nearly twice that of parents and teachers. Although teacher opinion remained about the same throughout the year, there was a small

FIGURE 3.5 Students Seem Bored

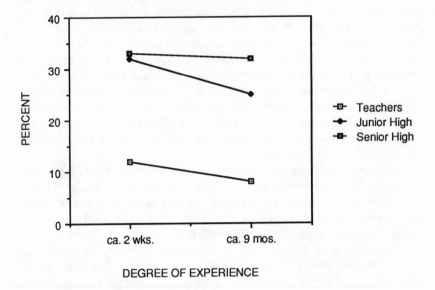

DEGREE OF EXPERIENCE

FIGURE 3.6 Channel One Is Too Simple

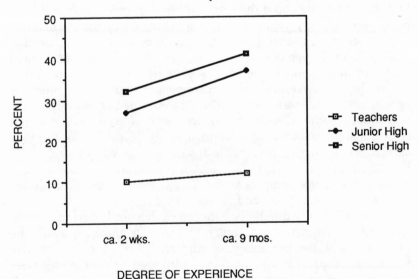

DEGREE OF EXPERIENCE

FIGURE 3.7 Channel One Is Too Complex for the Short Broadcast Time

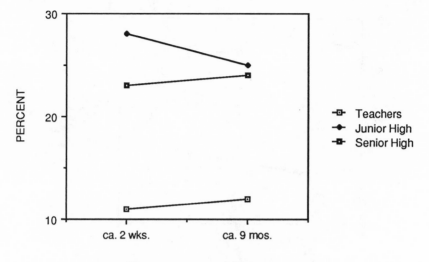

decrease in agreement among students and a small increase among parents (see figure 3.8).

This next section is about the advertisements. Figure 3.9 measures the perceived level at which advertisements are actively discussed with students for reasons of critical consumerism.

Students and teachers were asked about classroom discussions while parents were queried about discussions outside of the school setting. Fewer students than teachers perceived active discussions of advertisements in school, while parents jumped from 70 percent to nearly 100 percent at the end of the year. The adults seem to perceive that more attention is being paid to the ads at the end of the school year, while students followed a slightly opposite path.

Figure 3.10 displays the percentage of people who are not convinced that exposure to Channel One in school translates into learning about critical consumerism.

A higher percentage of both students and teachers agreed with this at the beginning of the school year than did at the end. In general, as teachers and students gained experience with Channel One, they were less inclined to believe that it teaches critical consumerism.

Figure 3.11 reflects the percentage of people who believe that the ads have too much influence on students.

Less than 50 percent of teachers, students, or parents agreed at either survey time that the ads have too much influence, but the

FIGURE 3.8 Encourages Thinking about the News

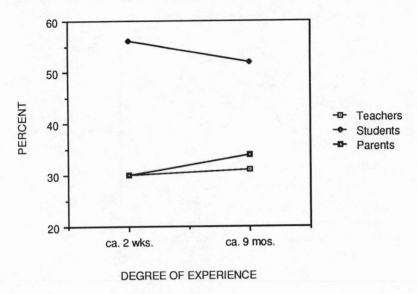

FIGURE 3.9 We Discuss Advertisements

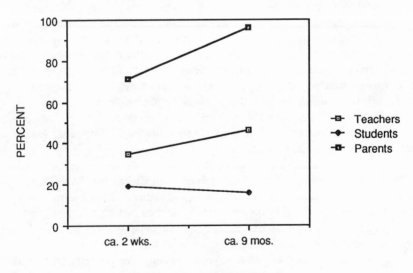

FIGURE 3.10 Not Convinced It Teaches Critical Consumerism

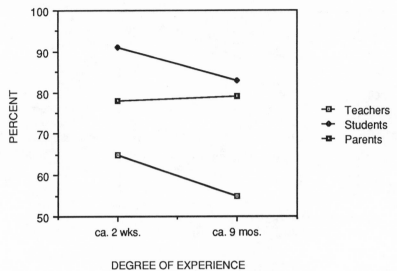

FIGURE 3.11 Ads Have Too Much Influence

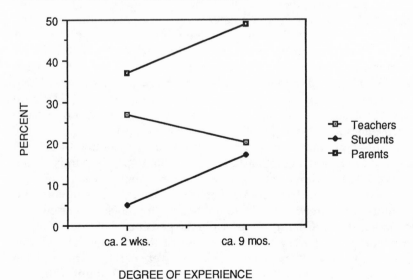

FIGURE 3.12 Ads Are the Same As Those on TV

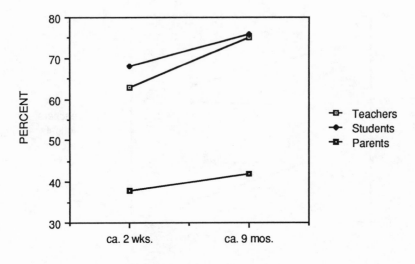

DEGREE OF EXPERIENCE

percentage of parents and students who agreed with this statement increased as the school year progressed.

The next two queries about advertisements raise the questions of whether the ads are the same as those on television as seen at home, and whether the ads are pretty truthful about the products. Figure 3.12 shows that, after living with Channel One ads over the course of the school year, a greater percentage of teachers, students, and parents agreed that the ads were the same as those viewed at home. Even though opinions did not fluctuate very much from the beginning to the end of the year, approximately 40 percent of teachers, 30 percent of students, and 15 percent of parents believed that advertisements are pretty truthful about the products (see figure 3.13). It is curious that teachers seem to be less skeptical of the advertisements than are the other two consumer groups.

In an attempt to measure the dichotomy of whether or not ads belong in schools, figures 3.14 and 3.15 take opposite stands, while figure 3.16 is meant to confirm the opinion of figure 3.15.

First, figure 3.14 reveals that the percentage of students and parents who agreed that ads do not belong in schools increased after experience with Channel One, while the percentage of teacher agreement dropped. A very small percentage of students agreed with this statement, while the most vocal objectors were parents. The opposite statement in figure 3.15 confirms this pattern of thought. Students

FIGURE 3.13 Ads Are Pretty Truthful

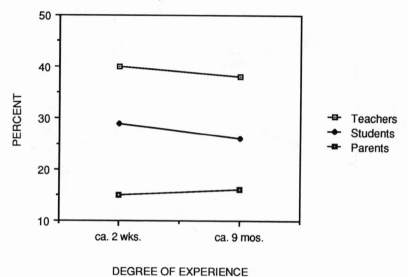

FIGURE 3.14 Ads Do Not Belong in School

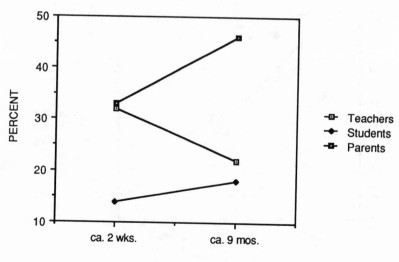

FIGURE 3.15 There Is Nothing Wrong with Ads in School

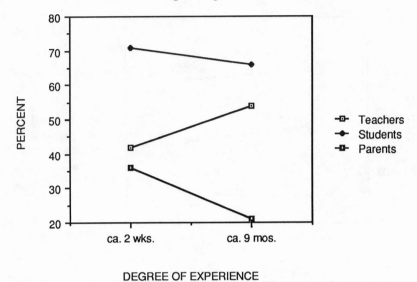

DEGREE OF EXPERIENCE

FIGURE 3.16 Ads in School Are OK

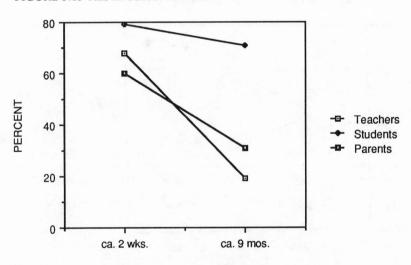

DEGREE OF EXPERIENCE

FIGURE 3.17 Causes Students to Read More News Magazines

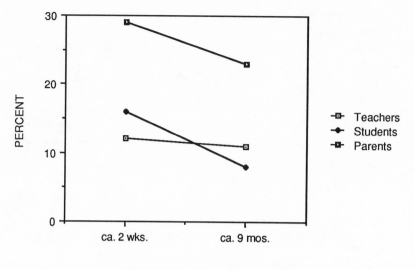

DEGREE OF EXPERIENCE

were likely to agree that there is nothing wrong with ads in school, while parents disagreed, and teachers floated around the midpoint. A higher percentage of people in all of the groups agreed at the beginning of the school year than at the end that ads in school are okay (see figure 3.16). Something happened during the course of the year to modify their initial opinion.

One possible side effect of viewing Channel One could be an increased interest in news consumerism. Figure 3.17 reveals that, at the end of the year, a lower percentage teachers, students, and parents believed that Channel One causes students to read more news magazines.

Figures 3.18, 3.19, and 3.20 report consumer behavior rather than consumer beliefs. Teachers, students, and parents were asked how many times per week they read news magazines and newspapers, and watched television news. Each question then tallied the percentage of people who engaged in this behavior at least three times weekly.

Figure 3.18 reveals an end-of-year increase in the percentage of parents and students who read news magazines three times weekly, while it reflects a decrease in teacher involvement. Figure 3.19 shows quite a split between students and adults in newspaper reading. Despite the split, the percentage of students and parents who read

FIGURE 3.18 Reads News Magazines at Least Three Times Weekly

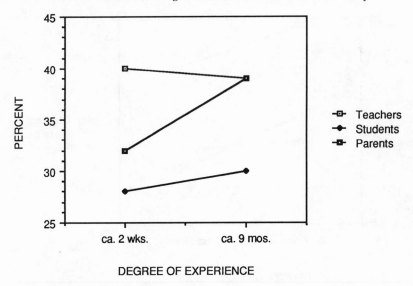

FIGURE 3.19 Reads Newspaper at Least Three Times Weekly

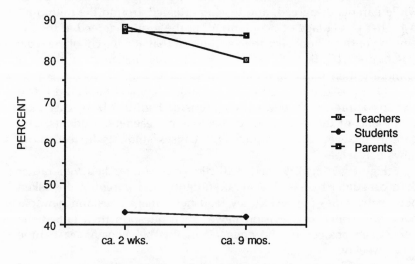

newspapers at least three times weekly remained relatively stable, while the percentage of teachers engaged in this activity fell about 8 percentage points on the end-of-year survey. Also, increased percentages of parents and students viewed television news at least

FIGURE 3.20 Watches News at Least Three Times per Week

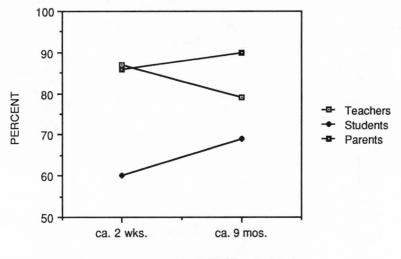

DEGREE OF EXPERIENCE

three times weekly, while the percentage of teachers dropped as the school year progressed (see figure 3.20).

The remainder of the figures treat overall response to Channel One. Figure 3.21 reveals that a larger percentage of teachers than students or parents agreed or strongly agreed that Channel One is a very good, quality teaching tool. In addition, teachers showed increased support, while the percentage of support among students and parents decreased during the school year. In general, approximately 80 percent of teachers believed in the quality of the broadcast, while only 50 percent of the students did so.

A large percentage of teachers liked the broadcasts, while a smaller percentage of students liked it (see figure 3.22).

A breakdown of students reveals that more senior-high than junior-high students liked Channel One very much.

A comparison of groups shows that teachers were most enthusiastic about continuing Channel One. They were followed by students, and then parents (see figure 3.23).

The adults lost some enthusiasm during the school year, while students picked up some interest. A breakdown of students shows a higher percentage of support from senior-high than junior-high school students, but senior-high interest decreased as the year progressed while junior-high interest increased (see figure 3.24).

Indeed, senior-high students made several verbal comments toward the end of the year about the program being geared to "babies."

FIGURE 3.21 Very Good Quality Teaching Tool

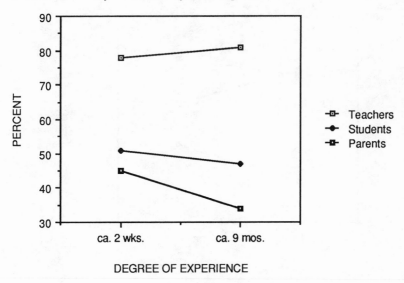

FIGURE 3.22 I Like Channel One Very Much

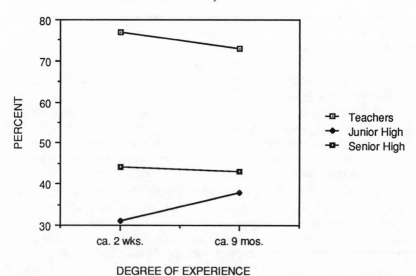

FIGURE 3.23 School Should Continue Channel One

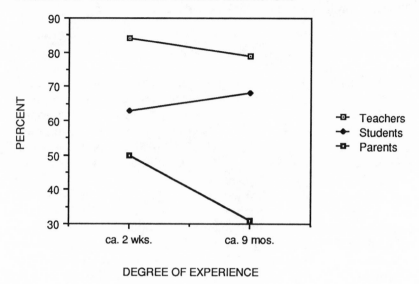

FIGURE 3.24 Should Continue Channel One

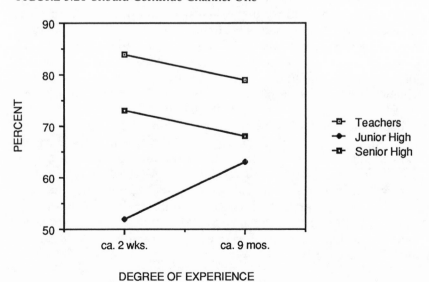

Perhaps they would not have felt this way had they not known that the junior-high students received the exact same broadcast.

CONCLUSIONS

The decision to adopt Channel One was based on opportunism rather than on curricular content or specific curricular need. Schools were interested in receiving something at a low cost, and personnel were especially excited about the possibility of receiving equipment and cabling. In some cases, teachers were disappointed because equipment configuration prevented them from doing the types of activities that they had envisioned.

Despite initial complications surrounding installation of wiring and equipment, teachers seem to like the broadcasts. Their positive response appears to be related to the high-production value of Channel One, and to their belief that it might improve knowledge of current events and geography. A good share of teachers claimed that Channel One itself is not great, but the resulting enthusiasm for related activities arising from exposure to Channel One makes time devoted to it worthwhile.

In most cases, Channel One was implemented as a stand-alone topic rather than in accordance with curricular goals. There appeared to be little class time devoted to preparing students for the broadcasts nor for discussions following the programs. Students' attention to and involvement with reading newspapers did not seem to increase over the course of the school year and, when they did read newspapers, they reported an interest in sports, comics, and leisure sections. A larger percentage of students read news magazines toward the end of the school year, but they did not perceive Channel One to have influenced that increase of activity. Increased numbers of students watched television news more frequently toward the end of the school year, but teachers experienced a drop off.

Although teachers' organizations at the national level have opposed Channel One, teachers at the local level support continuation of the broadcast. Because this local-level support does not seem to emerge from any evidence about curricular gains, one must ask whether teachers are taking the time to think critically about the educational value of the programs. Shallow implementation strategies revealed in this study suggest that teachers' motives for liking the broadcast are suspect.

Informal, spontaneous interviews with students after they had some experience with Channel One revealed more enthusiasm for the program at junior-high levels than at senior-high-school levels. The survey data do not confirm this, but they do show a trend in this direction. It is possible that senior-high students liked the broadcast more than they were willing to verbally admit among their peers. To do so might be considered as "uncool." Teachers had a more favorable assessment of broadcasts than did students or parents.

Parents had several opportunities to view broadcasts. A minority of parents responded to the survey, and a favorable number of those who did respond indicated a lack of substantial knowledge about the program. This lack of knowledge probably influenced parental response rates as well as the types of responses which parents gave. More parents responded to the second round of the survey. This suggests that more parents became aware of Channel One or developed an increased interest in following its activity during the school year. Whatever the reason for attentiveness, parents objected more strongly to advertisements as the school year progressed.

After several months of experience with the program, teachers and high-school students seemed to lose some interest in Channel One, while junior-high students gained enthusiasm for the broadcasts during the school year. A clear majority of all groups agreed that their school should continue to receive the program.

Research should continue to follow implementation strategies and opinions of key people involved with the broadcasts. In addition, effectiveness of programming should be followed closely to determine whether Channel One is effective as a teaching tool. One would hope that Channel One will be compared to other similar teaching resources. Further, social effects of implementing the broadcast were evident in this study, and they are bound to emerge in different ways as Channel One continues. These social effects should be closely monitored and evaluated.

REFERENCES

Cambre, M. 1987. A reappraisal of instructional television. Syracuse, N.Y.: ERIC Clearinghouse on Information Resources, Syracuse University.

Cuban, L. 1986. *Teachers and Machines: The Classroom Use of Technology since 1920.* New York: Teacher's College Press.

Fullan, M., and A. Pomfret. 1977. Research on curriculum and instruction implementation. *Review of Educational Research,* 47:1. 335–397.

Goodlad, J. 1975. *The Dynamics of Educational Change.* Toronto: McGraw Hill.

Knupfer, N. N. 1988. Teachers' beliefs about instructional computing: Implications for instructional designers. *Journal of Instructional Development* 11:4. 29–38.

Rogers, E. M. 1983. *Diffusion of Innovations,* 3d ed. New York: The Free Press.

JOHN C. BELLAND

4

Is This the News?

Channel One, the Whittle Communications classroom news service, has been the subject of much controversy. Most of the debate over this controversy has generated more heat than light. Whether the following analysis of the discourse in one week of Channel One programming will shed any light on the nature and significance of this communications phenomenon will depend on many things— who you, the readers, are; what types of new pressures the current governmental climate is placing on schools; what alternative news services are or will be provided to schools; what new possibilities the technological bounty provides; and many other factors. I hope, however, that this detailed look at the information communicated during a week of Channel One broadcasts will encourage thought-ful reflection on the impact of this recent commercial excursion into the classroom.

I will return to the substance and aesthetics of the commercial messages in the process of the analysis, but let me first remind you that commercialism in the classroom is not new. Teachers have turned to commercially sponsored materials for at least the past fifty years.[1] Catalogs of "free and inexpensive materials" really could have been called, "Catalogs of commercially sponsored materials." These films, filmstrips, booklets, charts, and the like bore commer-cial messages and often slanted the information contained in them to encourage the purchase of commercial products. Sometimes, these commercial messages could be viewed to be benign to both the learner and the society,[2] but most of the messages—such as those about infant nutrition which promoted the use of commercially prepared infant formula—had deleterious effects on people, society, and the environment, while they probably made the sponsors of the materials additional profit.

In so far as Channel One broadcasts are viewed by students as just more commercial television programming, I could also claim that Channel One commercialism is less likely to produce ill effects than those of the materials previously described. Channel One commercials are creatively produced, youth-product-oriented messages, some of which have been also used at later times during the breaks between cartoons or other "youth programming" on the commercial networks. However, Channel One is a loud voice in the privatization of information which, in itself, is a manifestation of the "collapse of the public sphere in the United States" (Jansen 1991, 8). If free access to information is the cornerstone of democracy, we might be a bit worried that 98 percent of cities in the United States have only one newspaper, fewer then twenty companies conduct the overwhelming majority of the magazine business, eleven companies account for most of the sales in the book industry, and three companies dominate broadcast television news (Jansen 1991). Under this concentration of communications resources, communications and education become basic industries, similar to steel and transportation. In such an environment, "access to control over the production and distribution of knowledge becomes potential . . . for social conflict" (Jansen 1991, 8).

By examining the communications discourse in Channel One— the news, the features, and the commercials—we can see how these contribute to the phenomenon of Channel One. Then, we can estimate whether this phenomenon is a major step in the privatization of information.

SELECTION OF PROGRAMS TO ANALYZE

Channel One programming is prepared in weekly cycles. In fact, the feature stories each day are sections of the theme for the whole week. On the other hand, the news stories for each day are determined by Whittle Communications' editorial view of what are the important and current world events. These are treated independently on a day-to-day basis. In any event, I believed that it would be appropriate to analyze Channel One only in weekly units. I viewed many weeks of programs, finally obtaining tapes of three weeks of broadcasts from spring 1991. From these, I attempted to pick a "typical" week, that is: (1) a week which did not involve cataclysmic world events, and (2) programming which used "standard" production techniques for Channel One. In addition, I decided to select a week in which one of the feature stories involved material with which I had some expertise—technology. In other words, I was not trying to focus on the bizarre, the unusual, or the abhorrent. Rather, I wanted to look at Channel One as it is presented to students day-in-day-out and week-in-week-out. Whether I have accomplished this, others will have to judge.[3] Television scripts traditionally present the audio on the left and the video on the right. Because we read from left to right, I decided to take up matters related to the audio first, even though I am personally more interested in the pictures.

THE AUDIO

The News

Each daily segment of Channel One opens with a "teaser"—a couple of statements providing a preview of the feature stories to be presented later in the broadcast. This is followed by a few seconds with no spoken language while the animated logo is shown.

The lead story. The anchorperson delivering the news stories introduces herself or himself—"I'm. . ."—and begins the lead story with "Leading the news. . ." The lead story is usually the longest story on each day with text ranging from a high of just over 175 words to a low of less than 50 words. The style of each lead story is journalistic. Each one begins with a statement which could be described as a headline or a lead sentence or some combination of the two as listed below:

MONDAY "U.S. Marines take on a new noncombat role, joining the relief efforts for cyclone victims in Bangladesh."

TUESDAY "A South African judge finds Winnie Mandella guilty of kidnapping."

WEDNESDAY "President braces for battle over his controversial nominee to head the Central Intelligence Agency (CIA)."

THURSDAY "A historical political development involving one of America's closest allies."

FRIDAY "A historic day on Capitol Hill, as the Queen of England addresses our nation's congress."

Each of these statements is different in style and communicates varying amounts of information. Most of them are more wordy than desirable for a print headline and far too wordy for a typical TV news sound bite. On the other hand, they seldom provide the characteristics of a lead sentence (who?, what?, where?, when?, why?). If capturing and holding the attention of adolescents is really the purpose of Channel One, it is curious that news stories begin with weak statements which might receive Ds or Fs in a beginning journalism class. In addition, these statements are spoken while the video displays the anchor rather than any video from the event which might serve to depict the information and grab attention.

Returning to variation on the form, style, and quality of the lead statements on different stories, I couldn't help but wonder whether the editorial staff had developed any standards for the text of the news. Some of the variation may be provided by editing and other input of the anchorpersons who alternated on news presentations each day. However, the Tuesday and Thursday statements delivered by the male anchor are both the most and least informative among them. In addition, the use of the grammatical pattern "a historic. . ." on successive days suggests that copy is written under the guidance of some policy on usage.

The body. The body of each news story varied from what I would estimate to be one short paragraph of information to a maximum of three paragraphs.[5] Most of the stories provided background information about locations and names of important persons involved in the story. The information is presented in digest form consisting of a series of generalizations with an occasional short quote from a major person in the story.[6]

In general the news vocabulary was unremarkable. There was no obvious attempt to oversimplify the words chosen, nor was there a large number of words which would be difficult for or unrecognizable by students in middle or high schools. Words such as *contingent* or *paramilitary*, which might have been considered as difficult before the Persian Gulf War, were probably familiar to students by the time these broadcasts aired.

Perhaps the most notable feature of Channel One news is that it rarely takes up half of the broadcast time, and, thus, communicates little more than headlines. No story that I examined would be accepted as satisfactory work from a high-school student in a standard English or journalism class.

I raised the question: "Did the text express the essence of the story?" A full analysis of this question goes beyond the scope of this critique, because it would require the analysis of documents as well as stories and analyses in both print and electronic media. However, I believe it is safe to say that no story presented more than a cursory snippet about any event. This may not be any worse than the practice of commercial news broadcasts in some cities which purport to present "The World in a Minute," but if teachers use such material, I hope they use it to encourage problemitization and critique, not as content.

Here is an example of a complete news story from the week of Channel One broadcasts which I analyzed.

> Finally, Britain's Queen Elizabeth arrived in Washington Tuesday. During a twelve-day stay in the U.S., the Queen will address Congress, attend a baseball game, and possibly bestow honorary knighthood on former Desert Storm commander, General Norman Schwartzkopf.
>
> Early in World War II, then 14-year-old Princess Elizabeth used a radio address to calm young people's fear. [Cut to actual World War II recording of Princess Elizabeth's voice with black and white photo.] "We know, every one of us, that, in the end, all will be well."

This story was broadcast on Wednesday and, obviously, was taped before the Queen made her address in which she was hidden from the view of television audiences by the height of the lectern and the microphones on it. There was nothing presented which reflected the uniqueness of the Queen's making that speech to Congress, and attaching material from World War II does not seem logical. I suppose Channel One writers were searching for something to relate the Queen to youth, but if an editor were hoping for unity in a story, those hopes were not fulfilled.

Information presented in these news stories was generally from a conservative point of view. The overriding tone was that governmental justice must prevail, and that youth should (perhaps even unquestioningly) obey the adult authorities. In addition, the news stories were presented as if the information in the stories had achieved closure. There was no indication that matters presented were subject to further exploration, study, or analysis. Finally, there seemed to be no sense of humor in the reporting. Adults did not have to laugh at themselves to survive doing things which were silly or immature. I submit that all of these qualities make the texts of Channel One news classic instruments of information capitalism.[7]

The Features

Feature stories during the week of programs which I analyzed focused on technology and continuing episodes in an "Around-the-World Field Trip." I was curious about what aspects of technology would be examined and what values would be either stated or implied about this topic. In a vague way, the lead sentence summarizes well the approach of Channel One to technology, "If you think that high tech can't get much higher, think again." Part of the second sentence continues, ". . . how it's [technology is] making our lives safer, more efficient, and more fun. . . ."

The first story concerned technology in music as represented by three short segments from work in the Media Lab at the Massachusetts Institute of Technology. The pattern of this story and other technology feature stories was that the anchors began with two paragraphs of general narrative followed by an explanation from an MIT student. The anchors and two more students alternated to complete the story. Topics were the computer design of "new musical instruments" and computer improvisation of music. A segment on technology jobs focused on acoustics research. The MIT student from the first feature segment ended this story by stating, "You have to like music. You have to like toys. You have to like solving problems, making things work."

In this story, there was no information communicated about the struggle which contemporary musicians—both composers and performers—have with just what is the nature of music. Is music still organized sound, or is music sound which is simply bounded in time? Issues relating to the interrelationship of technology and skill—which could be explored very powerfully in the context of technology in music—were not even hinted at. Technology in music was presented as the development of some new toys to play with—the "gee whiz" syndrome.

The second story concerned developments in high-definition television. Most of this story focused on the process of regulation and marketing for broadcast television. The ending of the story involves a very strange transition. After mentioning that U.S. consumer electronic sales in 1990 were more than $30 billion, the anchors say, "So there's a lot of money to be made in HDTV—or so people hope." They continue, "There's something very sexy to being involved in new technology." Then a new face appears saying, "We're the special-effects supervisors. . . ." This last portion talks about (and shows) a bit of what one can do when images are imported into computers and manipulated.

The third story concerned the U.S. space program; the fourth story returned to special effects, but this time for Hollywood movies; and the fifth story concerned the 911 telephone system and its interaction with paramedics. The 911 story did deal with ideas of technology involved in saving life, but, ironically, it featured human heroic acts required to use the technology. I suspect that most adolescents were already well-informed about 911 through the much more extensive stories presented on "Rescue 911" on prime-time commercial television.

Nowhere in this series of feature stories on technology were there any concerns expressed for the male-gendered hegemony or the ecological impacts of technology. Instead, they reflected the notion that technology is an exciting, always beneficial process which could take every person on something more exhilarating than a carnival ride. Every idea was communicated with the tone of "Isn't this marvelous?" High tech was the equivalent of high purpose and high spirit.[8]

Three other features were part of the "Around-the-World Fieldtrip." The stories concerned an archaeological dig on a Mediterranean island, elephant training in Thailand, and a king's burial site in Turkey. These stories followed standard travelogue conventions.

The final two features described two adolescent boys, one of whom has been publishing a small magazine about teen life. The other has developed virus detecting computer programs, one of which was used by U.S. Senate staffers. These vignettes provided each featured teen the opportunity to "show and tell" his project. The text of the narrative was about four paragraphs long—much longer than most of the news stories—and was very convincing to this middle-class adult. However, I could hear in my mind some adolescents I know saying sarcastically, "Oh sure!" as these teens were promoted as exemplars.

In general, I submit that the Channel One features are better produced than the news stories. These features share the same conservative value-orientation with the news stories, but include more factual detail and more direct expressions of the people featured in the stories. As such, they might be more appropriate as discussion starters or triggers for an investigation in the library. Perhaps Channel One would be a more appropriate service to schools and youth if it just broadcast features. Alternatively, it might do a better job with the news if it just did news and eliminated the features. Maybe doing ten minutes of news is too expensive for Whittle Communications. It is tempting to suggest that, rather than trying to do two jobs, an organization ought to try to do one job well. On the other hand, doing the news well in the Channel One format might be even worse than the present format.

The Commercials

In contrast to the other ten minutes of each Channel One broadcast, the two minutes of commercials place very little emphasis on text. Thus, they are more properly discussed below under video.

THE VIDEO

The News

Channel One begins with shots of inviting scenes from the stories to be presented, followed by a short, computer-generated "flying logo" sequence, and then a cut to the anchor presenting the first story. Video which depicts aspects of the story quickly replace the talking head. The video for some of the stories seems to be file footage which represents some general aspect of the locale for the story or some other similar event. Ordinarily, however, the video is at least as well-related to the story as that found on network television news.

On stories from locations which might be unfamiliar, very effective maps are used with an image zooming in on the particular area of focus in the story (see figure 4.1). Names of important people who also might be unfamiliar were superimposed over their images long enough to ensure recognition and to allow students to recognize the spelling of the names (see figure 4.2). The production quality of the story video and graphics was very high, and the assembly of anchor, video, and graphics was well-integrated into the program itself.

The news and features on Channel One are presented by two anchors—a young woman and a young man—who alternate for each story. They are dressed in teen clothes appropriate for youth in a middle-class predominantly white, suburban high school, even though they look considerably more mature (early 20s maybe?). The male anchor is black but with facial features more usually associated with whites. He has "Chicklet" teeth, a wide smile, and a conservative haircut (with every hair in place). The female anchor is white and also conservatively dressed. Her face is comely and expressive with the "standard" smile mitigated by slightly unevenly spaced teeth (refreshing, I think). The performance of these anchors was extremely well-polished, giving me the impression that retakes and editing

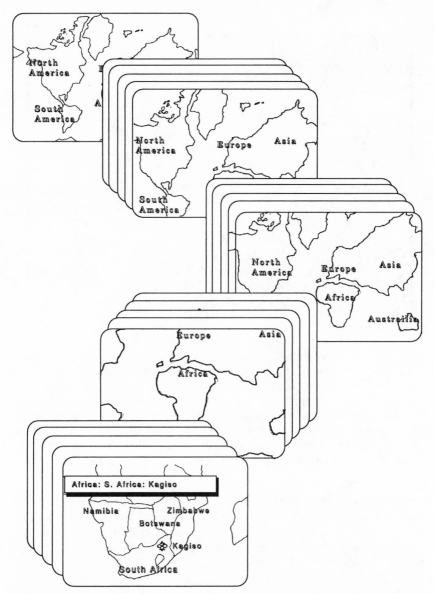

FIGURE 4.1 Effective Use of Zooming. Channel One provides an excellent use of media in its use of map zooms. It begins the zoom by displaying a map of the world and then zooms in to the particular part of the world which is the setting for the story. As the end of the zoom nears, the specific location is marked and labeled. The research of Gavriel Salomon and others suggests that the zoom is a powerful means to encourage the mental processes of relating parts to wholes, and that of singling out details.

FIGURE 4.2. Name Overlays and Image Composition. Channel One places the name of persons in the news and feature stories in the picture for a few seconds so that viewers can see the spelling of the name. This probably eliminates confusion for many viewers who might have read a name in the print media but can't relate it to the pronunciation. In this drawing, representing a frame from the feature story on archaeology, the male anchor is shown in a superior position in the upper left of the picture. This relationship of males to females was consistent throughout the week of programs I critiqued.

were probably used to ensure this. Thus, in contrast to the broadcasting of television news on the commercial networks in which the anchors work live, the Channel One production is probably taped in separate segments and assembled in postproduction.

The Features

The feature stories about technology presented males as the ones leading the way in technology. These males were young, well-scrubbed, and articulate. The video showed not only talking heads of them but also showed them doing something relevant to the topic.

As part of the field trip, the feature stories presented the anchors alternatively as visitors to the locales. In one story, the male anchor featured the work of a female archaeologist. The other stories in the week I analyzed overwhelmingly showed males in the key roles.

The production quality of the features was excellent, using a variety of camera angles and camera movements to maintain a high degree of visual interest. There was tight integration of the visual with the narration and plenty of close-ups that the viewers would be able to see important people, scenery, or activities clearly. One of the episodes reminded me of the style of *60 Minutes* segments, while others seemed unstereotyped in format.

The most prominent negative aspect of the features presented during the week I reviewed was that of the valorization of male roles. The only relief from the male dominance of featured roles was that of the archaeologist. Even in that sequence, the male anchor led the discourse with his questions and was shown in a physically superior position (See figure 4.2). Gender issues are far too important to be discussed in this brief paragraph. An adequate analysis of the gender phenomena on Channel One would probably require the analysis of a full season of material. However, the features included in the week I reviewed should alert educators to the possibility of more widespread imbalances.

The Commercials

Because of the production process used by the producers of Channel One, the commercials were seamlessly integrated into the flow of the program. Earlier examples of Channel One which I have seen did not have this quality. In fact a feature called the "Pop Quiz" surrounded the commercials for the first year. In several instances, I did not know whether I was viewing a commercial until the product itself appeared. I asked my own adolescent children to view the same programs to see if they would recognize the commercials from having seen them on commercial-open broadcasts, and they claimed that the commercials used in the Channel One segments I showed them had not yet appeared in the shows which they watch. I felt a bit embarrassed by being so completely fooled by the beginning of these commercials and angered by the way in which a sophisticated production technique was able to impose the commercial message.

The first group of commercials appear after the series of news stories. Because the number of news stories varies somewhat from day to day, the possibility of a commercial "sneaking up" on the viewers is great. What's more, in the context of a well-produced program, the commercials are still the most gorgeous production gems of all. The second group of commercials is placed between the main feature stories, but appear to be attached to the end of the first feature. I was often unable to tell at first whether the feature had ended or whether some additional feature information was coming. I did not check to see if this was an unusual problem, because the preceding features in the week I examined were about technology (including two segments on special effects).

The products advertised on one Channel One program were Gatorade, M&Ms, Trident, Right Guard, and Pepsi. All of these—as do all the other products I have seen advertised on Channel One—fit well in the mainstream of American popular consumer culture. Adolescents are probably already consumers of most of these products. Thus, many adults may view this commercial exposure as having little effect on youth.[9] In any event, the commercials are gems of creative video production, and, if they don't teach the viewers to consume the products, they surely do teach that snazz and slickness make arresting television.

WHO CARES

It has been said, over and over, that a good teacher can take any situation and make it into a productive and important learning experience for her or his students. I believe that this is probably true. However, I don't think that this should be a reason for a teacher to take the time for Channel One away from learning experiences which occur *only* in schools. In-depth learning experiences are essential if we are to develop a generation of people who are not only informed participants in a democracy, but who also are able to analyze critically the information and experiences which confront them.

Channel One is certainly within the realm of contemporary American popular culture, and, as such, is one possible vehicle for the discussion and critique of that culture. However, most—if not all—learners have sustained and powerful experiences with that culture for many more hours each day then they spend in school. Channel One as already analyzed can be seen as providing experiences which are more abbreviated than those available from commercial network news programs, but ones which are certainly not unique. Thus, the discourse about popular culture can probably be much more productive during school time, if it draws on the experience of learners from out-of-school hours rather than spending additional time in school just experiencing more of the same.

One purpose of school might be to encourage the thought that one minute or so is insufficient time to experience a significant world event, even if pictures *are* worth a thousand words. Students must learn to seek out alternative sources of information, and to compare the sources for similarities and discrepancies. They must decide whether the similarities are caused by accurate reporting or by manipulative, propagandistic control of information. They must judge among a variety of opinions about events.

Now that teachers are allowed to videotape Channel One, it is possible to place the Channel One version of a particular story in the larger context of electronic and print news versions of the same story. Learners could challenge themselves to compare, contrast, analyze, and synthesize the information. They could also judge the long-range importance of particular stories and infer the criteria used by various news media to select the stories they report. However, no matter how intellectually stimulating, this work could not be encouraged by Channel One for at least two reasons. First, the taping might eliminate student exposure to the advertisements. Second, if the advertisements are taped, critical analysis of advertising would become an interesting classroom pursuit. Neither alternative would incline advertisers to buy time on Channel One.

Channel One might also be interesting educational material for those students studying television production. Some of the production elements are unique in the present broadcasting environment, such as the seamless integration of the commercial messages. Comparing the programs from day-to-day could provide a media studies course with a continuing stream of new material, much of which is handled in a standard format, but some of which would demonstrate unique production creativity. Again, this small audience could not possibly be attractive to the advertisers.

The only audience of interest to Whittle Communications for Channel One is mass captive audience of adolescent students in school. It is my belief that this audience is the one which would be unethical for educators to deliver to them. Teachers and students have more important things to do with the time spent in school.

Regardless of my critiques or those of others, Channel One is out there and in place. It challenges us, as educators, to refocus on a number of issues which have been around for years gathering dust at the margins of our discourse. These "old chestnuts" take on new urgency because of the opportunities afforded by the Channel One initiative. It is these old issues, now new again, to which I have directed attention in this critique.

- What is the place of so-called free and inexpensive materials in the classroom?
- What is the function of journalism in a free society?
- What is the responsibility of citizens in a democracy to fully inform themselves?
- Can the privatization of information and discourse ever be compatible with public discourse?
- Should impoverished school budgets limit teachers and learners to so called free sources of information?

Much work remains to be done. I hope that this critique is just the beginning of an extended critical discourse.

NOTES

1. Many would view the textbook as "commercially sponsored" information because it is prepared to serve market forces (such as the Texas Schoolbook Committee) rather than scholarship. If so, teachers have been held hostage to commercialism for half a millennium.

2. The conventional wisdom seemed to be that, as long as the materials helped the learners achieve the stated objectives for a course of study, they were acceptable and appropriate. This notion is disturbing when examined in retrospect.

3. I am indebted to Dr. Thomas McCain, professor of Communications and director of the Center for the Advanced Study of Telecommunications at The Ohio State University, for access to tapes for my critical review.

5. Because I did not have access to the scripts of the programs I studied, I had to rely on a transcript prepared by transferring the audio content from videocassette to audiocassette, and then using a dictation transcriber to type the text. My ideas of reasonable paragraph breaks were conditioned, not only by the text, but also by pauses taken by the anchors in the narration.

6. A Bush quote on Monday was, "That was a good sign," which would have been a ridiculous 1 ½-second sound bite, if the producers had let the audience hear Bush's voice.

7. There is the frightening possibility that journalism students are taught these days that journalism is a branch of the entertainment industry. If this is so, the mindless nature of the news stories may make a lot of sense. Another equally disturbing possibility is that, in the context of information capitalism, the purveyors of information don't want adolescents to know anything of substance.

8. An elegant critique of this unquestioned acceptance of technological change was written by William Taylor and Jane Johnson in the 85th *Yearbook of the National Society for the Study of Education*. (See The references).

9. In other broadcasts of Channel One, "pump" athletic shoes are advertised, leading me to wonder if adolescent consumerism is being pushed too far in the context of the classroom. If innercity school systems are tempted by the offer of "free" equipment from Whittle, the pressure on these youth to deal dope or steal in order to support the "need" for "pumps" should surely be considered by school boards before signing on to Channel One.

REFERENCES

Bagdikian, B. 1990. *The media monopoly.* Boston: Beacon Press.

Barry, A. 1989. Advertising in the classroom: The controversy over Channel One. *Journal of Visual Literacy* 9:2 35–67.

Hoffman, L. M. 1991. The meanings of Channel One: Curriculum, instruction, and ethics; history, control, and rhetoric. Paper presented at the Annual Conference of the American Educational Research Association. Chicago, Ill., April 6.

Jansen, S. C. 1991. Collapse of the public sphere and information capitalism. *Inquiry: Critical Thinking across the Disciplines.* November 8–11, 23.

Postman, N. 1985. *Amusing Ourselves to Death: Public Discourse in the Age of Show Business.* New York: Penguin.

Schudson, M. 1978. *Discovering the News.* New York: Basic Books.

Sears, A. and T. McCain. 1991. The television teacher debate: Educators' attitudes toward commercial television news services. Columbus, Ohio: Center for the Advanced Study of Telecommunications, Ohio State University.

Taylor, W. D. and J. B. Johnson. 1986. Resisting technological momentum. In *Technology and Education*, eds. J. A. Culbertson and L. L. Cunningham. 85th *Yearbook of the National Society for the Study of Education.* Chicago: University of Chicago Press.

5

Advertising and Channel One: Controversial Partnership of Business and Education

Since its inception, Channel One has continued to stir considerable controversy. Produced by Whittle Communications of Knoxville, Tennessee, Channel One is a ten-minute teen-oriented news program, with an additional two minutes of commercials. In order to receive the program, schools are given the use of television monitors, a satellite tuned to Whittle's signal, and a VCR to record it. The controversy has revolved around the presence of commercials within the classroom, the quality and format of program content, and the relationship between business and education in setting school curriculum. This chapter chronicles the main debate and explores both specific advertising concerns and the larger issue which underlies them namely the appropriate role of business in education.

GROWTH, PROFIT, AND CONTROVERSY

After two years in development, the Channel One program was piloted in six test-market school systems across the United States in 1989. The project was launched nationally in March 1990. By June 1991, it included more than eighty-seven hundred schools in forty-seven states and the District of Columbia, and a viewing audience of about 5.4 million students—an estimated one-third of the nations' thirteen-to-eighteen year-old population (Manuel 1991, 68). By March 1993, the program was reaching 375,000 classrooms nationwide, a figure reflecting more than 40 percent of all secondary schools and more than eight million students. The program was dubbed "Channel One" by Chris Whittle, who founded Whittle Communications in 1970 and brought the company from revenues of $3 million in 1976, to more than $152 million in 1989 at the beginning of the pilot program, and to $210 million by June of 1991. By August 1992, Whittle was predicting revenues of $3 billion by the end of the decade (Donaton 1992, 34). From the beginning, both Whittle and Channel One have been denounced and praised. Few opinions on either the man or the program have fallen between the extremes.

Those who have condemned it have taken direct and decisive action against the program. By the time of its national launch, for example, seven states already had taken steps to keep Channel One out of the schools, and most major educational associations had declared their opposition to it. New York and California banned the show from public schools after the pilot series. North Carolina put a moratorium on contracts. Rhode Island invoked a law against it, and several other states actively urged school boards to not subscribe to the program (Hammer 1990, 53). In response to pressure, California's Pubic Media Center, a nonprofit public interest agency went so far as to sponsor a full page ad in *The Sacramento Bee* and California editions of the New York *Times* criticizing Channel One and including clip-out coupons to send a state senator and Channel One advertisers (Channel One Fight 1990, 8).

Yet, despite the competition and growing criticism, some school systems have stood firm in their support of Whittle's program. Texas, for example, has more than 700 schools committed to Channel One, and Gahr High School in Cerritos, California—which participated in the pilot study—voted in mid-October 1990 to reinstate Channel One despite the warning by the State Superintendent of Public Instruction to cut off state funding to schools that use the network (Palmer 1990, 64). Later reports indicated that Whittle had spent $640,000 over an eighteen-month period to California lobbyists and other professional persuaders to place its program in the public schools (Stein 1991, 11).

To fully understand the nature of the controversy, one must become aware of what Channel One offers, the role that commercial interests have traditionally played in the schools, the current financial plight of the schools, the vested interest which advertisers have in the consumer market represented by school-aged children, and consequent educational concerns ranging from media content and use within the classroom, to control of the curriculum decision-making process.

INITIAL APPEAL

In a policy briefing paper released in December 1990 in response to a study commissioned by the Washington state legislature, Whittle Communications spokesperson David Jarrard, succinctly declared the uniqueness of Channel One in relation to the growing competition in instructional television (ITV) as *Equipment*. Neither CNN Newsroom nor public television provides schools with the equipment to receive and use their programming in the classroom. Both services provide quality programming, but it is like having a lot of gasoline and no automobile. Both have to be available to get anywhere" (Jarrard 1990, 3–4).

To Whittle—and to many of the educators committed to Channel One—the issue of advertising is "incidental," merely a means to the end of integrating their schools more fully with the technological age of the "real world" (Jarrard 1990, 2). To opponents of Channel One, the roughly $50,000 worth of equipment represents a seductive lure which masks the blatant sale of a student audience to teen-product advertisers and an irresponsible handing over of part of the curriculum to vested interests.

CHANNEL ONE PILOT PROGRAM

The Channel One pilot program ran from 6 March 1989 to 14 April 1989. Produced in Los Angeles by Susan Winston, a former producer of ABC-TV's *Good Morning America*, the twelve-minute video newsmagazine program was beamed by satellite to six pilot schools: Gahr High School in Cerritos, California; Eisenhower Middle School in Kansas City, Kansas; Billerica Memorial High School in Billerica, Massachusetts; Mumford High School in Detroit, Michigan; Withrow High School in Cincinnati, Ohio; and Central High School in Whittle's own Knoxville, Tennessee. Participating schools were given outright approximately $50,000 worth of technical equipment, including monitors, a satellite dish to receive the signal, and a VCR to record programming.

In a format essentially unchanged today, the twelve-minute program was targeted to twelve-to-eighteen-year-olds, featured eighteen-to-twenty-four-year-old anchor personalities, and consisted of a fast-paced mix of information/entertainment news, in addition to teen-targeted commercials. The following typical format outlines the premiere program of the five-week pilot series.

CHANNEL ONE PROGRAM

• Upfront: Summary of world and US news. Report on UN Security Council meeting on terrorism . . . savings and loans rescued . . . Dukakis will not seek fourth term in Massachusetts . . . space shuttle update . . . India lowers voting age.

• Flashback: New Mexico becomes 47th state Jan. 6 1912.

• Focus: Christine Higgins—daughter of hostage.

• Fast fact: 52 American hostages released Jan. 20, 1981, as Reagan is sworn in.

• Commercial (30 seconds)

• Fast fact: World's largest high school is in Calcutta.

• Commercial (30 seconds)

• Segment of five-part feature: The environment.

• Pop quiz: Which is older, the Pyramids or the Great Wall of China?

• Commercial (30 seconds)

• Fast fact: Arachibutytophobia is the fear of peanut butter sticking to the roof of your mouth

• Commercial (30 seconds)

• Feature: Carl Lewis or British autoguide or actor Johnny Depp.

• Pop quiz answer: The Pyramids, by 2,000 years.

• Features: Malcolm-Jamal Warner introduces U2 music video in a tribute to Martin Luther King.

• Tease: Alyssa Milano (for upcoming five-part series)

(Source: Whittle Communications)

CRITICAL RECEPTION

To some educators participating in the pilot series, bringing television into the classroom in this manner seemed a positive move in procuring valuable learning tools and placing them directly into the hands of those best able to use them. Robert Calabrese, school superintendent in Billerica, Massachusetts—where sixteen-hundred high-school students viewed Channel One—called it "a dynamite program—just a dynamite program" (Carton 1989c, 1). Cecil Good, director of data management for the Detroit public school system— where Channel One was seen by twenty-five hundred high-school students—saw the presence of a few commercials to which students are already exposed in their own homes a little enough price to pay, because only three percent of all schools had a satellite dish, and only one in ten classrooms had a television set (Landro 1989, 17). Advocates were quick to point out that teens were already seeing almost one hundred different commercials on network television each day and watching an average of about fifteen thousand hours of television between the ages of six and eighteen—about two thousand hours more than they spend in school. "We're always watching commercials," Cerritos, California, student Danny Diaz commented when interviewed (Carmody 1989, 16).

Many supporters have also defended the news offerings as inherently sound educationally. Kenneth Rossano, a senior associate with the Massachusetts Higher Education Assistance Corporation and a member of Whittle's council of advisors, comments, "I have seen schools using Channel One in various locations around the country, and I have yet to see one where it didn't stimulate students to discuss current events" (Palmer 1990, 64). One student from Billerica—sounding somewhat like a commercial for Channel One— commented, "I really didn't know why the Berlin Wall was built. Today, Channel One told me." Another classmate commented, "I didn't know Churchill pretty much provoked them to build the wall" (Raposa 1990, 5). Whittle advertisements for Channel One capitalize on this political naiveté, highlighting grotesque examples of student ignorance. One ad, for example, cites a student who thought Jesse Jackson was a baseball player and silicon chips were snack food.

Thus, faced with the alternative of using only print materials for current events and having no video equipment, many educators have seen the trade-off in gained television monitors as an educationally sound boon to their financially hard-pressed systems. "There really is a trade-off," commented New York educational psychologist Helen Boehm, who specializes in advertising to children. "My child didn't see the inauguration because there was no television set available at the school. The idea of access to that technology is very exciting" (Walsh 1989, 31). Whittle representatives have made sure that the trade-off is clear to local educational interests. Between 1989 and

1991, Whittle officials attended meetings of about 30,000 local and state school boards (Channel One comes 1991, 27).

Yet, others are worried about "selling out" education and have voiced arguments which have persisted. Numerous educational administrator and teacher associations, parent organizations, and child advocacy groups—such as Action for Children's Television—urged parents, teachers, and child-development experts to "scream bloody murder" (Carton 1989c, 1) about the commercial intrusion. According to Bella Rosenberg, special assistant to American Federation of Teachers President Albert Shanker, "The students are literally a captive audience, and it raises some fundamental ethical issues for a public school system that is essentially the steward of public trust" (Landro 1989, 17).

The American Association of School Administrators stated outright at its annual meeting in early March 1989 that the airing of commercials breached "certain ethical principles in education," and, at their annual meeting, the board of the National Association of Secondary School Principals likewise adopted a resolution opposing any commercial advertising in the classroom. The National Parent Teachers Association both voiced its opposition and encouraged letters opposing Channel One to Congress, the Federal Communications Commission and Whittle himself ("Major school groups" 1989, 5). Manya Unger, president of the National P.T.A., summed up the heart of the issue for the press. "We are opposed to making the availability of that technology contingent upon subjecting a captive audience to the promotion of commercial products" ("P.T.A." 1989, D17).

From the outset, Channel One divided educators into two opposing camps, with educational associations addressing theoretical and ethical concerns on one side, and educators in the field coping with financial pressures and lack of video equipment on the other.

NATIONAL LAUNCH

The decision to launch Channel One nationally, despite the growing criticism, was made primarily because of the enormous profit potential of the enterprise in terms of advertising sales, the positive feedback from schools participating in the pilot program, and the results of three research studies. Those studies were a tracking study while the pilot program was in progress, a commissioned Gallup poll to determine attitudes toward the project, and an independent but fortuitous Roper poll in which, after being read a brief description of the project, 57 percent of all those pulled and 75 percent of those polled who were already familiar with the concept, said they would be in favor of having Channel One in their schools.

At completion of the studies, Whittle dubbed the Channel One experiment "the most successful TV launch in the last twenty years," and field representatives began aggressively recruiting school systems across the country, with a national-launch goal of one thousand schools by March 1990, and a projected eight thousand schools by 1992—a goal which was already contractually exceeded by 1991. According to Whittle spokespersons, this represented an initial outlay of approximately $200 million. To earn a profit, the enterprise would have to earn $85-to-$100 million each year. By October 1989, Whittle had sold more than $149 million worth of commercials in three- and four-year contracts, with $51 million for 1990—more than half the launch revenue projections (Donaton 1989, 83). By the end of 1992, two of every five secondary public-school children were watching Whittle-sold commercials. To put these figures in competitive "news" perspective, the ESPN television network sold only $10 million worth of commercials in its first year, and Turner's CNN network only $24 million.

RESULTS, INTERPRETATION, AND CHANGING TERMS

According to Sara Fortune Rose, spokesperson for Whittle Communications, Whittle's first tracking study—"an educational assessment" test designed by professors from St. John's University and Hoffstra—indicated "a significant ability on the part of Channel One to facilitate the dissemination of new information among students."

According to statistics made available by Whittle on the private study, more than eleven thousand students participated in the multiple-choice test, which was administered by teachers at the six pilot schools and five control group schools of similar size and population. The test included 169 questions on current world and national events covered in the general media as well as information contained only in Channel One newscasts. According to news releases, Channel One students showed "significantly higher" correct responses on 138 questions. (Educational research 1989, 1–2).

Yet, closer scrutiny could lead to somewhat different conclusions. The test treated only those items chosen as significant by investigators. Conclusions suggested by the investigators related only to Channel One's "ability to build knowledge and information memorability over time"—an ability perhaps attributable to the impact of the television medium, rather than to Whittle's programming effort itself. Above all, it has also been argued whether information on the world's largest high school, Johnny Depp, U2, and fear of peanut butter sticking to the roof of your mouth is worth remembering at all.

Thus, "statistically significant" within this context may ironically provide the best curriculum argument against Channel One. During the pilot test in Billerica, Massachusetts, at least twenty students, administrators, and teachers, informally interviewed by this author agreed that the subject content of regular classes was being at least partially determined by the content of Whittle's news program. This, in effect, changes the basis of course-content decisions from proactive to reactive, and move the locus of curriculum decisions from schools and teachers themselves to Whittle Communications. Now firmly in place in Billerica schools, Channel One has since spurred many teachers to attempt to integrate media literacy into a variety of curriculum areas.

A second study, conducted in 1989 by Gallup for Whittle Communications on attitudes toward Channel One, consisted of twelve mall intercept surveys of 528 teenagers aged twelve to eighteen, 254 parents of teenagers aged twelve to eighteen, and 264 individuals without teenaged children, as well as a stratified random telephone survey of 1,007 adults, aged eighteen and older, based on the sample and used to represent adults living in telephone households in the continental United States. The mall intercept survey used random sampling, showed respondents a videotape of an actual program, and immediately thereafter interviewed them. Because this was not a true random selection of individuals, a telephone survey was used as a baseline comparison between individuals who had seen the Channel One program and those who had only heard of it.

After viewing the Channel One program, interviewees were told that two minutes of commercials were included in each daily program to students, that the equipment consisting of "satellite antenna, color TV sets, and VCRs for each classroom" was donated to the school by the broadcasting company; that the schools were "free to keep the equipment" and "to use it for any other purpose"; and that, in return, "students would be required to watch the twelve-minute program, including news, features, and commercials, each day." They were then asked to rate (excellent, good, fair, poor, or no opinion) each of the following: the idea of their own high schools participating in such a program; the quality of the news program; how well they liked the program; how interesting it was; how important they perceived the content to be; and how relevant the content was to its audience.

The results of the survey showed that, given the premises previously stated:

- 79 percent of teens, 86 percent of parents and 86 percent of nonparents thought the package offered a good or excellent idea for the schools;
- 53 percent of parents and 58 percent of nonparents thought the package would be a good or excellent idea for their child at school;
- 57 percent of teens, 70 percent of parents, and 70 percent of nonparents thought the program news content was somewhat better or much better than average;
- 29 percent of teens, 30 percent of parents, and 27 percent of nonparents like the program very much;
- 34 percent of teens, 67 percent of parents, and 52 percent of nonparents thought the program content was very interesting;
- 42 percent of teens, 52 percent of parents, and 43 percent of nonparents thought the news and features were very important;
- 57 percent of teens, 66 percent of parents, and 67 percent of nonparents thought the program to be more or much more relevant to the lifestyle of teenagers;
- 56 percent of teens, 65 percent of parents, and 64 percent of nonparents thought the time taken by the commercials was about right, as opposed to too long or not long enough;
- 40 percent of teens, 37 percent of parents, and 39 percent of nonparents thought the news program being shown with commercials was very acceptable;
- 38 percent of teens, 55 percent of parents, and 49 percent of nonparents described themselves as "very interested" in seeing these programs at teenagers' schools.
(Gallup study 1989, 3–16).

This approval—much publicized by Whittle as substantial support for Channel One—also necessitates qualification, because respondents were not made aware that, while it is true that schools were given installed equipment outright after the pilot study, "color TV sets" referred to in the survey were actually monitors rather than complete and independent sets; satellite antennae were fixed to the Channel One station and therefore could not be used to receive other programs; and VCRs were not provided with each set, but rather as the central necessary mechanism for recording and distributing each program. Thus, although schools were free to use the equipment for any other purpose, the purposes to which the equipment could be put were clearly more limited than the statement in the survey might imply.

In using the study to sell schools and potential advertisers on Channel One as being highly acceptable and even desirable to the general public, Whittle also omitted the important fact that the terms offered to the schools in the pilot program significantly changed between the pilot program and the national launch. Equipment is no longer given, and substantial financial losses through repayment for wiring could conceivably be incurred if the participating school decides that the program is objectionable, inferior, or both, or if it decides not to show the program for the required total number of days. When any premise changes, the conclusions drawn from it may change as well.

Thus, while free hardware may have been the differentiating factor which caused initial interviewees to favor the project, it was never offered again after the pilot program. Thereafter, Whittle's field representatives offered only the initial free installation of cable wiring, and the use—but not the ownership—of a fixed satellite dish, a central video recorder, and a number of television monitors in classrooms.

In return, schools were asked to sign five-year contracts, with a three-year minimum and penalty pay-back of costs incurred. They were also required to expose all students en masse to the whole package of news and commercials for at least 155 of the 180 days in the school calendar. At the contract's expiration, the equipment was to be removed, and the school would be left with only the wiring. Feedback would, schools were told, be welcomed, of course. However, censorship would be limited to turning off the set not more than twenty-five times, including vacation periods.

By May the offer again was modified and substantially sweetened to accommodate educational and other concerns, although the "free" equipment of the Gallup poll was never to be offered again. According to Whittle, the finalized offer dictated that:

• Not all students would be required to watch the programming;
• No minimum school size would be required, but the percentage of the school population exposed to television monitors in designated classrooms could not to fall below a minimum of eight hundred students per school on a national average;
• Students exposed to the programming could be involved in other activities, only so long as these did not interfere with others' viewing; and

* The use of equipment would be provided, including:
* Color television monitors for classrooms;
* Two videotape recorders, one to record Channel One and the second for other stations;
* A fixed satellite dish; and
* Facilities to add a moveable dish at the school's own expense. (Whittle Communications Launches 1989, 1–3).

In addition, participating schools were also offered:

* A "Classroom Channel" reserving one thousand hours of free satellite time each year for educational programming, not in competition with Channel One, to run independently of Whittle Communications interests, with $500,000 set aside each year for "Classroom Channel" program usage fees; and
* An "Educators' Channel" dedicated to in-service and other educational programming for professional development of teachers with a link-up for national organizations to speak with their constituents. (Whittle Communication Launches 1989, 1, 2).

In return, schools would have to comply with a noncompetition agreement, whereby they would agree not to contract with competing companies with the same news/advertising format targeted specifically to teenagers. This would exclude such news programming as CBS *Nightly News*, for example, as it is not directed specifically at a teen audience, and CNN *Newsroom* because it does not contain advertising.

THE NATURE OF THE PARTNERSHIP

In addition to providing much needed equipment, the Channel One experiment also seemed to Channel One supporters to be a desirable first step toward placing the responsibility for financing education onto the private business sector—an area which stands to benefit considerably from quality education, but which currently does little to subsidize it directly. The pervasiveness of a variety of "Nation at Risk" educational warnings and the effects of economic recession combined to create an environment ripe for "business-education partnerships."

By the end of April 1991, the much-discussed partnership concept had become part of a major presidential campaign, "America

2000," which called for both public education reform and private corporations to become fully involved in the process. In the plan, President Bush—a long-time advocate of school choice and educational vouchers to spur competition—directly challenged private industry to fund a national competition to "reinvent the classroom." "Playing Catch Up," a *Newsweek* article devoted to Bush's appeal, cited five examples of innovative school programs around the country (Kantrowitz 1991). Of these, two are especially notable in relation to Whittle. In Denver, Colorado, teachers and the city school board completely rewrote their contract from ground zero and created a policy in which a committee of teachers, parents, the school principal, and a business leader would decide not only staffing and salary issues, but also the educational philosophy and the structure of the school (Kantrowitz 1991, 30–31). Because Whittle has long been an advocate of the authority of local school districts, gaining support for his Channel One program and publications almost entirely from that quarter was an ideal innovative turn.

An even more sympathetic partnership between business and education cited by Kantrowitz was a West Side Chicago school financed by Chicago-based corporations with 1991 costs of about $5,400 per pupil, and no tuition. With an eye to business, students here are taught French, Spanish, and Japanese, under the leadership of a principal whose full title is "principal and CEO" (Kantrowitz 1991, 31). If this seems somewhat remote from a single twelve-minute video news magazine with accompanying commercials, it should be noted that Whittle's initial Channel One venture into the schools quickly expanded to include broader, and even more profitable, ambitions as well. On 16 May 1991, Whittle held a Washington press conference to announce his own plan to reinvent the public school by setting up two hundred for-profit schools, and enrolling 150,000 tuition-paying youngsters by September 1996. According to Whittle's plan, by the year 2010, there will be one thousand Whittle campuses with about two million students, from the age of three months to graduating high school seniors. Estimated start-up cost of the project is $2.5 billion. Taking what he calls a "Buck Rogers" approach to the classroom, Whittle envisions fully utilizing electronic learning systems complete with computers, television monitors, CD-ROM, paint-board fax, and printers (Manuel 1991, 67).

To retrieve costs—and, undoubtedly, with an eye to presidential support of school vouchers, which could allow students to choose their own schools and bring alone their share of tax dollars to them— Whittle would initially charge $4,500 tuition, the average cost-per-pupil in U.S. public schools for youngsters aged one to six. In addition, he proposed free tuition for 20 percent of the students in "nonchoice" neighborhoods (Cohen 1991, 67). Whittle also has stated that he hopes to raise additional funds by selling new educational methods and curriculum designs. Whittle's ultimate goal besides profits? According to Whittle, nothing less than "to reshape education in America" (Butterfield 1991, 8).

To citizen-action groups seeking to cut taxes and the cost of education, and to the growing number of individuals dissatisfied with the quality of education in public schools, this prospect of business bearing at least part of the economic burden of education looks especially appealing. Detroit's Cecil Good frankly admits, for example, that the decision to participate in the Channel One experiment was difficult, but one in which financial considerations ultimately outweighed any objections. "This is the first time we've ever been involved in anything so commercially based," he says, but it "comes at an opportune time for us because we are in great financial straits" (Landro 1989, 17). Since the inception of Channel One, Whittle has been quick to point out that federal defense budget expenditures are ten times larger than funds slotted for education, and, in many states, annual textbook expenditure is as low as $20 per pupil (Whittle 1989, 48). As Billerica's Calabrese put it, "Somebody has to pay the bill for education, and commercials are the most direct way to pay" (Jordan 1989, 25).

The controversy surrounding the role within the curriculum of business in general and advertising in particular is not new. Harty (1979) in *Hucksters in the Classroom* reviews the evolution of a variety of attempts by outside agencies to infiltrate the public classroom, giving biased and sometimes misleading information in the service of corporate profits. In her report to the Washington state legislature, State Superintendent of Public Instruction Judith Billings also cites decidedly more aggressive attempts including a McDonald's school magazine which teaches children the environmental advantages of styrofoam packaging; Nutrasweet's "educational program" promoting the sweetener for weight control, without discussing any dietary needs or possible health hazards to certain people; Chef Boyardee's "good nutrition" package which teaches students to eat pizza and how to make recipes with Chef Boyardee products; and "Changing," a booklet from Proctor and Gamble which introduces girls to Always brand sanitary pads (Billings 1991, 1).

In fact, so varied and productive have corporate efforts at influencing children become over the years, that most school authorities and parents have already accepted pervasive product promotion in the schools. In a desire to improve children's reading habits, for example, parents and teachers have been quick to endorse Pizza Hut's BOOK IT! National Reading Incentive Program, which gives free personal pan pizzas to students meeting a monthly reading quota. Rent-free food films and print materials abound in the curriculum as well, with everything from *The Amazing Orange*, to *Sugar—The Necessary Ingredient*, to *The Great American Chocolate Story*, to "why potato chips are not junk food" (Bates 1989, 16).

Lifetime Learning Systems—whose president, Roberta Nusim, is a former high school English teacher—produces a variety of teacher kits for the classroom. One of the most widely used—entitled "Quality Comes in Writing"—includes a wall poster, a news story, a ballad, a diary, and worksheets on letter writing—along with an advertisement and the pervasive logo of Bic pens who sponsors it. Like Whittle himself, Nusim speaks in educational terms which euphemistically turn advertising into "real world" consideration. "As a teacher, I found the most interesting way for youngsters to learn was to introduce real-world materials. For instance, reading the ingredients off a cereal box can teach kids about nutrition. Once you've got them interested, you can bring them back to the curriculum" (Moore 1989, 39). This is an argument often repeated by Whittle spokespersons.

Although some of the educational material produced by corporate sponsors can look benign enough at times because of its genuine usefulness to educators, an understanding of the goals and strategies lying behind the material would give most curriculum decision makers pause for further thought. One Lifetime Learning Systems brochure expresses a more direct purpose, encouraging marketers to "Take your message into the classroom where young people you want to reach are forming attitudes that will last a lifetime. . . . School is . . . the ideal time to influence attitudes, build long-term loyalties, introduce new products, test market, promote sampling and trial usage and—above all—to generate immediate sales" (Hoffman 1991, 8; Consumer's Union 1990, 8).

One of the more controversial commercial sallies by business into the classroom has involved a curriculum produced by Philip Morris Companies, Inc., and released in 1991, entitled "The Bill of Rights: Protecting Our Liberty." Although no advertisements for cigarettes appear in the materials, many educators—attuned to the growing movement to ban cigarette advertising and of the subtle and ingenious forms in which advertising has appeared in countries where it has already been banned—eyed warily an implicit link between First Amendment freedoms and the freedom to smoke. The Massachusetts Council for Social Studies, for example, "sensing an agenda," refused a Philip Morris offer to cosponsor an exhibit of Bill of Rights replicas (Combs 1993, 45).

However, the answer to the exploitation of a ready youth market does not appear simply to be to shut business out of the schools entirely. As Alex Molnar has commented, "Educators could not keep business out of the schools if we wanted to . . . The questions before us are: What manner of involvement shall we support, and what shall we oppose and why?" (Molnar 1989/1990, 68).

Lee Iacocca, corporate superstar, is a long-time advocate of corporate support for education. In *Talking Straight* (1988) he calls for business support of education while, at the same time, espousing a separation between business interests and the schools. "Things are so bad [in current educational practices that] three out of four U.S. corporations are forced to train new workers in basic reading, writing, and arithmetic. It's reckoned that the lost productivity is tacking on a whopping $25 billion a year in costs to American industry. . . . as many as a hundred companies including Eastman Kodak, AT&T and Polaroid now offer courses" and spend "around $40 billion a year to teach eight million workers . . . [Yet] American business ought [not] usurp the role of our schools. I don't want to see Chrysler teaching fractions and world geography," he says. "Before you know it we'd have to offer gym, and field a football team." "What business can do," Iacocca claims, "is support out schools and make sure our teachers are tuned in to the real world" (Iacocca 1988, 233–244).

Iacocca, thus, makes a distinction among long-term educational interests, business needs, and educational expertise which is often blurred in the case of Whittle. In promotional material on Channel One, for example, to the question "Why is Whittle Communications qualified to provide this educational programming?" the response is that "Whittle has been an educational publisher for nineteen years." As proof, it cites "Connections," a "magazine on the wall" for high-school students; "The Big Picture," a poster for elementary schools; *GO!*, a magazine for junior-high girls; and *Campus Voice*, a magazine for college students. Yet, all of the publications are clearly marketing advertising tools with editorial material chosen primarily for high interest rather than for educational value.

The argument that Whittle is qualified to produce *educational* programming because of his expertise in marketing is spurious at best, and has led critics to respond to Channel One with skepticism or even moral outrage. Joel Rudinow comments, for example, that

Channel One and its research findings add up "to a flagrant display of duplicity in which the public rationale of support to struggling institutions of public education barely masks the patently obvious agenda . . . the business of creating efficient vehicles for advertising, pure and simple" (Rudinow 1989/1990, 71).

Molnar, too, argues succinctly that "if cooperation of a business in support of public education carries with it a quid pro quo that advances that business' special interests, then what we have is not a civic-minded contribution to education but a commercial transaction in which school children are, in effect, uniformed participants" (Molnar 1989/1990, 69).

Edward Rensi, president of McDonald's Corporation U.S. operations, has also expressed similar concerns, despite their commercial presence in the schools. He told multiunit food service operators at their 1990 annual conference that the video equipment-for-ads trade isn't a good one for the schools or its students. "Do we want the classroom to become the new competitive battleground for our companies?" he asked. "The right thing for us to do is to give schools the audio-visual equipment for education, not for competitive advantage" (Johnson 1990, 77). McDonald's Children's Charities spent approximately $2 million on a 1991 promotional program with the National Basketball Association, NBC, Turner Network Television, and Nickelodeon to encourage students to stay in school by offering such prizes as attendance at festivities during the NBA all-star weekend, including the TV special, for achieving perfect school attendance (McManus 1990, 61).

Channel One may even stand in the way of such civic-minded business support of education. Occupying a middle ground between a laissez-faire neglect and no-strings-attached corporate financial help, the presence of Channel One in effect makes it easy for corporations with products to sell to get both relatively inexpensive advertising and specifically targeted "captive" audiences. Why give money away if the mechanism already exists to get something for it in return?

REAL WORLD MARKETING

This "real-world" approach has, in fact, been a successful lynch-pin for selling Channel One to the nation's schools from the beginning. Whittle made the point directly in an extremely effective ad, placed in the *New York Times* just prior to the beginning of the

March 1989 experiment. "Here's a list of everyone willing to donate $250 million to schools," the headline reads. The "list" next to it is, of course, blank. Clearly, Whittle is not implying that *he* is willing to donate $250 million to the schools, but that "reality" means not only that teachers must tie curriculum into the real world's practical demands on knowledge and commonsense, but also that, in the real world, no one gives anything to anyone else for nothing.

In an article entitled "Commercials, Plus Education," in the The *New York Times*—later reprinted as "Channel One: Lesson in Reality" in *Adweek* on 6 March 1989—just as the pilot program was about to be launched, Whittle queries, "Where will schools get the necessary funds to educate students? My answer is that education-business partnerships could be a significant source." The partnership he envisions, however, is predicated on immediate financial profits for advertisers rather than on long-range profit to industry from better educated workers—which gives rise to concerns extending from Channel One to Whittle's plan for for-profit schools. Whittle explains, "Corporate funds could be provided through the development of partnerships between business and education in which each party receives *direct and immediate benefits*" (italics added) (Whittle 1989, 48).

Whittle readily acknowledges that the trade-off is fiscal. "Were this a perfect world, we would agree that government, not commercials, should provide this technology and programming, as it does in Britain. But in today's real world of $20 textbook budgets and tough fiscal constraints, two minutes of appropriate advertising is not a bad solution" (Whittle 1989, 48). Whittle thus makes it clear that the relationship is to be a business partnership rather than an educational one, and the description which he gives of the program is couched in marketing terms familiar to the "real-world" business and advertising community. In the same article, Whittle states that Channel One "will contain domestic and international news and features. Anchorpersons, much like the students themselves, will report in a manner relevant to teenagers' interests. In addition to helping teachers facilitate discussion, the program will be the only source of daily news for many students." From a marketing perspective, Whittle's statement hits the mark exactly.

What in Marketing 101 classes is called "the marketing concept" acknowledges that the raw product is something which gains its value from the degree of acceptability among consumers rather than from the long-term needs of society. This implies that the degree to which the product is seen as desirable depends on its ability to bring relief to a problem (for example "R-O-L-A-I-D-S spells relief") or to enhance the quality of the consumer's life (as in, an Ultra-Brite smile has "sex appeal"), and the degree to which the consumer can identify with the message (I get heartburn—I would like to be seen as sexy). When consumers perceive a need, have the means to buy the product, and the competition is either weak or absent, marketers see a "window of opportunity."

Channel One is Whittle's response to just such an opportunity, as are the for-profit schools he proposes to institute by 1996. Jill Savitt of the Center for the Study of Commercialism described it this way. "The schools are caught between a rock and a hard place. They don't have the money, and along comes this huckster with some fancy-schmancy goods. It's hard to say no" (Streitfeld 1992, A80). By March 1989, when Whittle introduced Channel One, the American public had already become acutely aware through a variety of media that American education seemed to be failing. A kind of educational panic had already begun over student illiteracy—both in reading and culture—and Whittle was quick to claim in promotional material that televised Channel One news could battle the type of ignorance that had high schoolers identifying the District of Columbia as a Central American country and Chernobyl as Cher's full name.

Participants in Whittle's pilot program were also quick to point out their own "suffering points"—problems requiring relief—as they defended their participation in the project. Dr. Stan Jasinskas, principal of Kansas City's Eisenhower High School, for example, commented in *Wyandotte West* that "Many students do not make themselves aware of the world in which they live," and that the most widely read newspaper for "a significant number" of his students was the *National Enquirer.* "I don't think [the trade off] is a drawback, I think it's a reality" (Billerica Beat 1989, 10). In addition to answering a suffering point, the program also has filled the perceived need for equipment. Rosa Maria Soldevilla, of the International Studies Academy of Withrow High School in Cincinnati, another participant in the pilot program, told columnist Jim Rohrer in a *Cincinnati Enquirer* interview after the first day's broadcast, "Do you know how long I tried to get a television monitor? Two years. We need this and we've never has it as a teaching tool" (Rohrer 1989, 3).

Considering the general public's frustration over problems of high school drop-out rates, drugs in the schools, cultural illiteracy, and an apparent lack of competitive work skills in an increasingly high-tech global marketplace, it is not too surprising that Whittle's program has been perceived by some to be a magic bullet for technological educational ills—or that its accompanying advertising would be seen only as a minor annoyance, an annoyance which, in fact, had already been accepted by the everyday "real world." Dr. Lionel Brown, principal of Withrow High School, faced with an "unbelievable" drop-out rate, "an epidemic" of drug and alcohol addiction, and a lack of technical equipment, put it this way: "The fact that a child sees a candy bar commercial is way down on my list of priorities . . . Nothing in America is free. It has to be paid for. I don't have a problem with [Channel One]" (Rohrer 1989, 3)

Thus, Whittle's window of marketing opportunity consists of an already accepted concept of a business/education partnership; a real and apparent need on the part of students for a wider world experience and perspective implied by "news;" a widely acknowledged suffering point and perceived need on the part of teachers; a complacency about advertising because of its already pervasive presence in everyday life and within the school community itself; the instant affordability allowed by commercial support; ease of response to the advertising appeal; and the lack of competition in the field. In marketing terms, these perceived needs signaled the potential of a profit gold mine. It was this recognition which caused Ted Koppel to comment in an ABC-TV *Nightline* broadcast on 6 March 1989, that "it may be a breakthrough in education, but it is certainly a breakthrough in advertising, and a triumph in marketing."

MARKETING TO TEENS

Yet, none of this would have been successful if the package had not been made palatable to teens as well, for, as every astute advertiser knows, if the ultimate consumer doesn't like the product, all the hype directed at the middleman purchaser is worthless. For schools to "buy" the Whittle package, it was necessary to address, not only teacher and administrative needs, but also the issue of student interest as well. The combination of high teen appeal (teens are the ultimate consumer) combined with the free use of equipment (a benefit targeted to teachers as middleman buyers) completes Whittle's unique selling proposition. Both Whittle and his editor-in-chief, William Rukeyser, have readily confirmed that stimulating interest, not teaching, is the aim of the program, and that in-depth coverage of any one news item was intentionally never designed into its format.

Patricia Albjerg Graham, then Dean of the School of Education at Harvard, noted this particularly when she said that "If the point of this program is to inform young people, it may be a good entry point to get them interested. But it certainly does not replace serious study of geography, history, politics, and government" (Walsh 1989, 31). To many, this amounts to a fast-food approach to learning which encourages simplistic thinking about serious and complex issues. Massachusetts Education Commissioner Harold Raynolds, Jr., points to the format as working against education. "It's good if it gets children interested in what is going on in the world, but I don't think they're going to know very much if they depend on thirty-second sound bites" (Raposa 1990, 5).

TEACHING ADVERTISING

What this means in "real world" terms is that the responsibility for following up on interest segments and filling in the whole falls to teachers themselves—something which is a reasonable expectation in a curriculum structured by teachers and administrators. However, because individual schools can only react to Whittle's choice of news by complaining to the company or turning off the set, the questions of who controls the curriculum becomes a serious one. If no one alters the planned curriculum to follow up on the news program, it seems to be of little or no educational value to air it, and if teachers build into their lesson plans as accommodation to the daily Channel One program, it is clear that Whittle is controlling at least part of the curriculum for 40 percent or more of the nation's teenagers nearly every school day for up to six years—all well before his Edison Project schools are in place.

Educational content is, therefore, as much a key issue as the presence of advertising. Lead stories run about twenty seconds long and initially showed an even closer relationship to MTV. "It's just a series of boom, boom, boom, seven-second sound bites on the news with commercials interspersed," commented Jeremy Rifkin, president of the Washington-based Foundation for Economic Trends, which assesses the impact of emerging technologies (Carmody 1989, A16). To keep interest high, in-depth news coverage is deliberately avoided in favor of a fast-paced, upbeat style more closely related to commercials than to serious news programming, and creating a uniformity of style and content which ultimately gives advertising more impact. More specifically, within the program, psuedo-educational material has become recast in the mold of advertising itself.

At least one study, for example, shows that the form and content of the program cannot be separated, and that, because of the regular pattern of development, stylistic unity, and tight structure of the program," the form and style of Channel One serves the purpose of the program's producer to encourage, in fact require, students to watch the entire program, including the commercial material, thus guaranteeing to sponsors that the product will be delivered to the student 'market' " (Erdman 1990, 12).

Because of this structure, Erdman suggests, teachers cannot readily intervene, with the result that "the program dramatically affects the traditional relations of classroom and lesson control," with the teacher "now truly subordinate to the medium" (Erdman 1990, 13). If Erdman's conclusions are correct, the stated educational goal of the program is defeated by its own format while, at the same time, the advertising goals are most effectively achieved.

Educationally, what remains is only high interest value, entertainment, and commercial impact. In order to get and keep teens' attention, the Channel One news format has kept an exclusively teen-interest slant, features seeded with high-color rock stars, and teen anchors with high personality profiles who comment superficially between news and trivial pursuit pepperings called "fast facts." In a student poll done early in the pilot launch, in which 92 percent of students at Billerica High states that they approved of the program, "a portion" felt the program was too short and too fast. Almost half thought more music was needed, and five percent wanted more sports coverage. Sixty-one percent admitted they paid attention to the advertisements (Billerica Beat 1989, 3).

Because we have been generally conditioned to accept commercials within a nonschool environment, it is also easy to overlook the impact which the school environment itself has on reception of commercial messages. According to Rifkin, "At home, you can take the remote control and turn down the commercials, but this is a situation where [students] are expected to sit there" (Carmody 1989, A16). During the pilot—although not part of school contracts for the program's national launch—students were expected to sit quietly and attentively in homerooms and listen to the program. California Superintendent of Public Instruction Bill Honig called the program "forced viewing for profit" (Golden State 1989, 873). In its suit seeking to void contracts with Whittle within its borders claims, North Carolina has argued that compulsory school attendance laws "create a captive audience of millions of public and private school students for the advertising of commercial products and these laws could be exploited for [Whittle's] profit" (No Thanks 1990, 27).

The North Carolina Supreme Court has subsequently held, in a five-to-two ruling, that a 1969 law, which gives local school districts the right to choose "supplemental" instructional material, takes precedence over the right to a free education under the state constitution (Whittle Backed 1990, 8). Effects of such "supplemental" instructional materials demand careful study if their format conspires, intentionally or unintentionally, to give commercial messages prominence over education and to isolate teacher discussion from the viewing experience.

A *Boston Globe* editorial run the day following Channel One's premiere to 1,600 students in Billerica commented that "regrettably, the commercials appear to be the best part of the Channel One offering. . . . The news segments were lightweight, and appeared to have been concocted by a graphics team rather than a news staff. A feature on environmental problems seemed designed for elementary schools; a "Channel One exclusive" on Martin Luther King was really about the rock group U2" (Commercializing education 1989, 18). Journalist Ellen Goodman commented, "It is one thing when business is interested in young people as students. Quite another when they are interested in students as consumers. It is one thing when the marketplace supports the schools. Quite another when the schools become a marketplace." (Goodman 1989, 11). Bill Moyers, in a May 1989 interview with the *New York Times* saw larger implications. "You can tell a lot about a television producer if you know whether . . . he looks out and sees a nation of consumers or a nation of citizens. If he sees them as consumers, then the truth becomes that which sells, nothing more" (Sheinfeld 1989, 70). In 1991, the Center for the Study of Commercialism described Channel One and its Nike sponsor as two of the nation's "most excessive, intrusive and pushy marketers" (Nike 1991, 39).

Cognizant of the commercial controversy, some advertisers have begun to use a soft-sell PSA (public service announcement) approach to their commercial messages. Both Nike and Burger King, for example, have produced spots attacking the problem of school dropouts. Yet, subtly, these are tied to commercials already familiar to students, thus achieving maximum advertising value at the same time. Nike, for example, has used Bo Jackson and the familiar "Bo knows" theme as a clear carryover from their product commercials to promote the value of staying in school to learn a variety of academic subjects. It may also be true, as Erdman suggests, that these commercials "may actually intrude into the educational space of the program by becoming little lessons themselves" (Erdman 1990, 13). This further blurs the lines between educational and commercial messages and interests.

Yet, some educators, unaware of research other than Whittle's, see the presence of commercials as a plus within the school environment. For example, Joe Mancini, who is principal of Bishop Ready High School in Columbus, Ohio, comments "What better way to produce discriminating consumers than to have the students watch commercials with some faculty members?" (Zoglin 1990, 59) While this seems reasonable on the surface, it is debatable whether most faculty truly understand the sophisticated techniques used by advertisers to structure their commercials and, although some schools have initiated media literacy curricula, it is debatable how valuable a Channel-One-driven curriculum is in view of long-term educational goals.

The presence of Channel One does, however, provide an invaluable opportunity for researchers to examine the immediate and long-term effects of advertising on students in this age range. Yet, even though Whittle has commissioned a three-year research study on the effects of Channel One—begun in the fall of 1990 and continuing through the spring of 1993—none of the questions outlined by researchers deals with the negative effects of advertising on students—despite the social value of such research, especially in long-term effects in which little research has been done. Despite claims of the innocuousness of accompanying advertising, it is clear that advertising is not to be part of any Whittle testing program.

Instead, questions fit comfortably into the type of marketing evaluation done to refine the effectiveness of a product message or to gather data to promote the main product—namely, Channel One. To private business interests, however, Whittle speaks a different language, urging the Advertising Research Foundation and concerned business to develop new standards for advertising effectiveness, and to divert up to five percent of their ad budgets on research into the kinds of advertisements which work most effectively (Whittle urges 1991, D6).

UNIQUE SELLING PROPOSITIONS TO ADVERTISERS

Given the entrepreneurial success of the venture, it is not surprising that the advertising community has embraced Whittle's concept. Because of compulsory school attendance laws and ensured viewing audience contracts, Whittle can deliver to sponsors a demographically and psychographically well-defined target audience of eight million teens en masse, with no waste coverage. This is why a thirty-second spot on Channel One commanded $125,000 during the pilot program (Commercializing education 1989, 18); $117,000 in April 1991, a figure at least double the top rated prime time news program (Channel One tops goal 1991, C7); $150,000 in 1992; and a projected $200,000 in 1993 (Becker 1992). "Underneath everything that we do," says Whittle, "is the concept of targeted, high-impact, proprietary media systems. . . . Home-based media has dramatically declined as an environment for sending advertising messages. Place-based . . . helps you target" (Whittle Rips 1990, S2).

Environment is so important to message reception that product placement has become a multimillion dollar industry. Some films, for example, command upfront fees of well over $100,000 primarily because, according to Scott Dorman of Ted Bates Advertising, "most movies reach the very-hard-to-reach 12-to-24 year-old market." Sales of Reese's Pieces, for example, rose 62 percent after the release of *E.T.* (Sheinfeld 1989, 71). Not only does Channel One gain access to a generally hard to reach market, but it also offers advertisers a prime editorial environment for its product messages. Because the environment in which an advertisement is seen inevitably creates a positive or negative tone and is responsible to a great extent for product acceptance, appearance of the product name within the classroom setting both assures a captive audience and enhances the product image and message credibility. (Recognition of educational credibility is, for example, the primary reason for Whittle's hiring Benno Schmidt, former Yale University president, as Edison Project CEO.) The American Federation of Teachers has been quick to acknowledge the commercial power of environment. "By showing commercials, schools are implicitly endorsing the product" ("Is the classroom for blackboards or billboards?" 1989, 286).

This is why sponsors—aware that the target has a substantial disposable income to spend on products of its choosing—have gladly paid Whittle up to three times the cost of a network news spot. One Scholastic, Inc., brochure called the under-eighteen population "a giant spending machine," and noted that it spent more than $82 billion every year, and influenced the purchase of $142 billion (Moore 1989, 35). Dan Chew, marketing manager of Levi Strauss, one of the pilot program's original sponsors, described the program as "an intriguing, innovative way to reach parts of our primary target audience [of] fourteen-to-twenty-one-year-olds" (Reilly 1989, 76). Whittle's environment not only targets a lucrative market but also prevents the channel switching and commercial "zapping" which is generally so problematic in this age group, guaranteeing a quality of exposure which no other medium can match in this age group.

Among those advertisers to take advantage of this are Burger King, Colgate Palmolive, Columbia Pictures, Frito-Lay, Gatorade, Gillette, Kellogg, M & M/Mars, Magnavox, Nike, Nintendo, Paramount Pictures, Pepsi-Cola Co., Proctor & Gamble, Quaker Oats Co., Sprint, Taco Bell, Twentieth Century Fox, Warner Brothers, Warner-Lambert, and Vicks.

Another key advantage to sponsors is that Whittle's program provides a relatively clutter-free advertising environment—another primary concern of advertisers, because the more ads there are, the more difficult it is for a product to break through and grab the consumer's attention. To ensure that advertisers' concerns over the variables of clutter and competition are met, Whittle offers only two minutes of advertising per program and sells commercial time only in noncompeting product categories. The combination of editorial environment, target the audience, guaranteed exposure, category exclusivity and limited clutter is Whittle's unique selling proposition to advertisers in a highly competitive media marketplace.

This is why, despite concerns of many educators and parents, the issue has barely ruffled the ethical feathers of corporations and advertising agents. Madison Avenue media buyers direct over $120 billion worth of advertising dollars into a variety of media vehicles, and, for them, it's primarily a question of communication logistics. Micheal Moore, media director for top advertising agency D'Arcy Masius Benton & Bowles, for example, sees the idea as "A very interesting medium for reaching an audience that's hard to reach" (Landro 1989, 17).

Stephen Conroy, communications director at Della Femina McNamee WCRS-Boston, stated that "It's a terrific idea" and commented that "It's an age when [students have] got to take tests on American and world geography and have no idea not only what the capital of their state is, or who their senators are, but think that Calcutta is a team on the National Football League. If this helps teach, and get facts across in an interesting and meaningful way, I don't see why educators wouldn't endorse it." Bruce Kelley executive vice president of Ingalls, Quinn & Johnson, commented simply that it's "an excellent targeting opportunity" (Carton 1989b, 1). In his column, "At Close Range" for *ADWEEK*, John Carroll wrote a diary piece in which he appeared frankly bored by all the fuss, adding the epitaph, "John Carroll, creative director at KK&M/Boston, is like wicked glad he's not a kid" (Carroll 1989, 46).

COMPETITIVE ENVIRONMENT

Given the enormous profitability of the enterprise, it is not surprising that competition for Whittle's Channel One quickly appeared. Its main competition, Ted Turner's *CNN Newsroom* which has been beamed out to schools since August 1989, is a daily cable news program comparable in professional treatment, content, pace, and anchor personalities to Turner's regular Cable News Network fare. Although original news releases for *Newsroom* included two minutes of "underwriting messages" in an outline of proposed ad schedules, Turner apparently decided to eliminate the PBS-like sponsor messages after meeting with Gary Marx, associate executive director of the American Association of School Administrators (Colford 1989, 3). He apparently decided that, in view of educational opposition, the long-term good-will benefits to be gained from the donation of a service would be greater than the immediate financial profits. The Turner program first beamed out to all cable systems on 14 August 1989 at 3:45 a.m., EST, for later use in the classroom.

Although commercial-free and fifteen-minutes long, *Newsroom* was not developed specifically for teenagers, and Turner provides no equipment or service to the schools. Instead, he encourages local cable companies to provide access. Like Whittle Communications, however, Turner Broadcasting System also provides supplementary teaching guides and suggestions for incorporating news features into the general classroom curriculum. Because of the quality of news content and lack of advertising, the program immediately elicited praise in measure to the condemnation accorded Channel One. James Ogelsby, president of the National School Board Association, for example, has commented on the association's delight in this "important merger of business resources with our nation's educational system." The stamp of approval, although not outright endorsement, was also quickly given by the National Association of Secondary Schools Principals, the National Parent-Teacher Association, and the National School Boards Association (Carton 1989a, 59).

Meanwhile, a variety of other efforts aimed at bringing educational television into the classroom have also emerged. Cable's Art & Entertainment channel—which premiered in January 1989, just before Whittle's pilot program—provides a feature called *A&E Classroom* with daily, hour-long, commercial-free offerings in a variety of subject areas ranging from dramatizations of literary classics to sociological reviews of periods of history. *C-SPAN in the the Classroom* gives a realistic view inside the workings of government. All programming is of high quality and interest value.

Discovery Channel's *Assignment Discovery*, has been endorsed by the National Education Association, National School Boards Association, National Association of Secondary School Principals, American Association of School Administrators, and National Parent-Teacher Association, and has earned a host of major awards, including the National Education Association 1990 award for the Advancement of Learning through Broadcasting, a New York Film Festival bronze award, an Addy Award for excellence in graphics, and an International Monitor Award for best achievement in children's programming. In 1992, The Learning Channel initiated a similarly designed series of commercial-free preschool programs titled *Ready, Set, Learn,* from 6 a.m. to noon; *Teacher TV,* created by, for, and about teachers and coproduced by the National Education Association to share teaching techniques, ideas, and resources; and a series called *TLC Elementary School* designed for teachers of kindergarten through sixth grade.

Such programming would seem to confirm the view of John Krubski, vice president for local sales of the Television Bureau of Advertising who believes that television is fully compatible with and integrally related to advertising attempts to reach specific markets. "Something has to be the medium of America," he says. "TV will continue to be the glue that binds society as a whole" (Loro 1989, 48E).

Yet, even award-winning programming has educational critics concerned about the immediate and long-term effects of utilizing visual media for basic instruction in the classroom, primarily because television is a medium of passive entertainment rather than of active thought. As Joel Rudinow commented, "The active alert, engaged, inquisitive, creative, skeptical, reflective, habits of mind that education aims to encourage are hardly optimal for the reception of advertising. What advertisers want is a passive, unreflective, credulous audience, susceptible to the dictates of external authority" (Rudinow 1989/1990, 70). Neil Postman, who has been a leading critic of television in general, claims that higher educational aspirations can even be especially dangerous. "We do not measure a culture by its output of undisguised trivialities but by what it claims as significant. Therein is our problem, for television is at its most trivial and, therefore, more dangerous when its aspirations are high, when it presents itself as a carrier of important cultural conversations" (Postman 1985, 16).

Arguing that the epistemology created by television is inferior to a print-based one because it fails to promote serious complex argument—that is, argument characterized by coherence, reason, order, objectivity, and higher order reasoning—Postman warns that the visual image demands action and aesthetic and emotion appeal rather than rational thought. Instead of detachment and objectivity, it offers sensual excitement and emotional titillation outside of any coherent informational context. Ultimately, then, television functions not as as a "societal glue," but as a discourse in images which fragments facts and discourages the kind of abstract thinking necessary for long term cultural and economic survival.

From this point of view, what appears to be educational innovation in bringing television into the classroom may be really just another way of pandering to a growing appetite for entertainment and a decreasing tolerance for delayed gratification epitomized by advertising. Certainly, much of Whittle's Channel One programming and print publication is susceptible to this criticism. Advertising is fundamental and programming secondary. Many program items appear to be trivial at best, and news items are treated so quickly that it is impossible to explore connections or relationships. Getting and maintaining interest is paramount, while depth and complexity are avoided in favor of an entertainment format. The problem, Postman says, speaking generally, "is not that television presents us with entertaining subject matter, but that all subject matter is presented as entertainment" (Postman 1985, 87).

Yet, print, too, is not immune from criticism. For Whittle, in fact, television's role in target-marketing a "captive" audience is a natural extension of a larger, high-profit effort begun by Whittle Communications in 1980 and in the form of "magazine on the wall" advertising, which earned a record $80 million in two-year advertising contracts on its inception (Pomice 1989). By 1990, Whittle was publishing about twenty such "magazines," with more than 199 wall-media issues displayed on more than eighty-five thousand boards, which target both medical offices and educational institutions with information and advertising. About four-by-six feet in size, the posters use high-interest, action color photographs to grab attention and several short print articles to cover areas of immediate interest to the specifically targeted market segment walking through the corridors of high schools and colleges or sitting in the waiting room of the den-

tist's or doctor's office, where the average wait is twenty-seven minutes (Pomice 1989, 52). As of mid-July 1989, according to Jarrard, over
more than seventeen-thousand schools had agreed to hang posters
hawking such products as Prell shampoo, Crest toothpaste, and
Sure deodorant.

By 1991, however, at least some of Whittle's aggressive marketing techniques had backfired. Whittle's *Special Reports* magazines and
"Home Library" of booklets, targeted through doctors' offices, for example, sold $40 million worth of advertising in its first year (Landro
1989, 17). However, by August 1992, advertising's leading trade newspaper was saying, "Make no mistake. Chris Whittle is one of the best,
slickest salesmen in the business, as well as a marketing innovator
and iconoclastic media pioneer. But is he truly a media baron in the
making or a mere master of self-promotion?" (Donaton 1992, 30) Part
of the motivation for the question lies in Whittle's propensity for ex-
aggeration. Claiming, for example, that his *Special Reports* magazines
had an advertising recall 400 percent higher than any women's service magazine was attacked by media buyers at a host of advertising
agencies. When several charter sponsors pulled out, Whittle was
forced to reduce his initial six magazines to three, and then to one
every-other-month (Donaton 1992, 34).

In addition to other highly targeted, single-sponsor properties
such as wall media and product sampling kits, as early as 1989, Whittle became involved in publishing a controversial "Larger Agenda"
series of hardcover books authored by such well known figures such
as John Kenneth Galbraith and James Atlas, Donald Katz, Michael
Lewis, and George Plimpton. Sponsored by Federal Express Corporation, corporate ads appear between chapters ("For the record,"
1989). The first in the series—*The Trouble with Money*, a 94-page book
by William Greider, national editor of *Rolling Stone* magazine—
totalled eighteen pages of color ads, and was sent free to 150,000
"opinion leaders" in business and government in early November
1989. Criticized by such notables as *New Republic* columnist Robert
Kuttner, the enterprise has called into question, once again, the protection of journalistic, literary, and educational integrity from commercial pressures. The Whittle defense, predictably, centered around
the argument that the principle has, in fact, already been accepted by
the public and operating for years. Greider, for example, claims that
his book is "no different than doing a long essay for a magazine . . .
Have I sold my soul to Federal Express? My answer is, if advertising
corrupts writers, I lost my virginity a long time ago writing for newspapers and magazines" (Whittle books 1989, 72).

While Whittle has denied ever seriously considering getting into the educational textbook market, his pioneering marketing efforts through print media and Channel One in the schools, and his ambitious Edison Project to open two hundred for-profit Whittle schools across the country by 1996 and one thousand schools by 2010, leave the question open to speculation.

SUMMARY

Now the cornerstone of Whittle Communications, Channel One has grown from a six-school test market offering in 1989 to a highly profitable and sophisticated advertising vehicle reaching 40 percent of America's secondary school youth by 1993. In the process, it has proven to be a gold mine, for both Whittle and for its advertisers, who are offered a unique combination of category exclusivity, target marketing, positive editorial environment, and captive audience. Indeed, both the program's educational content and format are intrinsically linked to advertising's form, substance, and purpose. The reason for the success of the entertaining news program can be found in the combination of Whittle's marketing genius, the economic plight of the nation's schools, and the addiction of American youth to video communication.

Although Whittle's Channel One enterprise is unique, its significance lies in its effective combination of elements and commercial trends already present within our educational system and the society at large. If the major danger of the "business-education partnership" which Channel One implies lies in its confusion of long-range business interests with short-term marketing opportunities, it may also be true that there has been too ready of an acceptance of what Whittle has to offer schools—namely, visual media technology within the school environment without an adequate understanding of the educational and sociological implications, especially in terms of the power of visual language which advertising has mastered so well. The anatomy and impact of the visual message is still too little understood by most educators—educators who themselves have been taught through print materials and who have been lulled into a complacency about television's effects by its pervasiveness within the larger society.

Utilizing television's function both as commercial medium and a "societal glue," Channel one not only provides a gold mine for advertisers. It also acts as a force which subtly shapes educational curriculum toward Whittle-selected topics and into an overall "entertainment" orientation. In the process, it conditions more and more young people to accept the intrusiveness of advertising as a natural part of everyday life and to absorb its materialistic values and ethical practices as inevitable. Because Channel One's primarily visual mode of transmitting information may ultimately impact critical thought processes, turning potentially analytically active students into passive recipients of propagandized or commercialized messages, it demands and deserves highly critical national attention.

Still only a small piece in a marketing revolution, Channel One's commercial success cannot help but impact and, at least partially, direct the future of education. It is clear, for example, that the demand for technological resources within the schools will increase rather than the reverse. In view of the financial plight of the nation's schools and ever-scarcer economic resources to support them, more innovative ways of financing education will have to be found.

Although the increasingly aggressive presence of commercial interests in the schools is far from surprising in a nation already conditioned to accept advertising as a tolerable trade-off for the things which it desires, it cannot be ignored that a willingness to accept immediate and often subtle commercialism may be fundamentally destructive to the long-term goals of education, upon which the ultimate well-being of society depends. The controversy surrounding Channel One points, above all, to the necessity of reexamining our educational priorities and methods as well as to the advisability of clearly defining the limits of capitalistic enterprise within our educational system.

REFERENCES

Print

Bates, Stephen. 1989. First, this message. *The New Republic*, October 16. 16–18.

Becker, J. 1992. Chris and Benno's excellent adventure. *Vanity Fair*, August. 142–147, 172–176.

The Billerica Beat. 1989. Spring. 5:3

Billings, Judith. 1991. Report to the Legislature on Commercialism in Schools. Office of the State Superintendent of Public Instruction. January. Olympia, Washington.

Butterfield, Bruce and Joan Vennochi. 1991. After TV in classrooms, for-profit schools. *Boston Globe*, May 17. 1, 8.

Carmody, Deirdre. 1989. News shows with ads are tested in six schools. *New York Times*, March 7. A16.

Carroll, John. 1989. Diary of a Channel One kid. *ADWEEK, Eastern Edition*, March 27. 46.

Carton, Barbara. 1989a. Few neutral about TV show for classroom. *Boston Globe*, March 2. 1, 22.

————. 1989b. Pilot program brings news, and commercials, to high school classrooms. *Boston Globe*, March 4. 1, 8.

————. 1989c. CNN show for students catching on. *Boston Globe*, May 4. 57, 59.

Channel One comes under scrutiny in Texas. 1991. *Editor & Publisher*, November 23. 277.

Channel One fight in California. 1990. *Advertising Age*, June 18. 8.

Channel One tops goal. 1991. *New York Times*, April 5. C7.

Cohen, Muriel. 1991. Can Whittle-and profit-make it work? *Boston Sunday Globe*, May 26. 67.

Colford, Steven. 1989. Turner battles Whittle: Ad-free CNN Newsroom set for schools. *Advertising Age*, May 1. 3, 81.

Combs, Margaret. 1993. Political agendas in the classroom. *Boston Sunday Globe*, March 21. 42, 45.

Commercializing education. 1989. *Boston Globe*, March 6. 18.

Donaton, Scott. 1989. Whittle: Channel One is a hit. *Advertising Age*, September 18. 83.

————. 1992. Chinks showing in Whittle allure. *Advertising Age*, August 17, 1, 30–34.

Educational research finds students learn from Whittle's Channel One. 1989. Whittle Communications news release. Knoxville, Tenn. June 7.

Erdman, Barbara. 1990. Media Design and the educational experience, or what can formalism offer media design? Paper presented at American Educational Research Association, Boston. April.

For the record. 1989. *Advertising Age*, April 24. 71.

Gallup Study of Attitudes toward Channel One. 1989. Gallup Organizations, Inc. May.

Golden State. 1989. *The Nation*, June 26. 873.

Goodman, Ellen. 1989. Commercial school space for rent. *Boston Globe*, March 2. 11.

Hammer, Joshua. 1990. Golden boy's toughest sell. *Newsweek*, February 19. 52–53.

Harty, Sheila. 1979. Huckster's in the classroom: A review of industry propaganda in schools. Washington, D.C.: Center for Study of Responsive Law.

Hoffman, Lawrence. 1991. The meanings of Channel One. Paper presented at American Educational Research Association, Chicago, Ill. April 6.

Iacocca, Lee. 1988. *Talking Straight*. New York: Bantam Books.

Is the classroom for blackboards or billboards? 1989. *Consumer Reports*, May. 286.

Jarrard, David. 1990. Response to the second draft of commercialism on schools study: a policy briefing paper. Whittle Communications: Knoxville, Tenn. December 20.

Johnson, Bradley. 1990. School ads hit. *Advertising Age*, October 8. 77.

Jordan, Robert. 1989. Grade still out on school ads. *Boston Globe*, March 11. 25.

Kantrowitz, Barbara et al. 1991. Playing Catch Up. *Newsweek*, April 22. 28–31.

Landro, Laura. 1989. TV News Show Could Open School Doors to Advertisers. *Wall Street Journal*, March 4. 17.

Loro, Laura. 1989. Money moving toward more precise targets. *Advertising Age*, March 27. 48E.

Major school groups blast plan for commercial TV in classes. 1989. *Education Week*, March 8. 5.

Manuel, Diane. 1991. School reform-for a price. *Boston Globe*, May 26. 67, 68.

McManus, John. 1990. McDonald's, NBA team. *Advertising Age*, September 17. 61.

Molnar, Alex. 1989/1990. Business involvement in schools: Separating wheat from chaff. *Educational Leadership*, December. 68–69.

Moore, Thomas with Nancy Linnon. 1989. The selling of our schools. *U.S. News & World Report*, November 6. 34–40.

Nike, Whittle rapped. 1991. *Advertising Age*, May 13. 39.

No Thanks. 1990. *The Economist,* April 14. 27.

Palmer, Thomas. 1990. Channel One thrives despite its detractors. *Boston Globe,* December 5. 61, 64.

Pomice, Eva. 1989. Whittling the message into the medium. *U.S. News & World Report,* February 20. 52.

Postman, Neil. 1985. *Amusing Ourselves to Death.* New York: Viking.

P.T.A. opposes school TV plan. 1989. *New York Times,* March 3. D17.

Raposa, Laura. 1990. TV show brings news and ads to classrooms. *Boston Globe,* March 6. 5.

Reilly, Patrick. 1989. 7 Advertisers test Whittle's "Channel One." *Advertising Age,* March 6. 3, 76.

Rohrer, Jim. 1989. In real world, Channel One fills real need. *Cincinnati Enquirer.* March 8. 3.

Rudinow, Joel. 1989/1990. Channel One whittles away at education. *Educational Leadership,* December. 70–73.

Selling America's children: Commercial pressure on kids of the 90s. 1990. Washington, D.C.: Consumer's Union.

Sheinfeld, Lois. 1989. Dangerous liaisons. *Film Comment,* September–October. 70–72.

Stein, M. L. 1991. Lobbyist for California publishers' group also touting classroom tv. *Editor & Publisher,* September 7. 11.

Streifeld, David. 1992. Three years later, debate still swirls around Channel One. *Boston Globe,* May 3. A80.

Walsh, Mark. 1989. Channel One debut wins viewer plaudits but school groups pan "commercialism." *Education Week,* March 15. 31.

Whittle backed by court in North Carolina dispute. 1990. *Wall Street Journal,* March 5. A8.

Whittle books to have Fed Ex ads. 1989. *Boston Herald,* November 9. 72.

Whittle, Chris. 1989. Channel One: Lesson in reality. *ADWEEK,* March 6. 48.

Whittle Communications launches three channel educational network. 1989. Whittle Communications news release. June 8.

Whittle rips 'out-of-step' shops. 1990. *Advertising Age,* August 27, S2.

Whittle urges study. 1991. *New York Times,* April 10. D6.

Zoglin, Richard. 1990. Battle over classroom TV. *Time,* March 19. 59.

Interviews

Fortune Rose, Sara. Representative for Channel One. July 6, 1989. (Telephone).

Jarrard, David. Public Relations contact for Whittle Communications. July 6, 1989. (Telephone).

Koppel, Ted. Interview of Chris Whittle. *Nightline*. ABC-TV. March 6, 1989.

6

Reading the Ads:
The Bacchanalian Adolescence

Corn, corn comin' to you.
A fresh taste in corn chips
That's really new.
Corn crisp from Pringles.
You've got the fever . . .
For a fresh corn flavor . . .

New corn chips from Pringles,
The fresh corn fever reliever.
(Channel One, *Monday, April 9, 1990*)

As we approach the millenium, these are the sounds of the new public school curriculum.

If the authors of this book who conducted classroom research agree on one event, it is that students invariably watch the ads on Channel One, regardless of whether they watch the news. Classroom observers comment on the attentive gazes and silence brought about by these ads. However, the central question to be posed about the presence of ads in the classroom is not, "Will they have a negative effect on students?" The efficacy of advertising in this consumer culture needs no proof. The question to ask is, "What are they doing in the classroom?"

I have read several weeks of Channel One ads from 1990 and 1992, and I will describe my readings in this chapter. A call for evidence of the ads' detrimental effect on teens will also be discussed. Using an adapted reader theory, I will delineate the material base of these ads and provide a textual analysis of one representative ad. The context of modern and postmodern commercials will be used as a backdrop for the analysis, and a surprising Rabelaisian overtone to the ads will be noted.

The former California Superintendent of Public Instruction, Bill Honig, and a congress of parents, teachers, and students asked questions of Santa Clara's East Side Union High School District in a civil suit which worked its way to the state Superior Court (Fogel 1992). The school district—the defendants in the case—had disregarded a statewide ban on Channel One that Honig had issued, and they aired the daily news program in East Side Union's classrooms. The original position of California's Department of Instruction (DPI) was that students who viewed the program were being sold to advertisers. Most California schools are already wired for cable, and the ban was—for the majority—no hardship. While the ban was in effect, a new bill—similar to the New York law prohibiting coersive advertising in public classrooms—was initiated in the California legislature. Although the bill passed the Assembly, it failed to clear the state Senate. By the time the civil suit reached the Superior Court, Whittle Communications had joined East Side Union as a intervenor/defendant. (Fogel 1992). The state DPI sought a permanent injunction on two points of prohibiting the high school district from showing Channel One. The first contention was that the airing and viewing of the program was obligatory for teachers and students. The second point was "that the type of advertising contained in Channel One broadcasts is neither necessary nor incidental to a valid educational purpose . . . but instead amounts to a "sale" of the minds of students to Whittle and its advertisers in exchange for hardware for which defendant otherwise would have to pay in dollars"(Fogel 1992, 2).

Point one arose from the restrictive nature of the Whittle contract which mandated the showing of 90 percent of the news programs during the school year in every classroom that contained a Whittle monitor. The airing had to be during school time—not during lunch or recess—and students could not be excused to attend a study hall. If this contract was broken during the first three years of Channel One, the school would forfeit all donated hardware. Point two addresses the focal issue of this chapter—namely, "What are the ads doing in a public classroom?"

To assist himself in rendering a decision about point two, Judge Jeremy Fogel noted that East Side Union High School was in a low income district, and that "new and innovative means must be explored to provide resources to [low income] schools without the actual expenditure of funds." His decision rested on whether the impact of Channel One advertising could be called "incidental" to the educational process. After examining research studies presented by plaintiffs, he concluded that the impact of these ads could not be ascertained because "there does not appear to be convincing social-scientific evidence on this precise point" (Fogel 1992, 6). Again, the answer to a question fraught with cultural implications must be found, the judge believes, in scientific evidence. Perhaps he was looking for numbers. Yet, judges are versed in the daily application of specific social and cultural case facts to the principles of law.

Although, Judge Fogel ruled in favor of the defendant, he did call for some restrictions on viewing. He also called for a new study "to evaluate the impact of the advertising used on Channel One on the students who view it to assist the Court in determining whether such impact can reasonably be characterized as incidental" (Fogel 1992, 10). However, even without statistical evidence, advertisers—ever-tuned to the demographic glitch of the baby boomers—know that their ads make children consume. They are so confident about this fact that they are currently paying Whittle Communications $200,000 to place a thirty-second ad for their product on Channel One.

Probably no numerical proof can be amassed to convince Judge Fogel of the impact of classroom TV ads on students, and these commercials will become a part of the educational enterprise in the second most populous state in the nation. Their inclusion as curriculum is a central concern here. TV ads at home are not education, are not part of the curriculum, and are not given the imprimatur of the school district. At home, they are entertainment.

Gavriel Salomon (1984) found that students are used to being entertained at home by TV but, in the classroom, TV becomes instruction, not entertainment. Already eight million students in eleven thousand schools, almost one-quarter of all U.S. high schools, are wired to receive these TV ads along with the MTV-formatted current events program.

READER THEORY

Rather than seeking that elusive definitive measure of the effect of these TV ads on students, one could pose an alternative question. "How do these ads construct their subjects or position their viewers? In other words, just whom do these ads think their viewers are? To whom would one say 'You've got the fever for a fresh corn flavor . . .

Pringles, the fresh corn fever reliever'." (Channel One, Monday, April 9, 1990)

Channel One advertisments are texts that have been constructed with intent by producers. They contain socially constructed signs and symbols, and they are read and interpreted by viewers who have access to those signs and symbols. As such, an analyst can explore the readers, the ads, and their producers, or any combination of the three, by employing a poststructural reader theory. If an analyst is concerned with the way in which producers treat and address students in the classroom, he or she may find evidence of this treatment in the visual codes and verbal rhetoric of the ads themselves. Although this form of reading is a departure from the traditional content analysis that communication researchers conduct, it has more power to account for the presence of discourses within ads than does simple content analysis.

To ascertain the manner in which Channel One ads position their viewers, I have read several weeks of these ads and explored the textual and rhetorical devices used by designers and producers to map the subjectivities of their audience. I will describe my readings and provide a textual analysis of one representative ad. In this case, I am the reader, and my reading credentials are as follows: I have taught high-school English for nine years and am aware of the ability of adolescents to read visual and verbal texts; I have written about visual literacy and taught educational media and communications for nineteen years at the graduate and undergraduate level at a university; I have two children (male and female) whom I parented through adolescence. Before this reading, I will situate Channel One ads in the context of broadcast and cablecast TV advertisements.

Peopled with teens and narrowly targeted for adolescents in the classroom, Channel One ads constitute a new terrain on which producers map collective and individual teen subjectivity on a daily basis. Male and female teen bodies are objectified and commodified for student pleasure and consumption as they are pictured next to the product being sold. These bodies are being sold, because they signify that which is valued in teen culture. However, if ads simply reflected cultural habits, they would fail. (Note the manner in which Channel One ads fixate the gaze of high school students. They are attending, I believe, to learn new adolescent behavior, as well as to validate what they believe to be au courant.)

U.S. teens spend approximately $79 billion per year, and it is estimated that they influence parental spending of approximately another $44 billion in sales. (Mueller and Wulfemeyer 1991). Ads are on the cutting edge of popular culture. They assume leadership in setting style, and shaping habits and attitudes about appearance, behavior, and consumption. The ads on Channel One construct an adolescent world that invites students to participate in the pleasures of surprisingly homogeneous discourses (Ellsworth 1987). If the invitation is accepted, students could become subjects of (speakers and actors) and subjected to (recipients) of these discourses. They might employ the visual and verbal rhetoric of these discourses, while this rhetoric speaks through them. They might speak, act, and consume in the roles in which they are positioned by the ads.

They could, however, read against the grain of the commercials, and not accept the invitation to participate in these discourses.

THE CONTEXT OF ADVERTISING

In *The Culture of Narcissism,* Christopher Lasch writes:

In a simpler time, advertising merely called attention to the product and extolled its advantages. Now it manufactures a product of its own: the consumer, perpetually unsatisfied, restless, anxious, and bored. Advertising serves not so much to advertise products as to promote consumption as a way of life. It "educates" the masses into an unappeasable appetite not only for goods, but for new experiences and personal fulfillment. It upholds consumption as the answer to the age-old discontents of lonliness, sickness, weariness, lack of sexual satisfaction; at the same time it creates new forms of discourse peculiar to the modern age. It plays seductively on the malaise of industrial civilization. Is your job boring and meaningless? Does it leave you with feelings of futility and fatigue? Is your life empty? Consumption promises to fill the aching void; hence the attempt to surround commodities with an aura of romance; with allusions to exotic places and vivid experiences; and with images of female breasts from which all blessings flow. (Lasch 1978, 72–73)

Lasch clearly describes the work of advertisements in the modern world—for example, the construction and positioning of the unappeaseable consumer, and the work of creating new discourses about romance and commodities. He could have been describing television ads in the '70s that made standard appeals to the desire for love, health, security, confidence, and excitement—those states of being that are generally valued in our society. Modern TV ads, then and now, touted a product's ability to solve a problem, to lift someone from the doldrums. To reach this satisfying conclusion, advertisers first had to picture the doldrums, such as the antisocial state of a person with bad "morning breath." Modern ads are short narratives in which heroes and heroines overcome life's odds by the purchase and application of a product. These stories have a resolution.

The work of the reader of ads, as Kervin (1990) describes it, is to fill in the gaps, to make the connection between a product and what is valued. She contends that ads sell social values, and the goal for the reader is to achieve the valued state. Messages in ads are so short and intense that they must rely on the reader's knowledge of other social and cultural texts and signs and symbols contained in those texts. "Advertising, therefore, bridges culture and capitalism, combining social knowledge and market concerns" (Kervin 1990, 10).

Ad readers, I believe, are some of the most active viewers. They fill in narrative gaps to make sense of the commercial story by attending to the codified rhetoric of the audio track while threading their way through the abbreviated geography of the video space. More than other producers, producers of ads attend consciously to the job of constructing, positioning, and addressing their subjects. That is because these ads exist solely to make these subjects or viewers act. Few texts—such as ads and sermons—are designed solely to make their readers act. Producers of commercials, then, must rely on readers' knowledge of other cultural texts, such as those in mass and popular media.

TV ads are highly intertextual. They rely heavily on a viewer's knowledge of broadcast and cablecast programs. Verbal codified rhetoric and visual codes may be borrowed intact from these programs to assist the reader in making sense. For example, the modern Scope bad morning-breath ad borrows visual codes from sitcoms and other ads set in bathrooms. Visual codes are simply production patterns which arise in the course of shooting a scene within a particular format. On TV, some formats which have their own visual codes that shift over time are talk shows, sitcoms, sports events, MTV, and soap operas. Because modern TV ads must grab and hold the attention of the viewer, they mix visual codes from different formats.

Postmodern Advertisements

Christopher Lasch (1978) describes the change in advertisements which emerged in an age of modern texts. Modern literary and filmic texts were primarily linear. Their narratives were coherent and plot action was often subservient to the exploration of the psyche of the central characters. Technology was usually villianous. Modern texts generally had an Hegelian narrative direction of thesis, anti-thesis, and synthesis.

Visual and verbal texts of the '90s, however, are certainly post-modern and owe a great debt to Jorge Luis Borges who reestablished the primacy of the plot, but fractured the narrative while mixing fantasy with reality. Postmodern visual texts also owe a great debt to the Op and Pop Art movements of the '60s. Television which has the capability of producing fractured narratives and fragmented images spawned a quintessential postmodern text when MTV was initiated.

As Marshall McLuhan suggested, (1964) a medium in its infancy imitates the forms of a prior medium. Commercial TV initially imitated legitimate theater and Hollywood cinema until it discovered its original codes in the production unique to program formats. Production practices which emerged in 1981 with the creation of MTV significantly changed television's conventions and codes. Broadcast and narrowcast television conventions today are imitative of MTV. Also, the Children's Television Workshop has produced at least two educational programs—*Three, Two, One Contact* and *Square One Television*—which borrow MTV formats for their entire presentation. The organization of the news on Channel One—as well as most of the ads—is designed in an MTV format.

MTV and the postmodern text. High-school children—(eight million of whom are captive readers of Channel One)—have grown up reading MTV which was available to average sophomores since they were two years old. They are facile readers of music videos, most of which have fractured narrative lines, segmented images, and a panoply of TV formats. Within traditional narrative TV formats, directors follow camera rules, such as the 180-degree rule and matched cuts, so that viewers "know where they are" and can understand the geography of the space. By breaking the 180-degree rule and generously employing jump cuts, MTV tosses the viewer around in the geography of the space.

Those children whom I have interviewed for research projects have no difficulty reading these fragmented, jerky pictoral movements. In fact, they welcome the challenge to make sense of MTV shots, or to opt out of making sense and just let the images wash over them. For many it is a preferred viewing format.

Although this is an essay about how producers position adolescents, not how teens read TV, I will digress here to look at some teen viewing habits. The teens whom I have interviewed talk about two modes of watching TV. In the first mode, they deliberately make sense of what they see. In the second mode, they "zone out" and watch the screen for its escape value. One teen told me that "zoning" on MTV was like taking a drug. It is fantasy. It's many fast images, repeated over and over. I was told that it was something like watching the lines on a road zip by when one is speeding in a car. However, perception theorists—especially those who study the grammars of interpreting visual fields (Leeuwenberg and Buffart 1978)—would claim that, within the second mode, teens are unconsciously making sense of the fractured images that speed by them. Even when students are viewing in a passive mode, some learning takes place.

Broadcast and narrowcast television has shifted some of its advertisement time to the presentation of postmodern texts. I am sure that the decision to air postmodern ads was a collaboration of ad producers and network executives, not one that was foisted upon television by Madison Avenue. Consequently, some current ads have MTV formats with fractured narratives and fragmented images.

Another characteristic of these ads is the pecular elimination of picturing what Lasch (1978) calls the "age-old discontents of lonliness, sickness, and the like." Many postmodern TV ads display the "relieved state" which a product is supposed to produce, without presenting the prior state that the product was supposed to relieve. A postmodern ad on broadcast or cablecast television, therefore, is one that presents a fractured narrative with fragmented images of a trouble-free, often celebratory life. The conventions of production have been borrowed from MTV, but the creation of an idealized, pastoral life has been borrowed from select traditional codes of TV advertising. Whether modern or post modern, TV ads have always juxtaposed products with romanticized images of people and images from nature.

Many communication researchers who analyze advertisements today do not take into account the fact that postmodern ads call for post structural forms of analysis. The dominant analytical model is still content analysis which can describe the postmodern communication, but not account for it.

Kervin (1990) is one researcher who focuses on the reading of ads. While noting a shift in the argument presented in commercials from rational to emotional, she describes a new type of ad that she labels as "ambiguous." Although she deals exclusively with ads printed in magazines, she notes that there has been a recent spate of ambiguous ads whose objectives are unclear. They may contain blurred, black-and-white images. They often contain the face of a woman. They may depict an interactive scene between a man and woman, or they may juxtapose strange objects with the human form. They exist, she believes, to elicit a strong emotional response which is then connected to the product being advertised. The name of the product always appears. I would call these ambiguous ads postmodern in their form.

THE CONTENT AND CONTEXT OF CHANNEL ONE ADVERTISEMENTS

The majority of Channel One ads are made especially for the news program. This exclusive targeting brought about by a direct electronic pipeline to eight million teens—a 100 percent share of the largest teen audience ever assembled—prompts advertisers to spend production money on special ads. It is this unique group of ads that interest me, for they clearly display the producers' attitudes toward those eight million adolescents. They include ads for junk food, tennis shoes, jeans, candy, deodorant, acne medicine, shampoos, and other products.

In an excellent content analysis of Channel One ads, Mueller and Wulfemeyer discuss the frequency of product appearance. "Levi jeans were the most frequent . . . followed by commercials for candy . . . catsup . . . shoes . . . breath mints" (1991, 146–147).

Some companies, such as Burger King and Paramount Pictures, may not produce unique commercials, but simply air an advertisement that has appeared on broadcast or cablecast TV. It is surprising how many ads for commercial TV incorporate teens! There has also been a trend in Hollywood during the past decade to make adolescent films, just as there has been an increase of teen sitcoms and dramatic series on television.

There are also commonalities in the ads borrowed from commercial television. They usually picture some teens. They often picture people of color and white actors, whereas the Channel One ads usually incorporate only white teens. They are almost exclusively postmodern in their form—that is, with fractured narratives, fragmented images, heightened use of jump cuts, excessive use of dancing and singing, and startling juxtaposition of images.

That they are postmodern is important, because it indicates an awareness and a tacit agreement by the producers as to what appeals to teens and what forms of television they are prepared to read. However, the ads created exclusively for them draw upon a surprisingly narrow set of discourses. Yet, they construct a specific world of adolescence and provide a material base for depicting that world. It is distinctly Bacchanalian.

Teens are predominantly pictured singing, dancing, jumping, and riding in outdoor scenes where nature plays as large a role as do their bodies—that is corn fields, sand, surf, a garden wedding party, and garden dining areas. In this age of closed cars, they ride in open jeeps and convertibles. They cavort while riding, and hair streams in the wind. Whole bodies are displayed and fractured body parts are often juxtaposed with the item being sold. That item is often junk food, and the teens consume products in a celebratory fashion. Blond and dark-haired young women are pictured, but most close-ups are of blond hair cascading over a girl's shoulders and partially obscuring her eyes. Dark-haired girls are seldom seen in tight shots. Boys and girls are clothed in what might be considered fashionable in teen culture. Although boys bodies are sometimes objectified—such as in beach scenes—girls' bodies are clothed in tight revealing clothes and usually objectified. This fact is easily ascertained, because more female body parts are fractured and pictured without faces. This depiction was originally a pornography code. Adolescents pictured in these ads are almost exclusively celebrating and consuming. Nature is valorized, and no labor is depicted.

Textual Analysis

One Pringles ad is representative of the unique postmodern commercials made for Channel One. I will describe it here.

CAVORTING ON THE FARM

SCENARIO. In this thirty-second spot for Pringle corn chips, six teens (four girls and two boys) dance and play in a corn field. As the scene opens, one boy, standing in the middle of the corn field, is slowly detassling an ear of very yellow corn. The other is standing on a ladder propped against a silo. He has a paint roller in his hand, but is facing away from the silo and into the camera. Four girls, waving yellow cans of Pringles at the boys, arrive in speeding yellow jeep. Girls and boys come together. They dance and feed one another corn chips. Magically, the silo turns into a yellow can of Pringles. A large banner appears across the screen in block letters, "FEVER RELIEVER."

AUDIO. A musical jingle runs throughout this ad. The jingle compares corn chips to fresh corn and tells the students, "You have the fever for a fresh corn flavor." The rhythm and volume of the jingle gradually increase until they reach a "fever pitch." After the jingle ends, a rich deep male voice-over says slowly, "The fresh corn fever reliever."

VIDEO. The visual track is in the form of a music video. Although a story is told, dramatic narrative codes are abandoned in favor of MTV codes. Approximately seventy shots occupy the thirty-second slot. Very fast-paced cuts articulate the shots, half of which are not matched, but are jump cuts. The boys are dressed in jeans and T-shirts, but the four girls are dressed in tight bright clothes that call attention to their bodies. The two girls whose images occupy most of the music video are blond. Each wears an off-the-shoulder top. Their shoulders are bare. The pacing of the cuts increases as the rhythm of the music increases, until it reaches a fast-cut culminating scene. This scene is a very tight shot of a boy's lap. He is supposed to be seated in the corn field. His face is not shown. With one hand he holds a detassled ear of yellow corn erect in his lap. A female hand (no face) reaches for the corn. Magically, the corn turns into a stack of corn chips about the size of the ear of corn. The female hand plucks a corn chip, and the stack turns back into an erect ear of corn. By repeatedly intercutting the ear of corn held by the boy's hand and the female hand reaching for the corn/chip stack, the producer shows the stack of chips gradually diminishing. The scene closes with a close up of the girl's ecstatic face. The scene switches to the closing series of shots next to the silo where the "fever reliever" banner is rolled.

My purpose in conducting this textual analysis is not to suggest that adolescents use these abbreviated texts, among all visual texts they read, as guidelines for living. I am noting however, their rapt attention to them in classrooms. I am also questioning their presence in an educational setting. Producers of the Pringle's ad deliberately intercut two separate videos in the last scene to produce an erotic metaphor. Production techniques are not accidental. If teens are, at first, unable to read the erotic images, they will soon learn how to do so in this instructional setting. I am also not suggesting that teens suspend their celebration of life, nor that visual texts abandon equitable depictions of celebrations. I am suggesting that, if Hollywood and commercial television and classroom TV present only a Bacchanalian adolescence, then these images may assist teens in the construction of adolescence as primarily a party.

It may serve to confirm some already established notions. And where is labor in this depiction of life?

Rabelaisian Overtones

Some MTV presentations, such as rap videos, may be considered to be popular culture artifacts. Renato Resaldo (1989) likes to talk about culture taking place on the borders of a society. However, I like to think of popular culture as that which takes place on the borders of a society. In our society, rap takes place on the borders of popular music presentations on television, in concerts, and in film. It appears to break down old expected musical, rhetorical, and dance conventions by making startling new connections among the three. Of course, when musical innovations are appropriated by commercial television, advertisements, and Hollywood, they lose their ability to startle. They move from the borders and become mainstream. Yet, on the border is still this new Bacchanalian advertising format made exclusively for teens in classrooms and peopled exclusively by teens. Here is the material base for this new format. Here are juxtapositions of incongruent images which still have the power to startle.

"The most varied objects and phenomena of the world are brought into direct contact with food and drink" (Bakhtin 1981, 178). Phallic corn and snack chips are representative samples of the images on Channel One ads. Fragmented body parts are regularly displayed with incongruous objects, so that the human body clearly becomes the central material object upon which these abbreviated postmodern narratives are based. "In order to describe the human body . . . a mass of the most varied objects and phenomena are drawn into the body series" (Bakhtin 1981, 173).

Channel One ads continually juxtapose body parts and product images. New lives, solely of pleasure, are written upon the electronic bodies and into the electronic texts of these ads. Bakhtin (1981) speaks about consumption as a process tending toward stasis, and toward the present. As such, Channel One ads become stories about bodies in timeless acts of consumption.

It is clear that producers borrowed production conventions or codes from two sources, namely, MTV and postmodern TV ads. However, parts of each of these TV formats are Rabelaisian in content and structure, because they build their messages upon the material base of the body, they both juxtapose unusual images with fragmented body parts, and they valorize eating, drinking, and sexual activities. However, TV ads cannot completely abandon a structure that will appeal to those consumer-viewers accustomed to reading coherent modern text. So, the grotesque is eliminated and kept at bay, as it were, for the ultimate purpose of product sales.

The comparison of Channel One ads for teens to the works of Rabelais does not suggest that producers have read *Gargantua* and *Pantagruel* and imitated its structure. The comparison is, in fact, limited. The same modes of representation are used, but Rabelais, on the cusp of the Medieval and Renassaince world, had specific intentions. His project was to depict whole human beings, people who celebrated their bodies as well as their minds. He intended to break the corporeal restrictions of medieval literature and society (Bakhtin 1984). He tried to open up the conception of humans by depicting their physical and mental worlds. Although Channel One ads apply similar modes of representation, the result is the opposite. These commercials shut down, not open up, the representation of humans by depicting them only at play in a narrow set of Bacchanalian activities. Not only is the range of human action severly limited, but the actors are usually white and blond, further limiting the scope of human representation.

Although Channel One ad forms are derivative, both postmodern commercial TV ads and MTV have been directly influenced by Rabelais. These formats exist at the juncture of the modern and postmodern age in which postmodern texts seek to reclaim the validity of the body. Modern literary texts usually valorized the descent into the mind of white male heros, as in the works of Joyce, Kafka, Faulkner, Updike, early Roth, and others. Although they often included bodily and sexual activities, they were usually depicted because authors dared to break old taboos. Readers understood that it was the journey through the psyche that was central. Modern authors did not write about what has been called the "surface aspects" of characters' daily lives as described in the work of the U.S. minimalists (Beatty, Coover, Carver, Ford, and others), nor the visceral activities described in the work of the Fabulists (Borges, Vargas Illosa, Garcia Marquez, and others). Postmodern minimalists and Fabulists wished to shift attention away from Freudian processes to those concerned with the body interacting with everyday events. Literary styles, per se, do not directly influence the production of commercial TV formats, but they do offer a shortcut to understanding shifts in narrative techniques. They provide a way in which to decode the structure of narrative techniques in popular culture, and they certainly influence popular culture. As with the Channel One ads that I analyze here, TV ads respond to popular art and media styles, and they act as opinion leaders.

Because ads are the format of interest here, one might note that women's bodies have, for a long time and in both modern and post-modern times, been objectified in commercials. But as Kervin (1990) points out, while modern ads objectified women, they usually made rational appeals to the mind. Postmodern ads appeal to emotions, and make new and startling use of bodies.

Overview

Advertisements made for Channel One depict a Bacchanalian adolescent world peopled with white teens. This depiction reveals much about who the commercial producers think their viewers are, and/or about what they think their viewers value in life. Mueller and Wulfemeyer's findings concur with my reading of the ads. Most of the ads they viewed "featured young people enjoying themselves and the advertised products" (1991, 148). They also note the white world of these ads.

> Channel One commercials did not present an adequate racial mix of characters. African-American, Hispanic, or Asian domi-nant characters were rarely visible. Even the commercials that featured a large cast, more than 75 percent had only Caucasian characters. Such racially disproportionate presentations seem inappropriate for schools with racially mixed student popula-tions. (Mueller and Wulfemeyer 1991, 148)

They agree that these ads focused primarily on "leisure/pleasure, appearance/sexuality . . ." (Mueller and Wulfemeyer 1991, 149). They note that most commercials featured a dominant character who was Caucasian 87 percent of the time, and male 57 percent of the time.

I am grateful to Mueller and Wulfemeyer for uncovering a 1990 Whittle development document which places the issue of advertising in the classroom in context. I quote it here.

> Because of the age of its audience and the "educational environment in which Channel One is viewed, Whittle Com-munications recognizes that it has a special responsibility to the teenage audience." The advertising standards for Channel One state that it is important to present advertising which is truthful and tasteful, and not misleading or deceptive. In addition, Whittle Communications encourages advertisers to develop

commercials designed specifically for Channel One and lists some "proactive" responsibilities for advertisers.

A. Include a balanced representation of individuals from a variety of social, racial, ethnic, or gender groups.

B. Provide positive role models for all members of the viewing audience.

C. Include and portray individuals with physical and mental impairments.

D. Place an emphasis on the importance of education and remaining in school.

E. Communicate strong messages against all forms of antisocial behavior, including drug use, violence, prejudice, and the like.

What was the motive for writing these "standards"? Was it to sell a product—namely, Channel One—to school boards and administrators?

REFERENCES

Bakhtin, M. M. 1981. *The Dialogic Imagination*, ed. M. Holquist, trans. C. Emerson and M. Holquist. Austin, Texas: The University of Texas Press.

———. 1984. *Rabelais and His World*, trans. H. Iswolsky. Bloomington, Ind.: Indiana University Press.

Ellsworth, E. 1987. Media interpretation as a social and political act. *Journal of Visual Literacy*, 8:2, 27–38.

Fogel, J. 1992. Memorandum of decision. Santa Clara, Calif.: Superior Court of the State of California.

Kervin, D. 1990. Advertising and persuasion: From logical argumentation to seductive ambiguity. *Journal of Visual Literacy,* 10:2, 8–41.

Lasch, C. 1978. The culture of narcissism. New York: Norton.

Leeuwenberg, E., and H. Buffart. 1978. *Formal Theories of Perception.* New York: John Wiley and Sons.

McLuhan, M. (1964). *Understanding Media,* New York; McGraw-Hill.

Mueller, B., and K. Wulfemeyer. 1991. A framework for the analysis of commercials in the classroom: The decoding of Channel One. *The High School Journal,* February/March. 138–149.

Rosaldo, R. (1989). *Culture and Truth,* Boston; Beacon Press.

7

Form, Style, and Lesson: An Analysis of Commercially Produced School News Programs

Educational media forms are highly dependent on popular culture forms for aesthetic style and production techniques. In 1971, Charles Hoban recognized the influence of contemporary culture and school practice on educational film form, and acknowledged that educational media research had directed little effort toward examining issues raised by the production and use of this medium.

> That films reflect the culture of the society or cult of their makers is generally regarded as axiomatic. So is the corollary that American instructional film follow the "rules" of the subculture of American school instruction. Beyond these two statements, it is difficult to proceed, since very little analysis has been made of instructional films in terms of the values they portray and the "rules" under which they are produced and used. (Hoban 1971, 15)

To gain insight into the factors that structure the educational media experience, it is necessary to understand something about the medium itself, about viewer expectations, and about wider relationships of the medium within the culture. Each educational medium adapts the stylistic qualities and forms of the dominant modes of presentation for its own educational purposes, creating, in the process, educational forms and styles with their own characteristics.

It is important for educators to recognize that all learning experiences delivered through a medium that is also used as a popular entertainment form, provide an aesthetic experience as part of their motive for viewing, and draw on cultural expectations to communicate. Because most teachers are inadequately prepared to evaluate anything but the educational subject of media programs designed for education, how the formal and stylistic qualities within educational media interact to determine the type of instruction available to students and teachers is, unfortunately, rarely examined. The discussions of nationally available secondary-school news programs demonstrate this deficiency. There has been little evidence that teachers and administrators have evaluated the programs with any criteria other than the absence or presence of advertising segments, and the major concern of the debate within the education community has been over the policy implications of school-sanctioned advertising within the school curriculum. Educators have not analyzed the unified experience of the content and aesthetic design to determine how they construct knowledge, and what types of learning experiences are available through them.

My concerns, however, include questions about the relationship between, on the one hand, educational intent and form and, on the other hand, style in news programs produced for use in secondary-school classrooms and delivered via telecommunications technologies. My primary interest is in how the instructional intent influences form and style in the programs, and how the two school news programs structure the types of knowledge available in the programs. Using formalist methodologies, I have developed a model of the two programs—Whittle Communication's Channel One and Cable News Network's *Newsroom.*

THE FORMALIST METHOD

The formalist method has, most often, been discussed in relation to works of art. The formalist method of film analysis defined in the work of Bordwell and Thompson (1986) offers a model that can be applied to many media forms used in education, particularly those that include an aesthetic motive for viewing. This method is based on principles of formal unity and acknowledges that a media program is not simply a random group of elements, but, rather, its form is an "overall system of relations" that the viewer or participant perceives. (Bordwell and Thompson 1986, 24).

The formalist method is, for several reasons, an appropriate method of analysis for educational film, television, and many computer software programs. First, because these media forms use production techniques originating in the visual media, the analysis criteria available in formalist method can be applied directly to these programs. Second, an especially significant aspect of the formalist method is that it considers content, or subject matter, to be a unified part of the total formal system. Bordwell and Thompson explain that

> . . . very often people assume that "form" as a concept is the opposite of something called "content." This implies that a poem or a musical piece or a film is like a jug; an external shape, the jug *contains* something that could have just as easily be held in a cup or a pail. Under this assumption, form becomes less important than whatever it is presumed to contain (1986, 25).

Formalist analysis allows one to analyze the content in the programs as part of the form and to ascertain the entire experience offered by the programs.

CULTURE AND MEDIA DESIGN

A viewer's familiarity with a television genre or format—such as television news—is the result of a cumulative process. Viewers' expectations develop with repeated viewings, and viewers come to recognize the system of the format and its significance (Schatz 1981). Conventions determine what formal principles are recognized as belonging to a particular type of representation. For example, what makes one program a family sitcom and another an adult drama are formal and stylistic elements that are generally agreed upon and expected within our culture. Norms, however, are not complete sets of rigid rules, but a range of common traits that both the creator and the spectator recognize as appropriate within the work. Within a set of norms, there is also a certain degree of variation (Schatz 1981). What makes a program attractive is often the ways in which it diverges from the norms of its genre. For example, *All in the Family*—a late 1960s family sitcom—broke with the norm replacing the typical benevolent father figure with an arrogant and bigoted head of the family in the person of Archie Bunker. The variations within popular or successful television programs and films affect the evolution of the genre. An example of the way a genre can change over time is apparent in the mother-focused family sitcom genre by comparing the 1950s *I Love Lucy* programs to the programs of *Roseanne* in the 1990s. The formal norms of a particular educational medium are the patterns of formal principles regarded as typical for that medium. Norms can be determined for a general program type or genre, such as elementary-school-level skills development programs. Norms can also be determined for a specific programs series, such as *Newscast from the Past*, or *3-2-1 Contact*. Style refers to the repeated and salient uses of the techniques of the medium that are characteristic of a single program or of a specific series when the entire series is under analysis. Stylistic elements include scenic elements of setting, such as costume, makeup, lighting, and figure movement; framing elements of camera angle, height, and movement; and all aspects of editing and sound. The unified, developed, and significant use of particular technical choices creates a system within a program or series which is called its "style." Norms of program style are established when a pattern of stylistic features is regarded as typical for a program genre or an entire series. My study of the formal and stylistic elements of news programs produced for use in secondary school classrooms suggests, at several points, how the programs encourage specific activities on the part of the viewer.

When analyzing a program's formal system, it is necessary to understand the requirements of the form of the program in relation to the program's purpose. The formal system of the news program is organized around the need of the program to present specific new material in a clear manner, and, therefore, the form of the program can be analyzed around that purpose. In television news, the journalistic, or informational, subsystem combines with a stylistic subsystem to provide the larger organizational system of the total program. The subsystem of the "news story" is closely linked to the stylistic subsystem. For example, in the contemporary traditional news program, the anchor person functions both journalistically—as he or she introduces and describes news events—and stylistically— as the frequent appearance of the attractive, familiar, and trustworthy anchorperson provides program continuity and sustains viewer attention.

The consideration of techniques—such as cinematography, sound, editing, and the like—as elements within stylistic subsystems allows each technique within a program to be analyzed in relation to its function in the whole program. For example, when analyzing the functions of sound in a program, one finds that the anchor's commentary serves journalistically to develop the news story by simply stating facts, while on-location sound effects emphasize actions within the news story. The presentation of certain sounds concentrates our attention on actions that are particularly significant to the story. Sound devices also help unify the program and contribute to stylistic development. Repeated sounds—called "motifs"—are used to develop recurring themes. For example, a familiar musical motif often indicates the separation between news segments. These are just a few of the steps in the analysis process. A complete analysis details how every element shapes the program's form and viewer's experience.

To discover the norms of the secondary-school news program, I viewed regularly, over a six week period in the spring of 1990, programs from each of the two series: Channel One, produced by Whittle Communications; and *Newsroom*, available on Ted Turner's Cable News Network. I then analyzed two weeks of programs from each series, in depth and using formalist methodologies. I determined what was average and normal to each, and then to both. These programs—are developed—as are all television programs in a series—around a formula. Understanding the similarities between programs allows for an understanding of the experience of the school news genre. Understanding their differences provides a basis for comparison and contrast.

The 1989–1990 school year was the first year during which two series of secondary-school news programs were widely available to all schools via telecommunications technology. During this year, the programs' producers were competing for audiences and experimenting with program form and style. Because it was likely that the form of the secondary-school news genre would undergo potentially significant changes in form and style after the first year, I analyzed another two weeks of programs from each of the two series during the spring of 1991.

THE EVOLVING FORM AND STYLE IN THE SECONDARY-SCHOOL NEWS PROGRAM

My initial analysis indicated that the secondary-school news program made use of television's ability to attract, direct, and hold attention, and of the appeal and impact of the immediacy of fast-paced presentation styles. The genre used the traditional techniques of the news program—a pair (always male and female) of news anchors; the lavish use of cinemagraphic and sound techniques which functioned to direct attention; and the generous use of visuals, both graphics and on-location shots, to provide redundancy of information within the program content. Programs in the genre were divided into five to seven regular segments, each clearly identified and with a different content focus. Two to three current news items were presented in thirty-second "sound bites" in each program. The remainder of the program was devoted to more general current events or a more in-depth treatment of a topic of current interest, with the selection and treatment varying between the two programs. An analysis a year later indicated that the general form and style of the genre had not changed significantly. However, each of the two programs—*Newsroom* and *Channel One*—had evolved slightly in ways that continued to make the experience of viewing them significantly different from each other. Perhaps this indicates that the genre of the secondary-school news program is loosely defined, with each of the two series meeting the separate needs of very different producers.

NEWSROOM

My original analysis of the format of the CNN *Newsroom* program indicated that programs aired during the spring of 1990 very closely mimicked CNN's regular news programming in form and style. The opening segment identified the program as *Newsroom* and distinguished it clearly from the rest of CNN's daily programming. The introduction consisted of a brief, very fast-paced overview of that day's news items by a young female or male anchorperson. The introduction also included the *Newsroom* program's familiar opening background graphics of a rotating globe and historical news clips, and fast-paced synthesized music. The anchorpersons were present each day to open and close the program and usually introduced each new topic from the *Newsroom* anchor desk. Their presence was considered normal for the program—the absence of either anchor in any single program always resulted in an explanation of his or her whereabouts given by the remaining anchor. However, the young anchors rarely presented the news itself. This was most often done by a regular CNN adult reporter who was identified in the introduction to the segment, and was heard during the segment as a voice-over with the video footage.

On any given day during the first year's programming, the content and format of the program varied considerably. The fifteen-minute programs were made up of as many as nine segments or as few as five, with no apparent pattern established for the length of any segment or the focus of the daily topics. Time devoted to any topic varied from thirty seconds to three minutes. Segments regularly seen on the program included "Newsreel," a brief explanation of current news; "Quote of the Day," a quote from an historical or current figure relevant to current events; "Our World," news directly relevant to schools; "Future Desk," predictions of the future on such topics as the paperless office; "Flashback," a historical look at topics relevant to current news items; "Business Desk," news from the business world, such as the effect of computers on the clothing industry; and "On this Date," historical events occurring on the same date as the program.

Additionally, the events were almost always about male achievements in science and technology, or in dates of political relevance, such as those pertaining to military events. None of the ten programs that I analyzed for my initial study included references to achievements by women, nor were events of social or humanitarian interests covered.

While the majority of the segments covered topics with at least an indirect connection to the high-school curriculum—or to the personal interest of adolescents—I was surprised at how much programming time during the first year appeared to have been edited directly from regular CNN programming. Some segments—such as a feature on adult illiteracy in the Mississippi, the focus of which might seem to be more appropriate for an adult audience—appeared to have been lifted intact from the regular programming for inclusion in *Newsroom*. The regular appearance of the young anchors between the segments was the major unifying element for the program and confirmed its adolescent focus.

Newsroom programs aired during the spring of 1991 showed several significant changes in program form and style from those shown a year earlier. The new program format regularly included a segment called "Top Story," which discussed one topic from the current news in depth. In addition, the "Newsreel" segment—previously made up of three to five very short discussions of current events—devoted the entire two or three minutes to one topic. An additional third segment regularly devoted about three minutes to a current event or science feature. With these changes in format, almost three quarters of the fifteen-minute daily programming were devoted to current news events each day.

Although the major portion of the *Newsroom* daily news and current events segments still appeared to be edited from CNN adult programming—pacing and vocabulary level within these segments were consistent with adult programming, and the reporters were those regularly seen on CNN—the *Newsroom* anchors provided a transition into each of the segments with a repetition of significant names and through the display of color-coded and animated maps. The new program style included many visual aids to help clarify complex content. For example, in a fairly complex "Top Story" segment on arms control guidelines in the Middle East on 30 May 1991, text similar to subtitles in a foreign language film appeared at the lower portion of the screen. This text displayed, in simple sentences, the significant concepts heard in the audio portion. At least one segment of each program's regular segments seemed to have been produced specifically for the adolescent audience. This segment—usually "Our World," "Future Desk," or "Science Desk"— focused on teens and their activities or interests, and was most often placed at the end of the program to give the program a light-hearted or upbeat ending.

My initial analysis of *Newsroom* revealed a lack of program continuity, marked by a clear distinction between the program's segments which made it easy for teachers to select, tape, and use single portions of the program. More recent stylistic techniques give the program the appearance of a single unified program. Program unity, however, has not served an important function for regular CNN programming. The overall continuous form of CNN assumes that viewers are intermittent viewers. The short program segments are complete and unified within themselves so that viewers can start and stop watching as time and interest dictates. Originally, CNN designed *Newsroom* to be used in the same way. CNN made daily program guides available to teachers over several teacher-available on-line formats, such as *Learning Link*. Teachers taped the program during early morning hours, previewed it before class, and selected segments that were appropriate for their teaching needs.

In discussions with teachers during spring of 1990, I found none that regularly used *Newsroom* in its entirely. Thus, the new form of *Newsroom* will make it more difficult for teachers to select single segments for viewing.

CHANNEL ONE

Channel One, produced and made available by Whittle Communications, also provides a daily news and current-events program directed at the needs of the school curriculum. Channel One's programs are most often singled out in discussions of secondary-school news programs because they include commercial advertising. My initial analysis indicated that this was only one of many differences between the experience of watching *Newsroom* and Channel One. An analysis of the programs a year later indicated that the programs still offer a significantly different viewing and learning experience.

My initial analysis of Channel One in the spring of 1990 indicated that the program was produced to attract an adolescent audience. It did this in several ways. As with *Newsroom*, the Channel One series was unified by the appearance of a few regular young anchors. However, Channel One's young anchorpeople narrated the entire program, including some of the news segments, and provided much stronger elements of unity within each program, as well as between programs. While any given program may have had six or seven segments—comparable to the number in CNN's *Newsroom*—each program had a standard format of four regularly featured segments. They opened with "Upfront," comprising three or four short current news items, and were followed by "Focus," a more in-depth coverage of one or more featured current news stories. The programs then turned to the "World Class" segment, which was a week-long five-part series, devoted to one topic and addressed to adolescents. The weekly topics included Vietnam, sports, environmental problems, and learning disabilities. The program often concluded with a segment called "Endpiece," which continued a story from a previous program. During the first year, the two commercials were placed so that they did not interrupt the news segments and were, most often, clearly separated from the more substantive information section by "Fast Fact" and "Pop Quiz" segments. Because of the regular pattern of development and stylistic unity within each program, the viewer was encouraged to watch the entire show. By comparison, the more fragmented form of CNN's *Newsroom's* earlier productions allowed the viewer to break in or out of viewing at any time, with little disruption of program continuity.

The original form, style, and content presented by Channel One was designed to appeal to both adolescent viewers and their teachers. In fact, the news seemed to be manicured to appeal to them. Unlike traditional news programs, Channel One focused on the positive angle of most stories. The programs included few of the gratuitous shots of violence typical of the news genre. Many of the more tragic or specifically violent news events included each day in adult news programs—and in CNN's *Newsroom*—simply did not appear on Channel One. Ethnic minorities were represented often in the program and were presented positively. Although they may have spoken with a non-white dialect they were always articulate by white standards and were shown as sharing common concerns with the white middle-class youths.

Each news story was told from the point of the teenage school audience. For example, a story on a public transit shutdown included figures of how many high schools students were unable to get to school. A feature on the death penalty also included many interviews with adolescents. Through the program's style, the viewer was characterized as both a purposeful observer and as a participant, or at least peripherally involved in news and current events.

From a technical viewpoint during its first year, Channel One was educational television production at its best. Visual material was used to direct attention and clarify. Maps and labels were abundant and stylishly employed, with techniques such as flashing sections and zoom-outs to help the viewer understand the location of the story. Difficult names were both spoken and presented graphically. Teachers' guides were provided for the weekly series, with learning objectives identified and suggested activities given for different curriculum areas. While some educators criticized the quick pace of Channel One, the programs did not have the frenetically aggressive rapid flow of audio and visual tracks common to adult news programs.

An analysis of Channel One a year later indicated that, like *Newsroom*, it had changed. During the first year of programming, Channel One carefully separated the advertisements from regular program content and indicated their approach with the "Pop Quiz" segment which regularly asked a question before the ad sequence, and supplied the answer afterward. While these wrap-around segments kept the viewers watching through the commercials, they also soon indicated to viewers the next commercial segment. One year later, the program continued to be designed to wrap around the advertisements, but it did so in a variety of ways that made the approach of the ad less predictable, and the ad itself less recognizable. For example, the program continued to feature a weekly current-events topic which aired for three to four minutes each day, but it now introduced the topic in a short sequence immediately before the first commercial break. These unpredictable leads into the advertisement were designed to keep viewers' attention at least into the first few seconds of the advertisement. The ads themselves were designed to be less distinct from the news and current-events segments. Some ads mimicked the news program format with an anchor and authentic-sounding news information, which then continued to product endorsement.

Programs aired in the second year had a larger variety of segments, and the sequence of segments was less predictable. Ten- and fifteen-second-long segments—called "Planet Patrol" and "Earth Clock," and focusing on environmental issues—were regularly seen during a week when the environment was the feature topic. The segment "Pop Quiz," a daily regular the year before, was now sometimes replaced by other segments.

During its first year, the format of Channel One was very predictable. The new practice of varying the sequence of segments among programs functions to keep viewers' attention—especially second-year viewers who might have found the very predictable format of the first year to be monotonous. During its second year, the tone of the program was slightly less optimistic as programs focused on more topics with serious social implications—such as drugs, the homeless, and global effects of irresponsible environmental behavior.

Channel One was perceived by many as a daily news program, but, in fact, it presented very little current news. On each program, an average of about one and a half minutes were devoted to top news stories, with sometimes less than fifteen seconds devoted to an item. The majority of the daily program time focused on current events topics, such as AIDS or Japan.

During its second year, the form and style of Channel One continued to serve the purpose of the program's producer to encourage—in fact, require—students to watch the entire program including the commercial material. Thus sponsors were guaranteed that their products would be delivered to the "student market." The potentially objectionable and "tamperproof" qualities of the program were made more pleasing and tolerable by making each program unified and stylistically appealing to the audience of students and teachers. With programs designed in this way, Channel One positioned the student viewer as the "market" to be won. It did this by telling teens what they wanted to hear. It showed them that it's not such a bad world out there; that, even though there are problems in the world, adolescents could correct these problems by being good and caring people, as well as responsible citizens. It showed that teens across the United States and around the world have similar concerns and interests. It demonstrated that teens' opinions and actions are important, and that adolescents can have a positive effect on the world.

During its first year, the program presented a clear education agenda, with the commercials—so problematic for many—clearly separated from the main part of the program. Increasingly during the second year, many commercials actually intruded into the educational message of the program, either by their stylistic similarity to the program, or because ad space served a double function as snack-food-sponsored public-service messages which muddied the purpose of the commercial segments. Replacing commercials with educational content increased the credibility of the entire program as being educational. However, because the educational content of the public service messages was clearly labeled with the sponsor's logo, one function of the messages was product endorsement.

DISCUSSION

The genre of the secondary-school news program offers new resources for teachers and students. The genre of the television news format provides attractive and unique visual information, plus the opportunity for students to leave the classroom and go out into today's world to observe news events at a variety of inaccessible, exotic, and distant locations. It also presents learning experiences that are connected to the high-school student's experiences in a way that secondary-school programming has not done before.

Daily viewing is required of Channel One schools. However, stylistically, Channel One is also designed to encourage—almost compel—regular viewing. It offers a daily program, designed to be attractive to teens. It is also designed to meet—at least minimally—the current-events resource needs of teachers. However, in accepting the packaged program, teachers surrender an element of curriculum control. While teachers can interact with Channel One at the program's completion, the mechanical constraints of the video playback system make it difficult to select segments for reviewing or to save programs for future showing. With its formal and stylistic techniques, Channel One presents a lesson experience that excludes intervention from the classroom teacher. Just as it prevents the intervention of the teacher in the program, so it dramatically affects the traditional relations of student, teacher, and lesson. For twelve minutes, the teacher is now truly subordinate to the medium. The classroom experience offered to students is that of observer of messages clearly originating from outside the school and outside the teacher's control and design, rather than that of responsive interaction with teacher and lesson material.

The formal and stylistic changes during the second year of CNN's *Newsroom* programming makes it more attractive to students and teachers. An increase in segments both specifically designed for the interests of the teen audience and relating to curriculum needs are now included in the program.

There is much evidence in educational media literature—and from teachers themselves—that teachers don't often use an entire media package (Cambre 1987). Designers of educational television are now creating programs to accommodate teachers' strongly felt need to select segments from a program for their own classroom use. The capability to show a video segment more than once, when necessary to ensure a clear understanding is recognized as an advantage of the video medium. CNN's *Newsroom* supports this trend and continues to place control of the teaching experience in the hands of the teacher. While formal elements in the program make it unified and encourage continuous viewing, the feature segments are distinct within the program and lengthy enough to viewed individually. In some cases, the more complex treatment of topics warrants classroom discussion.

Both the form and style of *Newsroom* also serve the needs of CNN to develop, in today's adolescents tomorrow's viewing audience. With its emphasis on its parent network's programming, *Newsroom* continues to position the student viewer as junior-level or teen viewers of Channel News Network. As the young anchorpersons present segments from adult programming to their teen audience, the programs become training sessions for the larger adult CNN experience. High-school students learn that CNN is the best source for news.

CONCLUSION

This study was carried out with the understanding that there is a profound difference in the lesson experiences offered by each educational medium. It is important for media educators to recognize that all learning experiences delivered through a media form which is also used as a popular culture entertainment form provide an aesthetic experience as part of their motive for viewing. Researchers must begin the long-overdue task of analyzing that experience.

Additionally, it is important for more work to be done concerning the effects of the broader use of media in the culture, and how that use relates to viewer expectations in regard to educational media experiences. Because educational media programs are cultural products, the principles are determined by cultural conventions and expectations. Educational media forms are designed with popular formats. Thus, it is essential for educators to understand how these formats are designed, and that the types of aesthetic choices made by educational media producers determine the types of knowledge being constructed within the formats. This, in turn, affects the types of learning and teaching experiences which educational programs offer to our youth.

REFERENCES

Bordwell, D., and K. Thompson. 1986. *Film Art: An Introduction*, 2d ed. New York: Alfred A. Knopf.

Cambre, M. 1987. *A Reappraisal of Instructional Television*. Syracuse, N.Y.: ERIC Clearinghouse on Information Resources, Syracuse University.

Hoban, C. F. 1971. *The State of the Art of Instructional Films*. Stanford, Calif.: ERIC Clearinghouse on Media and Technology, Stanford University.

Schatz, T. 1981. *Hollywood Genres: Formulas, Filmmaking, and the Studio System*. Philadelphia: Temple University Press.

8

Whittling Away at Democracy:
The Social Context of Channel One

TAXES AND TELEVISION

We have entered a period of reaction in education. Our educational institutions are seen as failures. High drop-out rates; a decline in "functional literacy" (Kaestle et al. 1991);[1] a loss of standards and discipline; the failure to teach "real knowledge"; poor scores on standardized tests; and more—all of these are charges levelled at schools. All of these, we are also told, have led to declining economic productivity, a loss of international competitiveness, unemployment, poverty, and so on. Returning to a "common culture" will make schools more efficient, more competitive, and more open to private initiative (Apple and Christian-Smith 1991). This will solve our problems.

As I have claimed elsewhere, behind this is an attack on egalitarian norms and values (Apple 1993). Although hidden in the rhetorical flourishes of the critics, in essence, "too much democracy"—culturally and politically—is seen as one of the major causes of our declining economy and culture (Apple 1985).

As might be obvious, the conservative restoration is not occurring only in the United States. In Britain, Australia, and many other nations, similar tendencies are quite visible. The extent of the reaction is captured by Kenneth Baker, the former British Secretary of Education and Science in the Thatcher government, who evaluated nearly a decade of rightist governmental efforts by saying, in 1988, that "the age of egalitarianism is over" (Arnot 1990, 2). He was speaking positively, not negatively.

The threat that this represents to egalitarian ideas is never made explicit because it is always couched in the discourse of improving standards and quality in an educational system that is seen as in decline if not crisis (Arnot 1990, 3). This is especially the case with Whittle Communication's entire package of so-called reforms, from Channel One to Whittle's recent proposal to establish a national chain of private schools.

Channel One must be seen in the context of this conservative reaction. Its status as a "reform," and its acceptance in many schools, can be fully understood only as a partial embodiment of a larger conservative movement that has had a considerable effect, not only on education, but on all aspects of the common good (Raskin 1986). One of these effects has been to transform our collective sense of the roles which schools are to play in this society. While I shall discuss this in greater depth in the next section of this chapter, this has meant that equalizing the opportunities and outcomes of schooling has been seen increasingly, not as a public right, but as a tax drain. Public schooling—unless, as we shall see, it is defined as meeting the more conservative goals now in ascendancy—is too expensive, both economically and ideologically (Apple 1988a).

Among the major effects of this changing perception of schooling is that a large number of states have had to make Draconian cuts in education because of sharply diminished tax revenues and a loss of public support for schools. This has created a situation in which federal and state aid to local school districts—never totally sufficient in many poor school districts—has been less and less able to keep up with mandated programs, such as classes for children with special needs or those who speak languages other than English. It has meant that, for many schools, it will be nearly impossible for them to comply with, say, health and desegregation programs mandated by state and federal governments—to say nothing of other needs (Celis 1991a, B10).

Part of the situation has been caused by the intensely competitive economic conditions which business and industry are facing. Their own perceived imperative to cut costs and reduce budgets—often regardless of the social consequences—has led many companies to exert considerable pressure on states and local communities to give them sizable tax breaks, thereby "cutting off money needed to finance public education" (Celis 1991b, A1). Such tax exemptions are not new by any means. However, in the increasingly competitive situation in which companies find themselves, and in a context in which states and communities are justifiably fearful that businesses will simply go elsewhere, such breaks have, in the words of one commentator, "drastically grown" (Celis 1991b, B9).

State, city, and county governments "assemble packages that include the elimination or reduction of sales or property taxes or both, exemptions on new equipment, tax breaks for training new employees and reductions on taxes for school improvements" (Celis 1991b, B9). In some states, the rewards go further. In Florida, for example, companies even get tax breaks for fuel consumption (Celis 1991b, B9).

This has become a highly politicized area. Teachers on strike in the state of Washington included a specific demand to eliminate corporate tax breaks in their list of grievances. In Cleveland, the school system is facing an annual $34-million deficit. The school district has filed a complaint with the courts that maintains that it has been repeatedly damaged by tax breaks that the city has given to business in "the name of economic development" (Celis 1991b, B9).

The issues surrounding such breaks and outright exemptions are made even more powerful when compared to the withering criticism that the business community has levelled at the schools. This is coupled with the fact that business and industry have engaged in highly publicized programs of gift-giving to specific schools and programs (Celis 1991b, 9). Such gifts may increase the legitimacy of the business community in the eyes of some members of the public. Yet, it is clear that the amount of money involved in these public displays is considerably less than the taxes that would have been paid. The results are often all too visible in the classrooms of America.

For many chronically poor school districts, the fiscal crisis is so severe that textbooks are used until they literally fall apart. Basements, closets, gymnasiums, and any "available" space are used for instruction. Teachers are being laid off, as are counselors and support staff, including school nurses. Art and foreign language programs are being dropped. Extracurricular activities—from athletics to those more socially and academically oriented—are being severely cut back. In some towns and cities, the economic problems are such that it will be impossible for schools to remain open for the full academic year (Celis 1991a, B10).

The superintendent of schools of one East-Coast district puts the situation bluntly. "I think it stinks." Facing even more reductions in essential programs, he concludes, "Nobody seems to care. They just say, 'Cut the budget' " (Celis 1991a, B10). In the words of Harold Reynolds, Jr., Commissioner of the Massachusetts Department of Education, "We really are in a kind of catastrophic situation" (Celis 1991, B10).

In the context of such a financial crisis—one that is spreading even to more economically advantaged districts—even those school systems that know that corporate gifts almost never equal the amount that is lost in tax bargaining will, by necessity, look for whatever assistance they can get. A contract with Whittle Communications can seem to be quite attractive here.

The contract that is signed with Whittle for Channel One calls for schools to receive "free" equipment—a satellite dish, a VCR, and what amounts to approximately one television set for each classroom—that will enable them to receive the broadcasts. At the same time, schools must guarantee that 90 percent of the pupils will be watching 90 percent of the time (Hoffman 1991, 20). The program itself includes ten minutes of news and two minutes of commercials which must be watched every school day for three years as part of the contractual agreement (Hoffman 1991, 1).

The combination of free equipment and a content that most educators, community members, and the business community believe is important—the news—makes it difficult to resist. When combined with Whittle's aggressive advertising campaign—which portrayed Channel One as a crucial ingredient in the transformation of a stagnant and overly bureaucratic educational system that left its students unprepared for the "real world"—school officials can be convinced that allowing their students to be something of a "captive audience" is not a bad bargain (Hoffman 1991, 31). Whittle's partial success in this strategy can be seen in the fact that—while states such as New York, California, Rhode Island, and North Carolina have prohibited, regulated, or limited its use—nearly nine thousand middle schools and high schools have agreed to broadcast Channel One's version of the news everyday (Hoffman 1991, 4).

Economic crisis, a sense of public schooling being in serious trouble, a feeling that students are not being taught the knowledge that they need in order to be competitive—all of this creates conditions in which Channel One becomes acceptable. It can be seen by some educators, then, not only as a warranted trade-off among equipment, news, and an audience for commercials, but also as a legitimate reform that shows the way for cooperation between business and education. Indeed, William Rukeyser, executive editor of Channel One and a former managing editor of *Fortune* and *Money* magazines, puts the case this way: Channel One is a "test case for the viability of 'vigorous partnership' between business and education" (quoted in Hoffman 1991, 32).

But what kind of "partnership" is wanted? What kinds of reform are actually being proposed? Whose visions of education and society stand behind this movement? In what follows, I shall discuss this more general context in much greater detail, for one cannot totally comprehend the phenomenon of Channel One without situating it in the larger set of social dynamics that surround its production and reception.

REFORM AND CRISIS

In one of his most insightful arguments, the late philosopher Ludwig Wittgenstein reminded us that it is wise to look for the meaning of language in its use (Wittgenstein 1953). That is, words are given meaning by their use in particular historical periods and particular settings. Thus, don't ask what words mean in general. Instead, examine how they are being used in a variety of ways by different groups.

This principle is of special importance if we are to understand the meaning of the current movement to "reform" our educational system. In fact, with all of the discussion of reforming education in the popular media, in professional and scholarly journals, in government at all levels, and so on, we may be in danger of forgetting Wittgenstein's principle[2].

In the current context, what does reform talk do? How do Whittle's commercial initiatives in television—and now in private schools—fit in here? I do recognize that there may be serious problems with the curriculum and teaching that now goes on in many of our schools, and I have criticized them and suggested alternatives in a series of volumes (Apple 1985, 1988b, 1990a, 1993). However, I want to claim here that the way in which we talk about reforming education in general actually serves to divert our attention from many of the root causes of the problems which we are experiencing. As I noted in my introductory section to this chapter, in order to see this, we must focus both on the relationship between schooling and the larger society, and on the structure of inequalities in that society. The crisis we are facing in American society goes far beyond the school, and it will not be solved by blaming educators.

Part of the outline of this crisis is visible in the following depiction of the situation by Cohen and Rogers as they analyze the state of American political and economic life in the last 10 years.

The powers of the American state are now deployed in a massive business offensive. Its basic elements are painfully clear. Drastic cutbacks in social spending. Rampant environmental destruction. Regressive revisions of the tax system. [Looming trade wars.] Loosened constraints on corporate power. Ubiquitous assaults on organized labor. Escalating threats of intervention abroad. (Cohen and Rogers 1983, 15)

Of course, the fact that many people see a crisis does not mean that they visualize it in the same way—a point made very clear in Cohen and Roger's statement about governmental response just quoted. For progressive groups in the United States, the crisis is seen in the increase in poverty; in the defunding of the educational and social programs that took many years to win and are still so very necessary; in the attempts by rightist groups to impose their beliefs on others; in the widespread deskilling of jobs, the lowering of wages and benefits for many others; and the loss of whole sectors of jobs as industries engage in what economists call "capital flight" as they move their plants to other nations, thereby destroying whole communities in the process (Apple 1988b; Carnoy et al. 1984).

For powerful conservative groups, the crisis has little to do with this. The crisis is seen largely from above. It is simply an economic and ideological one. Profits and production are not high enough. Workers aren't as disciplined as they should be. We aren't competitive enough. People have begun to expect "something for nothing." All institutions, especially schools, must be brought more closely into line with policies that will "reindustrialize" and "rearm" America so that it is more economically competitive. The impact of this conservative definition of the crisis has had a truly major impact on official policy toward education (Apple 1988a, 1988b, 1993).

Nowhere is this clearer than in what was perhaps the most influential of all of the government-, industry-, or foundation-sponsored documents on the relationship between schooling and the economy. In "A Nation at Risk," the language leaves no false hope that education is performing anywhere near what is necessary. The report's authors state in their now famous quote:

Our nation is at risk. Our once unchallenged preeminence in commerce, industry, science, and technological innovation is being taken over by competitors throughout the world . . . [The] educational foundations of our society are presently being eroded by a rising tide of mediocrity that threatens our very future as a nation and a people. What was unimaginable a generation ago has begun to occur—others are matching and surpassing our educational attainments. (National Commission on Excellence in Education 1983)

The report continues:

If an unfriendly power had attempted to impose on America the mediocre educational performance that exists today, we might have viewed it as an act of war. As it stands, we have allowed this to happen to ourselves . . . We have, in effect, been committing an act of unthinking, unilateral educational disarmament. (National Commission on Excellence in Education 1983)

In these words, we see the crisis as reconstructed around particular themes of international competition, capital accumulation, and reassertion of toughness and standards. The crisis is *not* one of the immense inequalities that are so visible in American society. Instead, it is redefined by dominant groups to fit their own interests. It is the more general question—how do dominant interests work in the larger social context in which the role of education is now being dramatically changed?—that needs to be focused upon if we are to understand how many of the educational reforms now being proposed may embody social interests that many educators might not find to their liking.

In a chapter of this size, I can but note some tendencies that are reaching an advanced state or that loom on the horizon. The reader can find more detail and more supporting evidence in the references which I have included.

INDUSTRIALIZING THE SCHOOL

As I noted in the prior section of this chapter, we will miss what is happening in education unless we focus on the larger context in which educational change is occurring. There has been a breakdown of the largely liberal consensus that guided a good deal of educational policy since World War II. Powerful groups within government and the economy have been able to redefine—often in retrogressive ways—the terms of debate in education, social welfare, and other areas of "the common good" (Raskin 1986). What education is *for* has been transformed.

No longer is education seen as part of a social alliance which combines many minority groups, women, teachers, administrators, government officials, and progressively inclined legislators who acted together to propose social democratic policies for schools— such as expanding educational opportunities, developing special programs in bilingual and multicultural education and for the handicapped, and so on. A new alliance has been formed, one that has increasing power in education and social policy. This power bloc combines industry with the New Right and neo-conservatives. Much of its perspective has been incorporated within the Democratic administration as well, as it seeks to defend its shaky electoral position. Its interests are less in redressing the imbalances in life-chances of women, people of color, or labor. Rather, it aims at providing the educational conditions believed necessary both for increasing profit and capital accumulation and for returning us to a romanticized past of the ideal home, family, and school (Apple 1988a, 1988b; Giroux 1984; Hunter 1987; Omi and Winant 1986).

The power of this alliance can be seen in a number of educational policies and proposals that call for:

1. Voucher and choice plans and tax credits to make schools like the idealized free-market economy (Apple 1985);
2. The movement in state legislatures throughout the country to raise standards, and mandate both teacher and student competencies, as well as basic curricular goals and knowledge, usually by employing management and evaluation techniques originally developed not by educators but by business and industry (see Apple 1990a 1990b; Kliebard 1986);
3. The increasingly effective attacks on the school curriculum for its antifamily and antifree-enterprise bias, its secular humanism, its lack of patriotism (Arons 1983), and its supposed neglect of the knowledge and values of the Western tradition and of "real knowledge" (Apple and Christian-Smith, 1991); and, very importantly for my discussion here,
4. The growing pressure to make the perceived needs of business and industry into the primary goals of the school (Apple 1985; 1988b).

In essence, the new alliance in favor of the conservative restoration has integrated education into a wider set of ideological commitments (Shor 1986). The objectives in education are the same as those which serve as a guide to its economic and social welfare goals.

These include the expansion of the "free market," the drastic reduction of government responsibility for social needs, the reinforcement of intensely competitive structures of mobility, the lowering of people's expectations for economic security, and the popularization of what is clearly a form of Social Darwinist thinking (Bastian et al. 1986, 14). The effects of this on how we think about education are becoming clearer every day (Apple 1993).

As I have argued at length, the political right in the United States has been very successful in mobilizing support *against* the educational system, often exporting the crisis in the economy onto the schools. Thus, one of its major victories has been to shift the blame for unemployment and underemployment—and for the supposed breakdown of traditional values and standards in the family, education, and the paid workplace—*from* the economic, cultural, and social policies of business and industry *to* the school and other public agencies (Apple 1985; 1988b).[3] The commitments embodied in the quotes from "A Nation at Risk"—commitments also so very clear in a multitude of other national reports on education and which stand behind its policies—bear eloquent witness to these tendencies.

This process is heightened by the federal and state governments which literally bombard the public with a particular selection of statistical data about the well-being—or lack of it—of our society. I say *selection* here because the United States Government sets up "great manufactories of 'facts' and 'figures' " that are distributed to the public (Horne 1986, 189). These are usually economic and serve to construct a view of reality as fundamentally revolving around the economics of profit and loss, and of accumulation and profit (Horne 1986, 189–190).

In the process, the value of education is reduced to economic utility (Apple 1988a, 1988b). Other goals—such as critical understanding, political literacy, personal development, mastery and skill, self-esteem, and shared respect—are beside the point or "too expensive" (Bastian et al. 1986, 157). The issues of care and connectedness—which feminists have so crucially reminded us count so critically in building a society based on the common good—are disenfranchised as well (Gilligan 1982). Schools are to do one thing for society. They are to primarily function to supply "human capital," to underwrite "the promise of individual success in competitive labor markets and national success in competitive global markets" (Bastian et al. 1986, 21).[4]

At the same time that what education is for is being drastically reduced to its role in reaching the economic goals established by the new alliance, the schools have witnessed a steady internal increase in the use of procedures of standardization and rationalization that accompany this change in goals. Increasingly, teaching methods, texts, tests, and outcomes are being taken out of the hands of the people who must put them into practice. Instead, they are being legislated by state departments of education, state legislatures, or other centralized authorities. This process has been supported or stimulated by reports such as "A Nation At Risk" and many more current ones.

The effects have been widespread. The tendency is for the curriculum to be rationalized and industrialized at a central level focused largely on competencies measured by standardized tests. It also became more and more dependent on predesigned commercial materials and texts written specifically for those states with the tightest centralized control and, thus, the largest guaranteed markets (Apple 1985, 1988a). This results in the deskilling of teachers. When individuals cease to plan and control a large portion of their work, the skills essential to doing these tasks well and self-reflectively tend to atrophy and are forgotten. The skills that teachers have built up over decades of hard work—setting relevant curriculum goals, establishing content, designing lessons and instructional strategies, individualizing instruction based on an intimate knowledge of students' desires and needs, and so on—are lost. In many ways—given the centralization of authority and control, and given the transformation of the primary mission of the school into its mainly economic utility—they are simply no longer needed (Apple and Teitelbaum 1986). Just as critically—as I have demonstrated elsewhere—the fact that teaching, especially at the elementary level, has been socially defined as largely women's work makes the issues surrounding the probable deskilling of teachers even more important (Apple 1988b).

In the larger economy, this process of separating conception from execution and deskilling has been called the "degradation of labor." Importing these procedures into the school—as much of the conservative agenda wishes to do—can have exactly the same effects as when they are employed in industry. Those effects are a loss of commitment and respect, bitter battles over working conditions, a lowering not a raising of quality, and a loss of skills and imagination (Edwards 1979). Of fundamental importance is the conclusion that it has also ultimately reduced the power of employees to have any significant say in the goals and procedures of the institutions in which they work. All of this runs directly counter to what we are beginning to know about what will lead to effective education in schools (Bastian et al. 1986).

These types of interventionist movements will not only have consequences on teachers' ability to control their own work, but it is also becoming very clear that there are some very problematic results in terms of the type of content that is being stressed in the curriculum. This will also lead us back to Whittle. A simple way of thinking about this is to divide the types of knowledge which we want students to learn—perhaps construct and reconstruct is more appropriate here—into three analytic types: knowledge "that," "how," and "to."

Knowledge "that" is factual information, such as knowing that Madison is the capital of Wisconsin. Knowledge "how" refers to simple to complex skills, such as knowing how to use a library, engage in a crucial experiment, or how to inquire into the history of women in science. Knowledge "to" is dispositional knowledge. It includes those norms, values, and propensities that guide our current and future conduct. Examples include knowing to be honest, to have pride in one's racial heritage, to critically assess knowledge claims, or to see oneself as part of a democratic community and act cooperatively.

Each of these is important, but, if we were to place them in some sort of hierarchy, most individuals would agree that knowing an assortment of facts may be less important than are the higher order skills of critical inquiry. Both of these, in turn, are made less significant than they should be if the person is not disposed to use them in educationally, ethically, and socially important ways.

However, with the shift of control over content, teaching, and evaluation outside of the classroom, more and more of the focus is on those elements of science, social studies, reading, and other areas that can be easily measured on standardized tests. Knowledge "that" and low-level knowledge "how" are the primary foci. This is bad enough, of course, but in the process, even the knowledge "that" which is taught is made safer, less controversial, and stripped of its possible critical uses. Not only is this a formula for deskilling, but it is a contraction of the universe of possible knowledge largely into that which continues the disenfranchisement of the knowledge of women, of people of color, and labor (Apple and Christian-Smith 1991). Just as crucially, it also involves a radical simplification of the processes by which we come to fully know anything.

Yet, I do not want to avoid the question of knowledge "to." This process of increasing control can also constitute a very real transformation in what types of knowledge in each curricular area are considered to be legitimate, not only in terms of testability and reducibility, but also in terms of its social goals and the values that are embedded in them. With this in mind, let us examine a number of possible problems with the commercial news broadcasts that are aired by Whittle.

CLASSROOM REALITIES AND DOING THE NEWS

Many people have raised questions about Channel One's inclusion of commercials. From my arguments, it is evident that I, too, am deeply concerned. Yet, also at issue is the news itself. What will be reported? Whose news will be aired? Under what ideological umbrella will that news be presented?

How we think about something makes a difference. Let me give an example. We are now quite used to seeing pictures of disasters in which thousands of people lose their lives due to storms, drought, and so forth. We are told to think of these as "natural disasters." However, is this the appropriate way of understanding these situations? Or is it really a form of category error?

Take the massive mudslides that occurred in parts of South America in which large numbers of people were killed as torrential rains washed their houses down the mountain sides. A closer examination of this case reveals nothing natural about this at all. Every year, there are rains, and every year, some people die. This particular year, an entire side of a mountain gave way. The thousands of people living on it lost their lives—but they were the only ones. No one in the valleys—the safe and fertile land—died. Poor families are forced to live on the dangerous hillsides. This is the only land they can find in which to eke out an existence that is barely survivable. They crowd onto this land, not because they want to, but because of poverty and because of land-ownership patterns that are historically and grossly unequal.

Hence, the problem is not the yearly rains—a natural occurrence—but the economic structures that allow only a small minority of individuals to control the very lives of the bulk of the people of that region. Notice that this altered understanding of this particular problem would require a different practice. Not only would we send immediate aid to help the "victims" of the rains, but we would need to engage in a large scale program of land distribution to make it more equal.

The ability to understand this, to deconstruct and reconstruct what counts as "the news," is of great importance for teachers and students, given the way in which news is constructed on television. News is constructed usually as what disrupts the normal. Life is seen as "ordinarily smooth-running, rule- and law-abiding, and harmonious" (Fiske 1987, 284). If it is not, it ought to be. Such a set of norms is not descriptive. Rather, these norms are inherently prescriptive (Apple 1990a). They embody the values and beliefs of dominant groups by representing "a sense of what our social life ought to be, not what it is" (Fiske 1987, 284). The effects of this on our vision of people in other nations can be profound.

In his analysis of the ways the news presents Third World nations, John Fiske makes exactly this point.

> The unstated, ideological norms which made this conceptual strategy possible are those of *our* society. Negative events in another part of the world do not bear the same relationship to these norms and are, therefore, read differently. Third World countries are, for example, conventionally represented in Western news as places of famines and natural disasters, of social revolution, and of political corruption. These events are not seen as disrupting *their* social norms, but as confirming ours, confirming our dominant sense that Western democracies provide the basics for life for everyone, are stable, and fairly and honestly governed. When deviations from those norms occur in our own countries, they are represented as precisely that, deviations from the norm: in Third World countries, however, such occurrences are represented as *their* norms which differ markedly from ours. For the Western news media, the Third World is a place of natural and political disasters. (Fiske 1987, 284–285, emphasis in original)

What students and teachers are getting in the news, then, is quite important. It does not lessen the penetration of commercialism into the schools, but complements it. The news is often "bad". "Good" news is added to counterpose it, to set it up as a deviation from the norm, and of how this society is organized today. The fact that this normative assumption is unspoken, and is part of what we might call the hidden curriculum of the news which the students will see, makes it even more powerful (Fiske 1987, 285; Apple 1990a).

Of course, neither students nor teachers will be passive consumers of what Channel One broadcasts. They will actively construct and reconstruct the meanings of what is reported while watching and listening to it. Nor will all of these constructions of meanings be the same. There will be a contradictory assemblage of responses based on the class, gender, race, religion, and age relations in which people are formed (McCarthy and Apple 1989).

Yet, especially for teachers, this may be difficult given the intensification of their work. Teachers' work is becoming considerably more time-consuming. Only rarely is anything dropped from the curriculum. Instead, time and again, more is added. Given the steady growth of accountability measures and tests, the amount of paper work for which teachers are responsible is often overwhelming. Channel One enters this situation as one more addition. It is more than a little romantic to assume that teachers will be able to spend already scarce time on deconstructing the news.

Thus, as teachers' work becomes increasingly intensified, there will be almost no time to counteract the way in which the news is portrayed. I am not merely discussing what time pressures will be like in classrooms, although that will be of considerable moment. We must also focus on the lack of time outside the classroom as well. As I argued in *Teachers and Texts*, many teachers have very little time even to simply keep up with their respective fields. Given the immense pressures placed on them to do and teach more in their classrooms, they are having to rely more and more on outside experts, prepackaged curricular material, and standardized texts.

This pressure-cooker atmosphere spills over into one's time at home as well. As Andrew Gitlin (1983) documents, the amount of paper work that must be done by teachers has now reached such extreme levels that many teachers must often come in early in the morning and stay late after school, as well as facing up to two more hours of work at home each night, simply to keep up with the daily record keeping, grading, and so on. This situation has been exacerbated considerably by the current accountability movement from which one gets the impression that administrations, legislators, and economically powerful groups have tacitly said that, if it moves in classrooms, it must be measured.

I do not wish to be "cute" here. In such an intensified situation—when there is always more to do and less time in which to do it—it is unrealistic in the extreme to assume that most teachers will have the time and resources to expand on and/or reconstruct what Whittle Communications has determined is the news. Questions of immense interest her include: Whose news is it? What norms and values guide this news? What vision of society is being taken for granted?

PUBLIC VERSUS PRIVATE

However, it is not only at the level of social goals, the curricula, or teaching that the industrialization of the school has proceeded.

Channel One stands at the intersection of other tendencies here as well. Rightist movements have attempted to alter our very perceptions of schooling itself, turning them away from the idea of a common ground in which democracy is hammered out—an intensely political idea involving interactive notions of citizenship in a polity. Instead, the common ground of the school becomes based no longer on a set of democratic political commitments. Rather, it is replaced by the idea of a competitive marketplace. The citizen as a political being with reciprocal rights and duties is lost. In its place is the self as consumer, and schooling becomes a retail product (Bastian et al. 1986, 16; see also Giroux, 1984). Freedom in a democracy is no longer defined as participating in building the common good, but as living in an unfettered commercial market, with the educational system now seen as needing to be integrated into the mechanisms of such a market (Apple 1988a, Apple 1993).

I have already discussed the inherent weaknesses of these proposals, such as voucher plans and the like (Apple 1985, Apple 1993). The important point is to recognize the ideological reconstruction that is going on. It is also important to understand that, in the process of making the school into a product to be bought and sold—or in the case of Channel One, the students as a captive audience—we are radically altering our definitions of what it means to participate in our institutions. Participation has been reduced to the commercialization of all-important public social interaction (Hall 1986, 35–36). The unattached individual—one whose only rights and duties are determined by the marketplace—becomes ascendant. The ideological imprint of our economy is hard to miss here (Apple 1990a). There may be few examples more powerful or symbolic of this than is Channel One.

Convincing the public at large to see education as a product to be evaluated for its economic utility, and as a commodity to be bought and sold like anything else in the free market, has required a good deal of hard ideological work on the part of the rightist movements. This has meant that the citizenry must be convinced that what is public is bad, and what is private is good.

Hugh Stetton evokes the tenor of these claims when he says that

The commonest trick is this: of people's individual spending, mention *only the prices they pay.* When they buy a private car and a public road to drive it on, present the car as a benefit and the road as a tax or a cost. Tell how the private sector is the productive sector which gives us food, clothing, houses, cars, holidays, and all good things, while the public sector gives us nothing but red tape and tax demands. (Quoted in Horne 1986, 172–173, emphasis in original)

Perhaps the ideological comparison can be made clear when we realize that in the United States and Britain, for example, there is a tendency to treat welfare and other forms of public educational, health, or legal assistance as somehow not really deserved or as "abnormal." Yet, in countries such as Sweden, students are taught in their classes about the range of public benefits to which each citizen is entitled as part of one's very citizenship (Horne 1986, 175).

While the convictions of a majority of the American people may not have been totally swayed by such conservative ideological tendencies, it is clear that the processes of redefinition are part of the larger strategies involved in the conservative restoration. In fact, as recent polls have shown, there has been clear movement toward acceptance of some of the positions embodied by the rightist movements by groups within the larger society (See Bunzel 1985, Apple 1987).

WILL CHANGES IN SCHOOLS CHANGE THE ECONOMY?

Even with this brief analysis of the encroachment of economic interests, ideologies, and procedures into the educational system, a major question remains. Will the results in the economy be what the conservative alliance assumes if it is, indeed, successful in totally reorienting schooling? There is reason to doubt it, even with the "success" of certain initiatives, such as Channel One, within schools.

Others have called it a myth that "national economic growth and individual mobility are contingent on establishing more rigorous standards of educational competition" and by industrializing the school (Bastian et al. 1986, 8). In their own review of the history and current status of the relationship between education and the economy, the authors of a recent book proposing considerably more democratic changes in schooling show the other side of this argument (Bastian, et al. 1986). Rather than claiming that declining school performance is a major factor in declining economic performance, and rather than claiming that stressing high standards—defined by whom?—and discipline will somehow "restore economic productivity, competitive advantage, and job creation," the very opposite may be true. We instead may be creating a new elitism, one that will be justified by rhetorical artifice, but not by results (Bastian et al. 1986, 50).

The ultimate result of blaming the school, rather than the unequal structures generated by our economy and by our less-than-equal structures of political and cultural representation, will be the growth of discrimination and cultural elitism (Bastian, et al. 1986, 60). This will go hand in hand with the reproduction of a double-peaked economy in which those on the bottom will find their schooling is even more directly linked to low-waged, nonunionized, and largely futureless sector of labor market (Apple 1988b).

Bastian and colleagues summarize these arguments as follows:

> Economic realities do not justify the claim that a more competitive school regime will raise productivity and widely enhance job opportunities. The growing polarization of the workforce into a small professional strata and a large pool of low-wage, deskilled service and production workers indicates that our increasingly bureaucratized and industrialized education will mean more for a few and less for many, in terms of economic reward. The logic of today's marketplace is to lower expectations and limit chances for the majority of children, and competitive elitist schooling reinforces this logic. (Bastian et al. 1986, 163)

It is in this social context, and guided by this logic, that Whittle Communications' proposals for Channel One and for a network of schools for profit find their place. Such a logic might, of course, lead to a rearmed America. However, in the guise of the public good, a public largely consisting of the powerful will be the major beneficiaries (Apple 1988b, Apple 1993). Whittle will give his "free" equipment, and this will continue to cover the logic of lowered resources and the destruction of the economic and cultural base of local communities.

CONCLUSION

In this chapter, I have argued that education has increasingly become dominated by conservative economic and ideological interests that can lead, not to enhancing equality, but to its opposite. I have situated Channel One within the emerging relations of inequality in funding and power. In the process, I have pointed to the changing relations of power that have stimulated—and been stimulated

by—such "reform" documents as "A Nation at Risk." I also point to
the ideological shifts that have resulted. I have also noted that such
shifts in what education is for are not the only significant changes
that are occurring. We are witnessing important alterations in the
control of curriculum and teaching at the level of policy and practice.
This has also been accompanied by an attempt to not only enhance
the influence of economic needs on schools, but to make education
itself—as well as students—an economic product like all others.

In making these arguments, I have highlighted the negative
side of what is happening. This was done, not because I think
schools don't need improvements—of course they do—but, in part,
because of the fact that we are so often asked to ride on bandwagons
without paying sufficient attention to what other baggage might be
taking the trip with us. While bandwagons are certainly not new
to education, the current wave of "reform" could result in anti-
democratic tendencies, in worsening working conditions in schools,
in even less resources ultimately being given to education (even with
Whittle's free equipment), and to policies that will lead the public to
blame education even more for things over which it has little control.
Such outcomes would undoubtedly be a tragedy to millions of children, and to the teachers and administrators who now work so hard
everyday in uncertain conditions to provide an education worthy of
its name.

While I have painted a rather stark picture of a number of the
more damaging tendencies that are visible today under the guise of
educational reform, my argument is NOT that educators are totally
powerless or are only puppets whose strings are necessarily pulled
by large-scale economic and political movements and forces beyond
our control. Rather, I am asking that we do two things.

First, we must understand that, just as in the ways that natural
disasters are defined so that inequalities in land and power are reproduced, so, too, are recently proposed reforms of educational policy and practice—such as Channel One and Whittle's proposed chain
of private for-profit schools—often related to the reproduction of similar inequalities in hidden ways.

Second, I want us to be realistic. If ideological, political, and
economic forces are currently playing a large role in determining the
shape of curricula, teaching, and evaluation, then individual action
by educators is not enough. We can and must join together with
other groups inside and outside of education who are now working
to create schools that are more progressive in intent and outcome.
Channel One IS NOT the only answer to the economic and educational difficulties which we face.

To understand this, we must recognize that there are collective voices already in existence with which we can join, to which we can contribute something of value, and—perhaps just as importantly—from which we can learn. There are numerous groups throughout the country who are working in very uncertain conditions to build a more democratic education and a curriculum that responds to the knowledge of all of us, not only to those who, because of their power, have sought to shape teaching and curricula in their own limited political, ideological, and economic image.

These far-seeing organizations include the Rethinking Schools group in Milwaukee, where Fratney Street School provides a model for working with an ethnically diverse community of students, parents, and teachers in ways that empower all participants (Apple 1990b). It includes the justly well known Central Park East Schools in New York where the curriculum in all subjects is organized around a set of fundamental questions, one of the most important of which is "From whose perspective are we reading, seeing, and listening?" Yet another example is the recent efforts by the Rindge School of Technical Arts in the Boston area to combine science, technology, vocational education, and other curricula into a community-centered program based on integrating the problems which students are working on into plans for community development. (Rosenstock 1991).

To these can be added citizen advocacy groups such as the Southern Coalition for Educational Equity, Chicago Schoolwatch, and others who are engaged in defending and building upon the gains made in funding and control; in actively fighting the Draconian cuts which I discussed earlier; in democratizing curricula and teaching; and in making them more responsive. By forming coalitions with schools and groups such as these in the hard and time-consuming political and educational work to restore both a democratic vision and practice to education and the resources that support it in general, educators can more effectively participate in making what is clearly not a "natural" disaster but a social calamity into an education that is not a disaster at all (Apple 1993).

Educators cannot afford to stand above the fray, divorced from the structures of inequality in schools and the larger society that deny our citizens the values which they most prize. Channel One is a symbol of the results of these structures. Its roots lie in the conservative restoration we are experiencing and in the so-called opportunities this restoration has given to business to slowly transform our educational system into one more site for the generation of profit. Clearly, there is collective educational work to be done to counter the buying and selling of our schools, teachers, and students.

NOTES

1. The educational and political meanings of the term *functional literacy* are varied and are defined by different social agendas. Kaestle and colleagues (1991) have an interesting discussion of whether there has, indeed, been a sharp decline in functional literacy in the United States.

2. What follows is based on a larger discussion in Apple (1988c).

3. As many social analysts have argued, our type of economy must subvert traditional values and communities, and substitute an ethic of commodity purchasing and monetary status if it is to survive. Placing the blame on our educational system is a form of category error. (See Heilbroner 1985.)

4. Of course, the educational system of the United States—as well as that of other countries—has always had close links to the economy (Apple 1990a). However, this has just as often been a source of conflict, with many groups attempting to democratize both its goals and procedures. (See Apple 1993, Reese 1986, and Hogan 1985.)

REFERENCES

Apple, M. W. 1985. *Education and Power.* New York: Routledge.

———. 1987. Producing inequality: Ideology and economy in the national reports on education. *Educational Studies,* 18. 195–220.

———. 1988a. Redefining equality. Teachers College Record, 90. 167–184.

———. 1988b. *Teachers and Texts: A Political Economy of Class and Gender Relations in Education.* New York: Routledge.

———. 1988c. What reform talk does: Creating new inequalities in education. *Educational Administration Quarterly,* 24. 272–281.

———. 1990a. *Ideology and Curriculum* 2d. ed. New York: Routledge.

———. 1990b. Is there a curriculum voice to reclaim? *Phi Delta Kappan,* 71. 526–530.

Apple, M. W. 1993. *Official Knowledge: Democratic Education in a Conservative Age.* New York: Routledge.

Apple, M. W., and L. Christian-Smith eds. 1991. *The Politics of the Textbook.* New York: Routledge.

Apple, M. W., and K. Teitelbaum. 1986. Are teachers losing control of their skills and curricula? *Journal of Curriculum Studies,* 18. 177–184.

Arnot, M. 1990. Schooling for social justice: A new agenda for British education in the 1990s. Paper given at the 12th National Conference of the New Zealand Association for Research in Education. Auckland, New Zealand, February 15.

Arons, S. 1983. *Compelling Belief.* New York: McGraw-Hill.

Bastian, A., N. Fruchter, M. Gittell, C. Greer, and K. Haskins. 1986. *Choosing Equality: The Case for Democratic Schooling.* Philadelphia: Temple University Press.

Bunzel, J., ed. 1985. *Challenge to American Schools.* New York: Oxford University Press.

Carnoy, M., D. Shearer, and R. Rumberger. 1984. *A New Social Contract.* New York: Harper and Row.

Celis, W. 1991a. School districts reeling in weakened economy. *New York Times,* June 5. A1, B10.

———. 1991b. Schools lose money in business tax breaks. *New York Times,* May 22. B9.

Cohen, J., and J. Rogers. 1983. *On Democracy.* New York: Penguin Books.

Edwards, R. 1979. *Contested Terrain.* New York: Basic Books.

Fiske, J. 1987. *Television Culture.* New York: Methuen.

Gilligan, C. 1982. *In a Different Voice.* Cambridge: Harvard University Press.

Giroux, H. 1984. Public philosophy and the crisis in education. *Harvard Educational Review,* 54. 186–194.

Gitlin, A. 1983. School structure and teachers' work. In *Ideology and Practice in Schooling,* M. W. Apple and L. Weis, eds. Philadelphia: Temple University Press. 193–212.

Hall, S. 1986. Popular culture and the state. In *Popular Culture and Social Relations,* T. Bennet, C. Mercer, and J. Woolacott, eds. London: Open University Press. 22–49.

Heilbroner, R. L. 1985. *The Nature and Logic of Capitalism.* New York: Norton.

Hoffman, L. 1991. The meanings of channel one. Paper presented at the annual conference of the American Educational Research Association. Chicago.

Hogan, D. 1985. *Class and Reform.* Philadelphia: Temple University Press.

Horne, D. 1986. *The Public Culture.* Dover, N.H.: Pluto Press.

Hunter, A. 1987. The politics of resentment and the construction of middle America. Unpublished paper. Madison: University of Wisconsin, Department of History.

Kaestle, C., H. Damon-Moore, L. Stedman, K. Tinsley, and W. V. Trollinger. 1991. *Literacy in the United States.* New Haven: Yale University Press.

Kliebard, H. 1986. *The Struggle for the American Curriculum.* New York: Routledge and Kegan Paul.

McCarthy, C., and M. W. Apple. 1989. Race, class, and gender in American educational research. In *Class, Race and Gender in American Education,* L. Weis, eds. Albany: State University of New York Press. 9–39.

National Commission on Excellence in Education. 1983. A nation at risk: An imperative for educational reform. *Education Week,* April 27. 12–16.

Omi, M., and H. Winant. 1986. *Racial Formation in the United States.* New York: Routledge and Kegan Paul.

Piven, F., and R. Cloward. 1982. *The New Class War.* New York: Pantheon.

Raskin, M. 1986. *The Common Good.* New York: Routledge and Kegan Paul.

Reese, W. 1986. *Power and the Promise of School Reform.* New York: Routledge and Kegan Paul.

Rosenstock, L. 1991. The walls come down: The overdue reunification of vocational and academic education. *Phi Delta Kappan,* 72. 434–436.

Shor, Ira. 1986. *Culture Wars.* New York: Routledge and Kegan Paul.

Wittgenstein, Ludwig. 1953. *Philosophical Investigations.* New York: Macmillan.

9

Drawing the Line: Questions of Ethics, Power, and Symbols in State Policy and the Whittle Concept

In this chapter, I will examine the ethical and legal arguments given by the superintendent of education in California, the North Carolina Department of Education, and local school governing bodies in their struggle to set educational policy in response to Whittle Communications' offer of the Channel One program. In doing so, I will construct patterns that emerge from this inquiry and which focus on ethics, power, and symbolism.

The entrance of Channel One into high-school and middle-school classrooms implies more than just another means for the delivery of current events. It raises old arguments and debates concerning the purpose of education and the responsibility of schools to children, community, and the nation. The debates and struggles over policy by state and local authorities, as well as by special interest groups, have brought together ethical and moral arguments from the late nineteenth and early twentieth centuries with arguments arising from the current political discourse over excellence, equity, business partnership, and global competition.

The history of education in the United States is a story built around struggles for control of the school curriculum, and its construction, delivery, and evaluation (Kliebard 1987). By becoming part of children's educational experiences, Whittle Communications'

Channel One has also become an element in the continuous ideological debate over who is to control an institution charged with the socialization of children.

Historically, discussions and movements in curriculum theory and development have focused on how schools should prepare students to be more productive citizens in a democratic society (Kliebard 1987, Popkewitz 1987). The curriculum—which was to be scientifically developed—was to remain neutral and unbiased. Mass culture and the profit-driven interest of business were not intended to be part of the legitimate knowledge of schools (Popkewitz 1991). Before Channel One, the benefit to business was seen in terms of a more productive, flexible, and well-trained workforce. It was generally accepted that no business or individual should receive direct benefits from the public school project. By including advertisements in their twelve-minute program, Whittle Communications crossed that line separating neutrality and benefit (Action for Children's Television [ACT] n.d.).

An analysis of policy decisions in response to Whittle Communications' Channel One reveals debates constructed by various interest groups. Even though these debates have appeared to be centered on concerns of an ethical nature and the role of public education in protecting children from the evils of mass culture, they have actually emerged from historical and political struggles for control of the school curriculum. To refer only to a description of the pragmatics of policy making, frameworks, guidelines, or regulations situates the debate within a nonhistorical, technobureaucratic, positivist paradigm (Feenberg 1991, Popkewitz 1991). By unpacking educational policy debates within a historical, social, and political paradigm, the inquirer is provided with different ways of understanding educational policy.

If the debate on the Whittle concept—as manifested in Channel One—is moved outside the horizons of neutrality, technique, methods, and bureaucratic process, then questions centering on policy reveal a discourse which examines notions of power, benefit, and symbolism. In framing the debate in this manner, ethical and legal questions move beyond the debates over Channel One into broader philosophical discussions on the nature of schooling and its relationship to economy and interests.

THE DEBATE

Reaction to the Channel One project has, at times, been swift and aggressive. Action for Children's Television, a watchdog group concerned with children's television programming, has raised ethical issues in the relationship between the purpose of schooling and the self-serving interests of business. Traditional educational organizations—including parent-teacher associations, school boards, and national teacher organizations—have all raised ethical questions and warnings concerning the commercial purposes and effects of Channel One on schools and children.

Embedded in the Channel One program are the values of a mass-mediated culture. Advertisements provide images and stories that display various lifestyles, values, and social worlds that appear to be drawn from the natural world. Advertisements present products and social relationships, not as they are, but as others think they should be (Ellsworth and Whatley 1990, Goffman 1976, Masterman 1985, Muffoletto 1991, Newcomb 1982, Salomon 1981). Showing promotional material in schools that supports various behaviors of consumption and social relations counters the educational myth that schools are places where the only interest served is that of the individual student. As agents of a democratic state, schools are to remain disinterested, serving the interests of no particular group, and, especially, no particular business. To unmask that myth of disinterest would be to reveal the true nature of any educational system (Apple 1979, Muffoletto 1993, Popkewitz 1991). As long as the myth of disinterest is maintained, ethical concerns will appear to lack any economic, political, social, or historical context.

All materials become part of the schooling experience for both students and teachers when they enter the classroom. The Channel One program is no different. Arguments against Channel One have suggested that an ethical line was being crossed when individual school districts agreed to electronically distribute promotional materials in exchange for a current events program. By including two minutes of promotional material in its programming, the neutrality of schooling appeared to be violated. Even though questions over the program have addressed issues of moral, ethical, and economic boundaries, the more basic question has centered on the locus of power. The notion of power is critical to our thinking about Channel One because, whatever institutional body—public or private—controls the curriculum and its evaluation, also controls the schooling experience of children and teachers. In order to control the experience, they must also control what is let in and what is kept out. Institutions, such as special interest groups, are grounded within ideological horizons. They tend to let in only those visions which conform to an already defined world view (Apple 1993, Kliebard 1987).

Various state departments of education have taken different positions to the questions raised by Whittle's program. Some have constructed guidelines for districts to consider before entering into a contract with Whittle Communications (Michigan State Board of Education, personal communication, 6 May 1991; State of Wisconsin Department of Public Instruction, personal communication, 3 May 1990). Other states amended or proposed new state regulations to standardize and regulate local districts in their negotiations with businesses (Georgia Department of Education, personal communication, 10 May 1991; State of South Carolina, Department of Education, personal communication, 6 May 1991). Many states adopted a hands-off policy, letting local districts decide whether to enter into a binding contractual agreement with Whittle Communications (State of Idaho Department of Education, personal communication, 25 April 1991; Tennessee State Department of Education, personal communication, 29 April 1991; Texas Education Agency, personal communication, 30 April 1991).

For example, the New York State Department of Education considered both ethical boundaries and the medium itself as reasons for "fencing out" Channel One. The New York position is important because it address two concerns. First, it addressed ethical boundaries in school-business relationships. Second, it differentiates between delivery systems as electronic and nonelectronic. As the pressure on schools increases to become technological, more efficient, and more effective while using less economic resources, New York's position becomes pivotal and deserves some discussion.

On 6 April 1990, the New York State Board of Regents amended its rules about commercial activities on school premises. The purpose of the amendment was to outlaw commercial and promotional activity delivered through electronic means to public schools in New York State.

It was the expressed opinion of the New York State Board of Regents in a proposed amendment to the state constitution (1990) that, by entering into a contractual agreement in which children would be required to watch two minutes of promotional materials, overstepped the moral and ethical boundaries of public education. Part 23 of the Rules of the Board of Regents, "Commercialism in Public Schools" (BR 1.3), addressed the current debate on commercial ventures and promotional activities in New York's public schools. Of particular interest to our discussion is section 23.1 (b) which refers to electronic forms of delivery. The policy document defines commercial activity in this way:

Commercial promotional activity shall mean any activity, designed to induce the purchase of a particular product or service by students, or to extol the benefits of such product or service to students for the purpose of making its purchase more attractive, that is conveyed to students electronically through such media as, but not limited to, television and radio. (BR 1.3)

Section 23.2 of the Amendment to the Rules of the Board of Regents—"Prohibition of commercial promotional activity in the public schools"—further differentiates "commercial promotional activity" from "commercial sponsorship of school activities" by stipulating that declaring that

Boards of education or their agents shall not enter into written or oral contracts, agreements or arrangements for which the consideration, in whole or in part, consists of a promise to permit commercial promotional activity on school premises, provided that nothing in this part shall be construed as prohibiting commercial sponsorship of school activities (BR 1.4)

The focus on electronic delivery systems by the New York State Board of Regents is of critical importance. By focusing on electronic formats (television, radio, and computer-related technologies), the New York State Board of Regents did not "fence out" other forms of sponsorship. Schools under the amendment change could continue to enter into partnerships or agreements with businesses that, in some way, offered the school support or services in exchange for publicity or good public relations. Advertisements on the outfield walls of baseball diamonds, the name of a company on donated soft drink cups, advertisements in school yearbooks, product recognition on fund-raising activities, or partnership programs would still be allowed. The deciding factor for the State of New York was the nature of the delivery system and its format.

The New York State Regent's position is an attempt to maintain a set of ethical standards by "fencing out" commercial infusions into the state's curriculum and the minds of children for the benefit of business. However, educational policies and guidelines may shift with the social, political, and economic climate of the times. With limited and diminishing funds available for education—especially for schools located in low-tax-revenue areas—the ethical and moral arguments which "keep out" may, as a result of diminishing alternatives, shift to "let in." Schools may simply need the equipment and the program to promote a positive image in the community. A satellite dish, monitors in classrooms, and a current-events program—all at no cost to the taxpayer—may paint a picture of progressivism and opportunity to a community with few alternatives and limited futures.

As discussed earlier, the debate over Channel One has centered on ethical issues and the power relationships between state departments of education and local governing bodies. Whoever defines the parameters of the debate over responsibility for the welfare of children also has control over what is spoken and who is allowed to speak. Control over dialog, what is spoken, who speaks, and who is allowed to listen is a question of power. How that is played out at pragmatic and symbolic levels is a function of discourse (Cherryholmes 1988).

The debates in California and North Carolina were centered on ethical and legal concerns. Whoever permits access to classrooms through personnel and curricular materials does so under the cover of legal right and responsibility. What is understood, at times, as law concerning legal responsibility is actually a product of definition. I now turn to California and North Carolina as examples of argumentation on right and responsibility in both ethical and legal terms.

California

In California, former State Superintendent Bill Honig was supported by teacher unions, the state PTA, the California School Board Association, and others as he opposed the entrance of Channel One into California's public schools because of the commercial nature of the program and the loss of curricular control by educators.

In 1990, Whittle Communications supported a bill that would have changed the legal status of mandatory TV ads in the classroom. The bill failed (California Department of Education 1991).

In 1991, two bills—Senate Bill 741 and Assembly Bill 2007— were introduced to the California State Legislature. It was believed that the proposed bills would clarify the existing ban on operations such as Channel One.

Senate Bill 741 (1991) would prohibit "the governing board of a school district from entering into written or oral contracts that require advertisements, as defined, to be transmitted to pupils by any electronic medium during the school day, as defined" (California Senate Bill No. 741, p. 1).

Assembly Bill 2007 (1991) would require that "the fiscal penalties imposed by the State Board of Education for the failure to make up lost instructional time be based only on the number of students at each grade level in which the required minimum instructional time is not met" (California Assembly Bill No. 2007, p. 1).

Both of these legislative documents moved beyond setting of guidelines, frameworks, or policy to creating laws. However, neither SB 741 nor AB 2009 made it out of legislation.

Honig's argument against Channel One and similar business ventures in California public schools was built upon ethical and economic terms which resulted in a struggle for control over the classroom curriculum. Both SB 741 and AB 2007 tended to clearly define the territory controlled by the state superintendent of public instruction and local school-governing bodies. In its October 1990 meeting, the California State Board of Education stated a policy on the use of commercial products and services. The board's policy left issues concerning commercial interests and activities that surfaced by the Channel One program in the hands of local governing boards. The State Board of Education did not support Honig's position. The quest for control was not only between the state superintendent and local school districts, but also the State Board of Education. It was clearly a struggle between institutions for control in setting the agenda and direction of education in California (Popkewitz 1991).

In his argument, Honig states he believed that engaging in contracts with Whittle Communications conceded "control of the curriculum to an outside party who is not primarily interested in educating students but in selling advertisements" (California Department of Education 1990, 1). Second, Honig clearly communicated that watching commercials was not to be considered as an educational activity, thus positioning Channel One commercials as noneducational. Third, Honig's position was that the State of California is not in the business of selling instructional time or access to students.

In a 2 November 1990, memorandum to county and district board presidents, superintendents, and principals, Honig stated, "Nobody can seriously argue that watching commercials is an educational activity unless these are occasional ads viewed in the context of understanding persuasive techniques or as part of consumer education."

If this argument—which is similar to arguments made in other states—is to be accepted then the door is open for Honig's third position of instructional time. The November 2 memo continues:

With regard to showing the programs' advertisements during school time, Educational Code Section 46300 reads, "in computing average daily attendance of a school district, there shall be included the attendance of the pupils while engaged in educational activities required of these pupils and under the immediate control and supervision of an employee." (California Department of Education 1990, 1–2)

If the argument can be made that viewing commercials is not an educational activity, the state can then withhold funds which are linked to instructional time per child. For example, a fictitious high school of 500 students is considering signing a contract with Whittle for the Channel One program. Under Honig's economic position, that school would lose a large amount of instructional funding. The state could withhold an amount equal to 500 students (those viewing Channel One) times two (minutes per day) times 180 (number of school days) times a set amount for instructional time. That would equal nearly 180,000 total instructional minutes or 3,000 hours of instructional time over one school year. If the total program was deemed to be noninstructional, as it has been in other states, the amount of time and funds would be even greater at twelve minutes per program.

In an earlier 4 August 1989 California Department of Education news release, Honig also stated

I have determined that participation by public schools in proposals such as "Channel One" is not permitted by state law and the California Constitution. Based on California Education Code 46000, I can not pay schools to have their students watch commercials. Therefore, I will not certify as "instructional minutes" any time watching advertisements in any broadcast similar to that proposed by "Channel One." (California Department of Education 1989, 1)

Honig also positioned his ethical argument on the notion of public trust. "Parents entrust their children to our public schools. We have no right—*legally* or *morally*—to sell access to our students even if schools receive some benefit in return" (California Board of Education 1989, 1).

Honig's argument against Channel One draws upon ethical concerns and the role of the school in transmitting selected values while keeping out others. The leverage which Honig used was simply economics. By positioning elements of the Channel One program as noneducational, he could withhold funding. This effort to control districts by the state superintendent was undermined by the state Department of Education in its position that this was a local issue, not one for the state superintendent. The lines of conflict in California became very clear. However, where the line was drawn and who could draw it is still an issue of power.

In November 1992, in a case between the California Department of Education and East Side High School, a California trial judge ordered that the compulsory viewing of Channel One be limited to only those students who chose to watch it. As stated in a 26 March 1993 news release from the California Department of Education,

> The order was the first from a trial judge which limits the compulsory showing of TV commercials during class time anywhere in the U.S. While it is a step toward eliminating the issue of a captive audience, it does not deal with the more basic issue of misuse of the time set aside for learning and for which taxpayers spend millions of dollars per year. (California Department of Education 1993, 1)

The debate still continues in California, as in New York, over who is to control what experiences and knowledges that enter the classroom, and the extent, if any, of commercialism in public education.

North Carolina

Looking at the events in North Carolina offers the opportunity to analyze the policy and the law in terms of ethical and economic relationships (Berger and Luckman 1966, Popkewitz 1991). As in California, the North Carolina debate centers on the right of the State to influence or steer and control the actions of local school boards and schools.

Also, as in California, the North Carolina arguments against Whittle's program focused on ethical concerns over the compulsory viewing of advertisements by students, the questionable educational value of Channel One's advertisements, and the control of educational activity by individuals or corporations outside education.

In February 1990, and after discussing the Whittle proposal, the State Board of Education adopted a temporary rule

> . . . prohibiting local school boards from entering into a contract which (1) limits or impairs its authority and responsibil-

ity . . . to determine the materials to be presented to students during the school day; or (2) limits or impairs its authority and responsibility . . . to determine the times during the school day when materials will be presented to students (*North Carolina State Board of Education* v. *Whittle* 1991, 4)

Sections one and two of the ruling directly addressed the contract requirements that each program be shown in its entirety and at the same time each day. The ruling also addressed the issues of compulsory education and commercial advertising in stating that

Local boards of education are obligated to assure that students, as a consequence of the compulsory attendance laws, are not made a captive audience for required viewing, listening to, or reading commercial advertising. Therefore, no local board may enter into any contract or agreement with any person, corporation, association or organization, pursuant to which students are regularly required to observe, listen to, or read commercial advertising. (In Martin 1991, 3)

It becomes clear from this temporary ruling that the North Carolina board of Education held the position that acceptance or rejection of the Whittle proposal was under their legal domain.

In response to the board's temporary ruling over control of curricular decisions, the 1990 session of the North Carolina General Assembly did not side with the department of education. In fact, the decision was just the opposite. The position taken by the General Assembly, in the form of an amended state statue, empowered local districts to decide whether or not supplemental instructional materials could contain promotional materials. The amended state statute stated, "Local boards of education shall have sole authority to select and procure supplementary instructional materials, whether or not the materials contain commercial advertising . . ." (*North Carolina State Board of Education* v. *Whittle* 1991, 15).

The implications of this decision may reach further than the Whittle project. With limited local and state funding, the decision by the General Assembly opened the possibility of further school-business partnerships that included promotional materials. By giving control over these matters to local boards of education, the state board was removed from the decision-making process.

The conflict for control of the curriculum then moved from the state's General Assembly to the chambers of the North Carolina State

Supreme Court, where the decision was made to dismiss the Board of Education's complaint. The decision was later appealed and decided again in favor of Whittle (*North Carolina State Board of Education* v. *Whittle* 1991). The North Carolina Supreme court viewed Channel One as supplementary material which falls under the control of local school boards and not under the control of the State Department of Education. Both cases were heard in the State Supreme Court between the plaintiffs, North Carolina State Board of Education and Bob Etheridge, state superintendent of Public Instruction; and the defendants, Whittle Communications, the Thomasville City Board of Education, and the Davidson County Board of Education.

The North Carolina State Department of Education argued during the Supreme Court hearings that approving instructional materials that contained advertisements or promotional materials was a misuse of tax dollars. They estimated that the contract with Whittle is costing the taxpayers approximately $4 million per school year. This is based upon the amount of time students spend watching the program and the amount of tax money spent to maintain the public schools. The district contended that there was no extra cost to the district for showing the program. Concerning the spending of time (student time equates to capital), the Whittle contract for this district allowed for students to choose not to watch the program. Thus, the argument over the "spending of student time" was rejected by the majority opinion of the State Supreme Court.

Even though the court sided with the local district that the program was supplemental instructional material, and that students were not required to watch it, it is interesting to note that a dissenting voice from the majority opinion argued that the program itself was not instructional. His position is well worth mentioning in full.

> However, there is a serious issue as to whether Channel One is instructional. The evidence discloses that the students are not required to use Channel One in any way. They are not required to view it, and, during the time when it is being exhibited, every student in the school could absent himself from the showing of Channel One. How can materials be instructional if the students are not required to use them? Further, there is no evidence that any teacher or other person explains Channel One or uses it in any way while it is being exhibited or thereafter. No teacher expounds upon Channel One to any students, whether assembled to watch Channel One or in any other way. In short,

Channel One is not used as instructional material. Also, there is no evidence that students are tested in any way upon the matters broadcast over Channel One. No teacher questions any student concerning his viewing of Channel One, and no student is required to prepare an essay or other written material concerning Channel One. The students are not in any way required to demonstrate any knowledge of the materials contained in Channel One that they might acquire *en passant*. It is apparent that whatever is broadcast over Channel One is not "instructional" material, but more in the nature of entertainment which students might enjoy during recess. (Martin 1991, 7)

The guiding ideas about what is and is not instructional are based upon how individuals think about the roles and purposes of education. It appears from this one judge's opinion that teachers and students must be doing something—teaching, evaluating, or demonstrating—for an activity to be deemed as instructional. This perception of teaching and learning is couched in notions of work and efficiency which is rooted in the progressive education movement and the efficiency experts found in the early quarter of this century (Callahan 1962, Kliebard 1987). The ideas that must be considered in arguments such as those found in North Carolina are the sliding definitions of legitimate practice concerning instruction, learning, and the public good. Where those definitions are housed and how and when they are used is more a concern of power than institutional purpose.

The arguments provided by the local school district and the North Carolina State Department of Education reflect the historical ideological positions and relationships of each. In situating them within a historical institutional and social discourse of struggle for control of education within the contexts of ethics, economics, and power, the discourse on policy and law take on different meanings from one which is positioned as ahistorical, neutral, and serves no interests.

ETHICS, ECONOMICS, AND SYMBOLISM

This section will discuss ethics, economics, and symbolism as forms of discourse and power relationships. For, as Popkewitz (1991) suggests, the relationship between power and discourse acts to "steer" the construction of policy at the state and local levels.

Ethics

The ethical argument against self-serving commercial activities in schools centers on the historical roles and responsibilities of schools to protect children from the negative elements found in the social world. Through their curriculum and institutional organization, schools have acted as gatekeepers for keeping out selected world views and values and letting in others. This pedagogic and institutional role not only legitimated a narrow spectrum of knowledge and meanings, but it also formed the relationships or the subjectivities of students in kinship to the dominant ideologies.

Falling back upon the ethical and moral foundations of education, opponents of Channel One argue that requiring children, as a captured audience, to view promotional, noninstructional, and value laden programs (meaning advertisements) is a breach of trust. A New York State Department of Education representative expressed it in terms of crossing boundaries. "Enough is enough. We had to draw the line somewhere." The argument from the California State superintendent and the North Carolina Department of Education also centered on this same issue. Agreements with Whittle Communications not only crossed a perceived ethical line, but raised questions concerning the rights of children and their accessibility via the new electronic medium.

Economics

Since the turn of the century, schools have been under pressure to be modern, efficient, and cost-effective. Institutions have had to consider ways of conserving funds through business-partnerships while finding the most cost-effective use of taxpayer's money. In constructing innovative strategies for the efficient use of funds, while still working toward the idea of educational excellence, educational agencies have had to reconsider the boundaries of legitimate behavior. Both California and North Carolina have provided examples of how economics and time can be used as a discourse of control. The economic-and-time arguments, both for and against the Whittle concept, has centered on two themes: the cost of technology, and student time as capital.

To be modern and technological schools have had to invest in expensive instructional systems, including hardware and software. The cost of hardware and software, its maintenance, and its support has always been a major problem for education (Cuban 1986). This has become more evident over the last ten years with decentralization of federal support for social programs and shrinking state budgets for education and other human services. This economic slump has hampered many districts and states from investing in and supporting video and computer technologies—that is, hardware, software, and system design—as well as human resources. Districts with larger tax bases and higher incomes have tended to provide different educational environments than do lower income areas. This environmental difference has caused inequalities in access to information and experiences (Apple 1979, 1982; Kozol 1991).

The educational inequalities caused by economic differences have forced districts to consider various offers from the private sector that take the form of school-business partnerships. Because of economic hard times and the general "loss of faith" in public education by the electorate, Whittle's offer of free video-related technologies, installations, and maintenance, along with a free current-events program, may be too much for many schools to turn down. As more than one school official reported to me, "We will put up with the commercials so we can get the equipment." It appears that the arguments used to outweigh the ethical and economic concerns of those opposing the Whittle program were based upon the perceived symbolic value of the hardware received, and its potential use outside the showing of the program.

Whittle's offer of technology and programming has lead state policy makers to address the issue of time as a commodity of exchange. The funding of educational programs originates from tax revenues from individuals and business on local, state, and federal levels. As part of the equity issue, many states disburse funds on a per-student, per-day basis. As the cases in California and North Carolina demonstrated, the perceived correlation between student time and money is a real one, and it was used to justify forming policy against contractual agreements with Whittle Publications. This perceived correspondence between time and money is one that deserves our attention.

The constructed relationship between time and money is present in many facets of our culture. Time is thought of as being tangible, and it is equated to money in our culture. Laborers exchange their time for money. While attending school for advance degrees or skills, individuals consider the loss of income endured by their removal from the marketplace. In the same light, students' time in elementary, middle, and secondary schools—which is purchased by the taxpayer—is equated to and expressed in terms of dollars and cents.

Since the late nineteenth century, concerns over efficiency, effectiveness, and accountability have dominated educational and business policy makers (Callahan 1962). Good policy is usually related to good business. Efficiency, effectiveness, and accountability is linked to control over the use of time and the effective use of resources and raw materials in the development of quality products. In education, the product is a productive and contributing citizen, which translates into working taxpayers.

How time is defined becomes an institutional instrument for control. The key in our discussion here is instructional time. Many districts—as in the state of Iowa—have expanded their school day by twelve or fifteen minutes to accommodate the Channel One program. This added-on time in some districts is not treated as additional instructional time but as a noninstructional or supplemental instructional time. In framing time in this manner, control over time shifts from state to local school levels. The cases in both California and North Carolina demonstrated how time may be labeled and categorized in terms of control. With time-as-money, control over the definitions of time is critical.

Viewing Channel One during noninstructional, locally controlled time, becomes a vehicle for maintaining local control of the content of some instructional experiences. As with instructional time, instructional materials must also meet the guidelines or frameworks designed by state departments of instruction. In moving Channel One to a period which is deemed as noninstructional or supplemental, the content is removed from meeting state guidelines and review. Local authorities can decide on a case-by-case basis what curricular materials will be used in their schools. Again, who controls the educational experiences of children is partly a definition of time and its perceived value.

As California, New York, and North Carolina portray, the consumption of student time, the ethical dimensions of schooling, and concerns for the control of tax dollars to support a commercial venture have forced policy makers to seriously reflect upon the implications of the Whittle concept for future relationships between education and business.

Symbolism

It is important that schools appear to be doing what we have come to believe they should be doing. For that to happen, the rituals, ceremonies, and appearances of schools must fit a certain image. For that image to be meaningful it must function on a symbolic level.

As Susan Langer suggests, the symbol functions as an instrument of thought (Langer 1942). The meanings of gestures, tokens, and artifacts may exist on many levels at once. The symbolic—not the "thing" itself, but the idea and its meaning—is paramount. The gestures and artifacts of priest, politicians, and others live in the social and historical world (Goffman 1976). They have become part of our refined consciousness. Who we are and how we think about ourselves and the outside world is formed by our social relationships to the meanings already attached to objects and social institutions (Berger and Luckman 1966). As a collective, their meanings work to inform our horizons.

On one level, Channel One offers schools and communities a visible symbol that functions to relieve concerns and to maintain promises. The satellite disk is more than an technological object. It is a marker that refers to "technology as progress." Schools that have historically existed with very little and have few markers of success can now point to their entry into the twenty-first century with no extra financial burden on the taxpayer. Schools that have been unable to offer the same programs as have others can now point to the Channel One program and the hardware installed in their classrooms. Because of low standardized test scores and concerns over the quality of educational programs and teachers, schools, and teachers can now point to Channel One as an innovation and quality educational program, implying that it will make a difference.

Meanings and practice at one point in time provide the horizons for future moments and rationales. Decisions to empower local school boards or to allow promotional material within instructional materials have implications for future actions in education as well as in other social arenas.

If the symbol is examined, if the social nature of its meaning is explored, and if the reality of the classroom is investigated, will anything be any different?

CONCLUSION

Conflicts between state and local school boards, parent groups, businesses, teachers, administrators, and other educational policy brokers over whose interests are represented and served in the curriculum are not new. Struggles over the curriculum have been a major part of the United States' educational experience (Apple 1979; Kliebard 1987; Popkewitz 1991). Positioning the controversy over

Channel One within that discourse will reveal institutional relationships and their quest for control of the schooling experience.

This chapter intended to locate the Channel One debate within arguments focused on ethics and power. Issues over ethics, economics, and symbolism have meaning only in relationship to other institutions, social events, and other discourses. As school administrators, teachers, parents, and school boards consider the ethical and educational issues associated with Whittle's program, the question arises over who has control of access to the minds of children.

Consider, for a moment, the possibility that the educational agenda is not set by special interest groups, educators, or administrators, but by a socially and historically constructed social consciousness concerning problems and their solutions. In doing so, how we may think about Channel One goes beyond a twelve-minute television program to larger, more demanding concerns. As a daily program found in thousands of classrooms and experienced by millions of students in the United States, Channel One is not by itself that important. However, what occurs because of Channel One does become important, not only for the students sitting in today's classroom, but in tomorrow's as well.

REFERENCES

Action for Children's Television [ACT]. N.d. *Classroom News and Commercials in the Classroom.* Cambridge: Action for Children's Television.

Apple, M. W. 1979. *Ideology and Curriculum.* London, Boston, and Henley: Routledge & Kegan Paul.

———. 1982. *Cultural and Economic Reproduction in Education: Essays on Class, Ideology and the State.* London and Boston: Routledge & Kegan Paul.

Berger, P. L., and T. Luckmann. 1966. *The Social Construction of Reality: A Treatise in the Sociology of Knowledge.* Garden City, N.Y.: Doubleday & Company, Inc.

California Assembly Bill No. 2007 1991–1992. Sacramento: California State Legislature. Senators Torres, Alquist, Dills, B. Greene, Keene, and Watson.

California Department of Education. 1989. Honig explains why channel one is barred from California schools. News release, August 4. Sacramento.

———. 1990. Channel One. News release, November 2. Sacramento.

———. 1993. Channel One case is appealed. News Release, April 21. Sacramento.

California Senate Bill No. 741. 1991–1992. Sacramento: California State Legislature. Assembly Member Lempert.

Callahan, R. E. 1962. *Education and the Cult of Efficiency: A Study of the Social Forces that Have Shaped the Administration of the Public Schools.* Chicago and London: The University of Chicago Press.

Cherryholmes, C. H. 1988. *Power and Criticism: Poststructural Investigations in Education.* New York and London: Teachers College Press.

Cuban, L. 1986. *Teachers and Machines: The Classroom Use of Technology since 1920.* New York and London: Teachers College Press.

Ellsworth, E., and M. H. Whatley. 1990. *The Ideology of Images in Educational Media: Hidden Curriculums in the Classroom.* New York and London: Teachers College Press.

Feenberg, A. 1991. *Critical Theory of Technology.* New York and Oxford: Oxford University Press.

Goffman, E. 1976. *Gender Advertisements.* New York: Harper & Row.

Kliebard, H. M. 1987. *The Struggle for the American Curriculum 1893–1958.* New York and London: Routledge.

Kozol, J. 1991. *Savage Inequalities: Children in America's Schools.* New York: Crown.

Langer, S. K. 1942. *Philosophy in a New Key: A Study in the Symbolism of Reason, Rite, and Art.* Cambridge: Harvard University Press.

Martin, J. 1991. *In re North Carolina State Board of Education v. Whittle Communications, Thomasville City Board of Education, and Davidson County Board of Education.* NC, No. 164PA90–Wake. April 3.

Masterman, L. 1985. *Teaching the media.* London: Comedia Publishing Group.

Muffoletto, R. 1991. Technology and texts: Breaking the window. In *Paradigms Regained: The Uses of Illuminative, Semiotic and Post-modern Criticism as Modes of Inquiry in Educational Technology.* Englewood Cliffs, N.J.: Educational Technology Publications.

———. 1993. Machine as expert. In *Computers in Education: Social, Political, and Historical Perspectives,* eds. R. Muffoletto and N. Knupfer. Cresskill, N.J.: Hampton Press.

New York State Board of Regents. 1990. Proposed for action. (Proposed promulgation of part 23 of the rules of the Board of Regents pursuant to section 101, 207, and 414 of the Education Law, and Article 8, Section 1 of the New York Constitution relating to commercial activities on school premises). Albany: State Department of Education of New York. January 30.

Newcomb, H. 1982. *Television: The Critical View.* New York and Oxford: Oxford University Press.

North Carolina State Board of Education v. *Whittle Communications, Thomasville City Board of Education, and Davidson County Board of Education.* 1991. NC, No. 164PA90–Wake. April 3.

Popkewitz, T. S. 1987. *Critical Studies in Teacher Education: Its Folklore, Theory and Practice.* London and New York: The Falmer Press.

————. 1991. *A Political Sociology of Educational Reform: Power/Knowledge in Teaching, Teacher Education, and Research.* New York: Teachers College Press.

Salomon, G. 1981. *Communication and Education: Social and Psychological Interactions.* Beverly Hills and London: SAGE Publications.

10

Two Rhetorics of Cynicism in Debates over Channel One: Two Riders in a Barren Landscape

Twenty-five centuries ago, when Platonic philosophy was proposed as a rejection of sophistic rhetoric and cynical satire, there began a long-running series of disputes over methods for deliberating moral questions (MacIntyre 1990, Shweder n.d.). These debates were attenuated in Western philosophy during the seventeenth century, when ground rules for discourse were greatly redrawn. In recent times, yet another battleground in the struggle over moral bases of public discourse has been the curriculum of public schools, over which many parties heatedly debate questions about what knowledge is of most worth.

A recurrent image in these debates is that of the marketplace. In this essay, I will discuss how this image informs certain kinds of rhetoric, which is to say, the detailed construction of deliberation (Fish 1990, 203–222; Vickers 1988). Two contrasting rhetorical positions will be presented, each of which may be called cynical but with significantly different implications. Some aspects of these differences, I claim, were infused into public schooling in the West from the outset, becoming more prominent as schooling expanded during the past two centuries. Finally, I will show how both versions of cynicism feature in recent debates over the place of Whittle Communications' Channel One in the school curriculum. Some of the most outspoken opposition to Channel One, it seems, continues an old debate between two closely related forms of moral deliberation, ancient and modern cynicism.

RHETORICS OF CYNICISM

Cynicism was first named in the works of Greek philosopher Diogenes of Sinope in the fourth century B.C.E. (Dudley 1967, Sayre 1938, Sloterdijk 1981). To him and his colleagues—collectively known as Cynics—the basis of moral deliberation was a divinely ordained but mysterious cycle of birth and death over which human action is powerless. They recommended that humans who would avoid delusion should steadfastly tell the entire truth about their impoverished situations. Cynics, for instance, readily condoned Socrates' bold confrontation with the Athenian jury that condemned him to die, because capitulation to avoid death would have been an abhorrence to cynical precepts.

In Greek philosophy, particularly in the cases of Socrates and Diogenes, *parrhesia* was a term associated with practices of unyielding honesty in defiance of convention. Although *parrhesia* is often associated with voluntary self-denial—such as vows of poverty taken by ascetic monks—Greek Cynics were less contrite in their ways. They actively sought to affront common moral standards by shamelessly standing in the marketplace lost in thought, dressed in tatters, eating dirt, sleeping in washtubs, defecating, masturbating, or copulating in public. For such willing disregard of conventions of self-presentation, the term *cynic*, or *dog*, was evidently first applied to parrhesiasts such as Diogenes. In turn, he regarded the deprecatory label as an ironic tribute. As he wrote to his father,

> Do not grieve, father, because I am called "Dog." . . . Although the name is not suitable, it is in a sense an honorable symbol. I am called a "dog of heaven," not of earth, because I resemble the former, living not according to opinion, but according to nature, free under Zeus. (Diogenes, quoted in Sayre 1938, 119)

Among Greek Cynics and their successors, moral deliberations were occasions for making unflinching witness to human insufficiency and divine authority. Living out their testimonies as mendicants, Cynics sought natural lives, which is to say, uncontaminated by extensive associations with fellow humans. They chose to abide like animals, aspiring to live closer to an entity called "nature" which they averred did not harbor illusions of wealth or power. As with most adherents of various types of asceticism, Cynics considered publication of tracts to be irreconcilable with their beliefs. Carrying their repudiation of the marketplace further than most monastics, Cynics had no sacred texts, rituals, or icons at all. The Cynics were opposed to any ideals save their vague idealizations of nature. They rejected any foundations for moral deliberation, holding that nature was inscrutable, and that ordinary human affairs were contemptible.

Emperor Julian the Apostate described cynical opposition to systematic philosophy, saying circa A.D. 360 that cynicism

> . . . has been practised in all ages . . . it does not need any special study, one need only hearken to the god of Delphi when he enjoins the precepts "know thyself" and "alter the currency." (Dudley 1967, ix)

Donald Dudley further summarized that

> . . . Cynicism was really a phenomenon which presented itself in three not inseparable aspects—a vagrant ascetic life, an assault on all established values, and a body of literary genres particularly well-adapted to satire and popular philosophical propaganda. (Dudley 1967, xi–xii)[1]

The rhetoric of the ancient cynics was therefore couched in interrogations of moral worth according to two imperatives: to "know thyself," requiring continuous self-critique; and, in parallel, to "alter the currency," involving continuous social critique. Cynical satires and sermons are caricatured in tales of a philosopher-beggar dressed in tatters, bearing a lamp in broad daylight to search for an honest man. Variations of this figure reappear in many works, notably New Testament portrayals of Jesus Christ taunting Pharisees or driving out money changers.

In its antique denotation of a mendicant philosopher who scorns and derides civil society, the term *cynic* meant someone who upheld high standards of goodness, "marked by an ostentatious contempt for ease, wealth, and the enjoyments of life." More recently, the term has mutated into meaning someone "disposed to disbelieve in human sincerity or goodness" (*Oxford English Dictionary* year, 1304).

Throughout this chapter, I will emphasize the antique meaning of these terms by capitalizing *Cynicism* and *Cynic*. Modern meanings of the terms will be indicated by lower case. Alternatively, Sloterdijk distinguishes these two meanings of the term by referring to Cynicism as *kynicism* (see Sloterdijk 1981, 101ff).

How did the cynical basis of moral deliberation and political critique turn from a metaphysical source—such as the oracle of Delphi—into a nihilistic one desecrating all gods? That mutation has involved a shift in the importance of the marketplace, the public space in which the Cynics first appeared and testified to a moral universe above and beyond human knowledge and material existence. Even though the gods were not public presences, it was assumed by the first Cynics that naturally immanent divinity could be made manifest amid the bustles of commerce and daily routine. Following the wide spread of Western European ideas labeled *Enlightenment*, the temporal discourse of the marketplace has come to overwhelm and absorb most variants of mysticism. Without gods, such as Zeus, as their master, cynics became dogs of a different type.

In effect, the discourse of the first Cynics placed into dichotomy two versions of reality, thus giving philosophers status to assert that one pole—namely nature as a source of spiritual and moral truths—was superior to the other of artifice, or social and economic verities. By the eighteenth century, relations between spiritual and economic norms had switched so that the marketplace now acquired superior status. In many intricate ways, materialism came to dominate moral discourse over a long duration. A specific aspect of this transition is evident in a change that takes place from the rhetoric of Diogenes to that of Hobbes and Descartes, in which vastly different notions of moral action emerge, to be further transformed in such influential European works as those by Adam Smith and Karl Marx. Rather than review these changes, I propose, in the next section, to illustrate some of their differences.

TWO RIDERS IN A BARREN LANDSCAPE

Two cynical parties to long-standing debates over moral deliberation are portrayed in Bob Dylan's song, "All Along the Watchtower," the lyric of which is constructed as a vicious circle so that the first lines,

"There must be some way out of here," said the joker to the thief.
"There's too much confusion. I can't get no relief."

follow the last lines.

All along the watchtower, princes kept the view
While all the women came and went, barefoot servants, too.
Outside in the distance, a wildcat did growl.
Two riders were approaching. The wind began to howl.

The song's narrative line is an endless loop in which there is constant confusion with no hope of escape. In the second stanza, however, the thief replies to the joker's exclamation of futility as follows:

"No reason to get excited," the thief, he kindly spoke,
"There are many here among us who feel that life is but a joke.
But you and I, we've been through that, and this is not our fate.
So let us not talk falsely now, the hour is getting late."
                                                    (Dylan 1968)

Dylan's song recounts two contrasting approaches to moral deliberation, both cynical but with very different purposes. First, there is the joker who lives on the edge of the marketplace to mock its currency. By contrast, the thief comes from outside the marketplace to take the currency. The thief is a predator engaged in a black market that is an underground double of the above-ground market. The joker is a peripheral, like the card in most games, a player who never wins. As a jester, he appears in court with no lineage, clad in motley that parodies the garb of those in power. The joker survives by making his patrons amused but not angry. He is, at best, a risky aesthetic. Despite his precarious position, he is loyal. In Shakespeare's *King Lear*, the Fool is the last retainer of the mad king, remaining at his side even after he loses all his power and wealth, so guideless as to ask him to ". . . keep a schoolmaster that can teach thy fool to lie. I would fain learn to lie" (Shakespeare year, 195–196).

Guile is the work of the thief, who lives by raiding the marketplace and resides outside its laws. The romantic figure of a legal transgressor as spiritual transcender grew more popular together with the development of centralized industrialized nation-states. By the nineteenth century, folkloric figures, such as Robin Hood or Jesse James, were portrayed on mythic quests to reclaim alienated lands, labor, or justice from modern marketplaces. The joker had powerful sponsors to insulate him from the market, but the thief—the more modern cynic—had to engage with it, construct doubles to it, and so contest the claims of economic life upon individual freedom. The joker retains tendencies to the life of denial and *parrhesia* espoused by ancient Cynics, but the thief questions the joker's honesty in living as a slave. Unlike Lear's Fool, the thief knows what lying is and how to lie.

In Dylan's song, the advice that the joker gives the thief, to "not speak falsely now" would not seem to be a platitude to an early Cynic, but rather as a corollary to their two imperatives. Along with knowing oneself and altering the currency, speaking the truth would be included in a cynical catechism to prescribe the most moral course of action in a world that is not controllable by moral precepts. Such a catechism could not become universal, however, without dissolving the marketplace within which the self and the currency are both defined. Cynical practices of self-criticism and social criticism, therefore, entail a degree of social separation which defines limits and purposes of intellectual discourse and practices. Thus, the song's two riders are depicted as outsiders as a distance from society, symbolized by the watch tower, marketplace or court.[2]

Rhetorics of cynicism and implied critiques are idiosyncratic reactions to social circumstances. However, it may very generally be said that these metaphorical figures and their social arrangements are set in a barren landscape, one that is divided along a boundary laid down during the seventeenth century, when Western thinkers formally abandoned divine law as a source of authority above and beyond the actions of nature and human society. This abandonment was announced by Hobbes as the superiority of social contract over natural right. In place of the "war of all against all" of humans in their natural state, Hobbes proposed that nation-states be organized rationally, in economic terms.

> The Value, or WORTH of a man, is as of all other things, his Price; that is to say, so much as would be given for the use of his Power: and therefore is not absolute; but a thing dependant on the need and judgement of another. (Hobbes 1985, 151–152)

Taking a step beyond the Delphic admonitions to "Know thyself" and "Alter the currency," the modern self—as proclaimed by Hobbes—is, in itself, a form of currency whose worth is set by social relations that resemble patterns of material supply and demand.

According to Hobbes, cash-nexus relations replace ancient conceptions of natural law as the basis of modern morality. Likewise, conceptions of self and society based upon traditional authorities such as the Delphic oracle are replaced by ideas of selfhood and nation based upon the precepts of natural science and mathematics. In

Hobbes' time of the European seventeenth century, modern Western values of self and society transformed the subjects of cynical critiques and testimony.

The ancient cynic sought refuge from the marketplace at its margins, turning to nature for evidence of divine ideals upon which to base critiques of self and society. The modern cynic must occupy different enclaves for moral deliberation, whether they are buffer zones, such as courts, schools or laboratories protected by law or custom; or gaps among these institutions in which self-reflection and social reconstruction can occur.[3] No longer a conceptual space reserved for gods and their prophets, nature becomes, then, an annex of the marketplace. The modern landscape upon which the joker and thief ride is barren of the sanctions of absolute divinity.

As Hobbes foretold, realignments of modern values are paralleled in widespread and frequent reevaluations of currency (Michaels 1986). The value of metal coins, long set by the monarch whose regal figure was stamped upon them, increasingly became associated with rates of exchange set by markets for the very metals. Michel Foucault says

> Whereas the Renaissance based the two *functions* of coinage (measure and substitution) on the double nature of its intrinsic *character* (the fact that it was precious), the seventeenth century turns the analysis upside down: it is the exchanging function that serves as a foundation for the other two characters (its ability to measure and capacity to receive a price thus appearing as *qualities* deriving from that *function*). (Foucault 1970, 174) (Emphasis in the original)

The emergence of mercantile, bourgeois social arrangements led to more fluid currency as well as pluralistic and contingent sets of values. Just as a new rhetoric of science was constructed to proclaim with mathematical certainty the laws of nature and society, there arrived a new rhetoric of cynicism. Rather than a voluntarily powerless outsider appealing to forces outside the marketplace, the cynic began to appear as a willfully powerful outsider overriding the limits of a marketplace. Not content to mockingly alter the currency, the modern cynic steals it.

Far from taking nature as a model of morality, the modern cynic distrusts all models, including the modernist ideals of scientific and social progress. Pushed to its extreme, modern cynicism can lead to nihilism, a state of continuous doubt about both self and currency.[4] As Friedrich Nietzsche, the most nihilist of modern cynics, aphorized

. . . truths are illusions about which one has forgotten that this is what they are; metaphors which are worn out and without sensuous power; coins which have lost their pictures and now matter as metal, only coins. (Nietzsche 1954, 47)

The Cynic of ancient Greece avoided the pit of nihilism by basing moral decisions on divine revelation, especially as manifest in natural processes. The modern cynic pulls up short of the nihilistic abyss by identifying material processes as relatively stable benchmarks in a godless world. For example, the value of gold—Nietzsche notwithstanding—may fluctuate but never becomes entirely devalued. Likewise, to a modern cynic, contingencies—such as processes of historical change, legal rules of a commonwealth, or disciplined observations of nature—while not necessarily absolute, are nonetheless sufficient bases for moral deliberations.[5]

Dylan's two riders—the joker and the thief—represent two modes of rhetoric that, generally, take a stance outside the centers of power. Both positions for deliberating the worth of the marketplace make specific reference to human fallibility and the limitations of convention. A third common feature of these rhetorical platforms is a highlighted conception of truth, impelling the rhetor to confess the poverty of human knowledge and action. The joker and the thief share their barren landscape with others who base their moralities on ideals such as God, nature, or history, but as critics and *parrhesiasts* they reject any means of escaping their plight by adhering to some such ideals. They accept the contingency of their situations, asserting their dependence upon others and assuming the eventual futility of all beliefs as well as their own.

After the seventeenth century, divine indulgence was no longer necessary for critiques and satires of marketplaces and their currency, because the currencies themselves had become standards of truth. "Alter the currency" had itself been changed to "Money talks." To modern cynics—anonymous and secretive—all that matters are the rules of the marketplace which take precedence over limits set by faith, law, or scruple. This idiom of moral deliberation—which Alasdair MacIntyre calls "genealogy"—is a form of realism set in opposition to religious idealism, which he calls "tradition," and secular idealism, which he calls "encyclopaedia" (MacIntyre 1990).

By adopting a genealogical idiom of moral deliberation, modern cynics adhere to three precepts: self-knowledge, social critique, and *parrhesia*. In moral deliberations informed by these rules, cynics do not escape the circularity of their situation. They reaffirm it. This idiom has some specific implications, particularly for discourses of schooling. In the following section, I present evidence of ancient and modern cynicism in the rhetoric of educators in the United States, showing how ancient tensions between nature and the marketplace were incorporated into the design and construction of mass public schooling.

CYNICISM OLD AND NEW IN SCHOOLS

How do rhetorics of cynicism occur in public schooling? Since the seventeenth century, modern schools have been constructed and maintained generally insulated from the marketplaces that surround them. Like the monastic cloisters from which they were derived, often in revolt against clericalism, schools were administered by state agencies as specialized enclaves. Secular European schools flourished with curricula based on conceptions of the classical seven liberal arts and without direct linkages to commercial or utilitarian purposes, except perhaps the law (Alexander 1990, Green 1990).

In the nineteenth century, after monarchies and theocracies had been toppled throughout Europe and the United States, schooling was transformed in ways that were suited to new conceptions of self, currency, nation, and God. At this time, professional educators came to be called a "classless profession," translating into school curricula the moral values of the Protestant churches. (Goodson 1988, Mattingly 1975, Tyack and Hansot 1982). The rhetoric of the "schoolmen" was thus devoted to social utility, but it retained an ascetic disdain for many human pursuits. As the leading promoter of common schools for all children and normal schools in which to train their teachers, Horace Mann took this position ardently and with eloquence.

> Every one, either from his own experience or from observations of others is made acquainted with the emotions of fear, hope, jealously, anger, revenge and the explosive phraseology in which those passions are vented. Now the diction, appropriate and almost peculiar to the coarser and more animal parts of our nature, is almost as distinct as though it were a separate language, from the style, in which questions of social right and duty, questions of morals, and even philosophy, when popularly treated, are discussed. (Mann 1839, 74–75)

The common schools, Mann and others maintained, were "bulwarks of democracy," but only if they treated "higher" subjects and avoided "coarser" topics and the sensational diction with which they were expressed. Educators such as Mann, in the ancient Cynical tradition, set out to serve the new republics by shunning the marketplace and its modern cynics who would knowingly manipulate popular passions.

It is not as though Mann and his peers advocated complete withdrawal from worldly pursuits. Rather, they upheld a Protestant ideology that predicated material prosperity as a consequence of the attainment of certain kinds of spiritual worth. Mann asserted that human progress depends upon the types of intelligence best cultivated in schools which are set apart from the marketplace.

> For the creation of wealth, then,—for the existence of a wealthy people and a wealthy nation,—intelligence is the grand condition. . . . The greatest of all the arts in political economy is to change a consumer into a producer; and the next greatest is, to increase the producer's producing power;—an end to be directly attained by increasing his intelligence. (Mann 1849, 67–68)

In other words, Mann's approach to schooling follows the two precepts of Greek Cynicism: know thyself through reflective deliberation, and alter the currency through social amelioration. Inverting the Cynical hierarchy that ranked philosophical idealism lower than naturalistic realism, Mann proposed that the schools cultivate an individual's capacity for abstract knowledge, reified as "intelligence." Carrying forward a traditional ascetic revulsion for worldly matters, Mann says that both production and consumption depend upon habits of contemplation without which ". . . an ignorant man is little better than a swine, whom he so much resembles in his appetites, and surpasses in his powers of mischief" (Mann 1849, 67–68).[6] Mann's rhetoric somewhat coincides with that of the joker in standing apart from political strife and commercial struggle, sacrificing power to maintain an unswerving commitment to truths revealed in empirical studies of nature as well as exegetical studies of doctrine. In Mann's rhetoric, common schools in the United States were dynamos of spiritual uplift and material progress, powered by ideas of moral worth labeled *human nature* (Curti 1980, Taylor 1989, 359).

In a fateful conjunction of ideas, the ideas and rhetoric of common-school reformers neatly dovetailed with tenets of physiological psychology developed in European research laboratories in the latter decades of the nineteenth century. The path from the labs to the schools was not smooth. There were debates among the "new" psychologists, pitting those who would keep the science of mind pure of practical applications against those who would apply psychological research for purposes of ameliorating social conditions. Most psychologists in the United States spoke out for psychological theories as intellectual bases for schooling practices. One of the foremost, John Dewey, declared

> We are overwhelmed by the consequences of the very sciences into which have gone our best thought and energy for these past few hundred years. We apparently do not control them, they control us and wreak their vengeance upon us. . . . The recourse of a courageous humanity is to press forward . . . until we have control of human nature comparable to our control of physical nature. (Dewey 1980, 53–63)

The remedies for social ills caused by technology in the marketplace, Dewey argues, are to be offset by technologies reserved for schools. Although "new psychologists," such as Dewey, defined conceptions of human nature that were compatible with Protestant ideologies and industrialized economies, they maintained crucial rhetorical distinctions that were older than Diogenes. Schools built along progressive lines would be enclaves removed from the marketplace, not to transcend it so much as to improve it and all social arrangements.

The technologies of applied psychology proposed by Dewey and other progressive educators would maintain the divisions that Mann advocated between "baser" and "higher" languages. While equipped to address social problems, schools would remain separate and distinct social institutions. If schools were, in Dewey's famous image, social arrangements in embryo, then they would seem to require a protective shell. As he later stated

> If our public-school system merely turns out efficient industrial fodder and citizenship fodder in a state controlled by pecuniary industry, . . . it is not helping to solve the problem of building up a distinctive American culture; it is only aggravating the problem. That which prevents the schools from doing their educational work freely is precisely the pressure—for the most part indirect, to be sure—of domination by the money-motif of our economic regime. (Dewey 1984, 102)

Dewey's formulation of the marketplace is, like Mann's, within an ascetic tradition similar to that of the Greek Cynics. Commerce is too close for schools to ignore, but remains too hostile to higher pursuits around which the curriculum should be built. Dewey was far from cynical in his indomitable optimism about prospects for improving the human condition through philosophical speculation, scientific experimentation, and democratic action. However, as a psychologist and philosopher, Dewey would share the same rhetorical platform as the joker: know thyself, alter the currency, and do not speak falsely.

Progressive educational reforms involved formulating intelligence as an individualized entity that was somehow distinct from utilitarian skills required to "make a living," that is to maintain one's body or earn money. Simply put, public-school teachers retained their authority over students but delegated their authority over children and citizens. As Thomas Popkewitz summarized, "A network of relations linked teachers' work, pedagogy, teacher education, and educational sciences. The epistemology gave reference to a rationally planned organization of schooling based on an individualization of social affairs and a secular notion of pastoral care" (Popkewitz 1991, 76).

Progressive educators—their ranks filled with men and women dedicated to education as a distinct and elevated profession—struggled over what types of vocational and technological knowledge were worthy of inclusion in school textbooks and professional preparation programs. Often, the terms of debate changed little if at all. For example, a concept of predestination central to Calvinist theology and similar to one that Plato advanced in *The Republic* turns up intact in early proposals for tracking vocational students. More often, advocates of various liberal and technical curricula were embroiled in continual controversies, including overt resistance by aboriginal and immigrant groups, despite overwhelming tides of assimilation, expansion, and institutionalization. There is no simple summary of these contentious curriculum debates that continue up to the present. As Herbert Kliebard has stated, what passes for contemporary curriculum is "a loose, largely unarticulated and not very tidy compromise" (Kliebard 1986, 29).

One reason that curriculum compromises are untidy is that much of the educators' discourse—using what Mann called "higher diction"—is at odds with much in the daily lives of teachers, teacher educators, and policymakers. In many curriculum theories—as well as critiques, satires, and social histories—schooling is described as contested terrain where children's bodies, popular culture, and the commercial marketplace are very actively engaged. In the words of one teacher writing about his feelings when he hears the word *education*, Garret Keizer said

> . . . few words make me as queasy as that one. When it does not smack of the most shameless professional jingoism, it bespeaks all kinds of mediocrity, fadism and quackery; it categorizes all kinds of people who have little to do with what I do in the classroom. (Keizer 1988, 105–106)

In a competition to select a Teacher of the Year, Keizer was asked to describe what he finds most difficult about his job. He said

> I am surprised that I did not answer "grading papers." Perhaps the nature of the competition prompted me to respond, "The struggle not to be cynical." That was not a cynical reply, however. A good part of the struggle not to be cynical is resisting the disheartenment of working in "education." (Keizer 1988, 105–106)

Keizer uses two contrasting meanings of cynicism in this passage. He is true to the Greek Cynic's devotion to honesty, but nevertheless wants to avoid the modern cynic's tendency toward nihilism. As anyone who has spent time in a teachers' lounge will attest, the moral idiom of everyday discussions about curriculum is closer to either version of cynicism than to any sort of idealism or pragmatism, however ingrained they might be in educational research and policy. Or, put in MacIntyre's terms, practitioners' curriculum deliberations more closely resemble Nietzsche's "genealogy" than Mann's "tradition" or Dewey's "encyclopaedia."[7]

Here, the problem of circularity takes practical form. How, without a binding, universally accepted moral tradition—or else a proven encyclopaedia of scientific bases for morality—can educators sustain coherent moral purposes for schooling? Although claimed, in principle, by some philosophers, no one has been able to show in practice how deliberation, reflection, and critique can avoid turning in on themselves, like ships without compasses, and lacking overriding abstractions such as God, the market, or nature. Nevertheless, without the solaces of religion or the regulations of commerce, educational deliberation requires a foundation, or what Richard Rorty calls "solidarity"—that is to say, "the identification with 'humanity as such,' . . . an awkward attempt to secularize the idea of becoming one with God" (Rorty 1989, 198).

In schools, millions of teachers are asked to believe, as Mann and Dewey did, that their work serves higher secular ideals which, in turn, undergird curricular deliberations and decisions. All the while, most teachers are dubious about those ideals and are inclined, like Keizer, to wonder whether values inherited from educators, such as Mann or Dewey, could possibly mean anything for children growing up in cultures that uphold many different and often conflicting values. As MacIntyre summarizes

> Insofar as the curriculum, both in respect of [moral] enquiry and in respect of teaching, is no longer a whole, there can be no question of providing a rational justification for the continued existence and flourishing of the whole. . . . The emptiness and triviality of so much of the rhetoric of official academia is a symptom of a much deeper disorder. (MacIntyre 1990, 227)

Despite utopian visions held forth by nineteenth-century educational reformers, the moral landscape of the late twentieth century is apparently more barren than many of their heirs would readily admit. In the guise of the joker, teachers face complex moral dilemmas every day choosing what is best, most useful, or most palatable to offer their students. Most of them will readily admit their frustration. Yet, they revert to traditional and official pieties when confronted by the rulers of marketplace or their doubles, the thieves of the underworld. Teachers speak out against "cynical manipulation" of schools or students, but the antagonism may not be a simple one. Perhaps it is, instead, a choice among related versions of cynicism. The rhetorical figure of the joker reappears in debates over curriculum, both familiar and unquestioned, and unable to lie but also unable to escape his predicament, especially when in dialogue with the thief.

In this section, I have contended that curriculum discourse in public schooling has long contained specific types of moral deliberation which employ idioms and traditions that are, in some respects, cynical. In the following section, I will discuss aspects of controversies that surround Channel One, to show how educators' varieties of cynicism may be in conflict—but not necessarily in contradiction—with that of certain inhabitants of today's marketplace. The joker and the thief have a great deal in common.

DEBATES OVER CHANNEL ONE

Channel One, a daily news broadcast to public schools, has been a topic of debates that often counterpose two rhetorics of moral deliberation in schooling. Briefly, Channel One's designer, Christopher Whittle, heads a corporation that creates and delivers specialized marketing services for businesses selling to consumers who can be precisely defined, or targeted. For such captive audiences as readers of college newspapers, airline passengers or occupants of physicians' waiting rooms, Whittle's term is "place-based marketing" (Kleinfield 1991, 33). In keeping with that specialty, Whittle Communications supplies television equipment free of charge to schools which place Channel One in the curriculum of social-studies or communications-arts classes. During daily broadcasts of twelve minutes that reportedly reach eight million students, news segments are alternated with commercial messages for which Whittle Communications obtains revenue. According to their own estimates, it took less than one year for Channel One to become profitable.

Channel One has met with widespread criticism in U.S. mass media as well as among school administrators, teachers, and policymakers (Friedman 1992, 188–192; Gallagher 1989, 88; Hammer 1990, 52–53; Hoffman 1991; Rowell 1990, 52–54; Walsh 1990, 4). The rhetoric of many critiques restates Mann's distinction between high and low diction as well as Dewey's plea for shielding schools from pressure by the money-motif of the surrounding society. Although the term *cynicism* has been offered in rebuke to Whittle's proposal, it is my contention, as already outlined, that debates over Channel One probably accentuate differences among two traditions of cynicism rather than place two disparate ideas into conflict.

Were we to ask the joker and the thief about Channel One, both could honestly say that, first, most U.S. students watch television programs attentively—some even obsessively. Next, that audiovisual aids are already often used and sometimes abused in U.S. schools. Furthermore, those schools already host many marketing campaigns, such as recruitment for colleges or military service, sales of student supplies, and myriad fund-raisers. Questions about Channel One that divide two versions of cynical relations with the marketplace are not whether students should be treated as consumers, but about the appropriateness of openly doing so within the customary curriculum.

These debates are not new. Progressive reformers in all industrialized lands since early in this century have proposed many curricula for purposes such as vocational training and life-adjustment. In most of these proposals, direct references to the marketplace are either suppressed or disguised. Nevertheless, many critics have excoriated the value of these curricula, notably in back-to-basics movements that erupt periodically in the United States and elsewhere (Cuban year, ch. 13; Kliebard 1986, ch. 9).

Other critics question the legitimacy of business and industrial initiatives in schools on political grounds, defending schools as bastions of equity in a marketplace dominated by exploitative competition (Harty 1979; Rist 1991, 30–31). While there are undeniable tendencies toward excessive zeal among men and women of commerce in any era, there are also good reasons to ask why schools deserve particular exemption from commerce, especially when selected sales and marketing campaigns are already welcomed, and most students, if not educators, eventually enter the marketplace.

Whittle's Channel One bases its case on the claim that media are already in great demand by teachers and students in modern schools. This corresponds to a classic distinction between selling and marketing. Selling is trying to get someone to want what you have, but marketing is trying to have what someone wants. The marketers of Whittle Communications are not wrong about the market. There is ample evidence that most students already watch television programs—including commercial ones—as in-school and homework assignments in most subject areas. Furthermore, Whittle and associates are convinced, as many educators are, that television is most students' preferred medium of information. As one school superintendent said, "You have to remember that the children of today have grown up with the visual media. They know no other way and we're simply capitalizing on that [with Channel One] to enhance learning" (Bikerts 1991, 18, quoting Robert Calabrese). In other words, Channel One provides something that students want and teachers could use. As Whittle Communications' editor-in-chief asserted, their program is "an especially powerful tool to help teachers remedy the woeful ignorance of American teenagers about current events, geography, and related subjects" (Rukeyser 1989/ 1990, 75).

Despite evident advantages, television programs may, nonetheless, be said to pose serious threats to traditional academic curricula. It is apparent that electronic media are significantly incompatible with the cardinal concepts of higher intelligence and critical thinking as defined by nineteenth-century educators (Ewen 1989, Ross 1991, Tichi 1991). As Sven Bikerts points out

. . . a communications mesh, a soft and pliable mesh woven from invisible threads, has fallen over everything. The so-called natural world, which used to be our yardstick of the actual, can now be perceived only through a scrim. Nature was then; this is now. And the great geographical Other, the far-away rest-of-the-world, has been transformed by the pure possibility of access. (Bickerts 1991, 14)

Boundaries that create Otherness are transformed by instantaneous mass contact. The enclaves designed by educators for pursuit of higher intelligence and critical rationality have been ensnared in a net which provides ways to synthetically experience far more than most children or adults ever actually could.

These artificial modes of experience are incompatible with natural events, but they are also incompatible with established artifices of linear thought and action enshrined in school curricula. Modern technologies of communication have significantly abandoned the model of transmission/reception that has dominated education since the coming of literary. Unlike the customary teacher delivering information from a position of authority, electronic communications involve complex and anonymous processes that match information to an audience's expectations with data familiar enough to catch its notice, but with enough novelty to capture its attention. This cycle of communications has been termed *resonance* by Tony Schwartz.

In communicating at electronic speed, we no longer direct information into an audience, but try to evoke stored information out of them, in a patterned way. . . . A "message" is not the starting point for communicating. It is the final product arrived at after considering the effect that we hope to achieve and the communication environment where people will experience our stimuli. (Schwartz 1973, 36)

Rather than a linear model of communications, resonance assumes a cyclical model, more attuned to a marketplace where goods and services float along with the currencies used to obtain them.

How have educators reacted to Channel One and the challenges it poses to schools as enclaves of higher intelligence and linear literacy? One response—in direct lineage to Mann or Dewey—would be to resist such proposals at all costs. For example, Joel Rudinow exhorts

. . . the best defense against Channel One and similar proposals is organized, informed and, most of all, *sustained* resistance by educators, particularly classroom teachers. These efforts must succeed. If not, one of the few remaining preserves in contemporary society will be penetrated and harvested as just another advertising market. (Rudinow 1989/1990, 73) (Emphasis in the original)

This response would ask teachers to defend public schools as "preserves," somehow above and beyond marketplaces, and protecting an ascetic tradition whose idealistic moral values are, as most teachers realize, difficult to sustain and impossible to impose on a pluralistic society.

A compromise response would be to adapt electronic media—such as Channel One—to fit traditional curricula, as John Olson proposes.

In the end, it is the teacher who renders materials truly educational by making them serve educational purposes—the cultivation of critical awareness and independence of mind. . . . These habits of mind run counter to the purposes of corporations whose very existence depends upon uncritical allegiance to their products and points of view. If corporations want to invest in materials directed at schools, that is their choice—they have a right to produce those materials. We have a responsibility to see them for what they are. (Olson 1990, 80)

This response calls for critiques of corporate sponsors, but omits critical examinations of schooling and the challenges faced by today's educators after the breakdown of "uncritical allegiance" to their own corporate product line of linear literacy, reified intelligence, and academic detachment.

Another type of response to Channel One's challenge to schooling would surpass the other two examples already given by turning to the three precepts of cynicism outlined in this essay: know thyself, alter the currency, and do not speak falsely. As Jay Rosen put it, Channel One's direct appeal to its audience, or resonance

. . . is the shift that should worry us. Not the waning of print and the rise of television, not the triumph of visual imagery over the word, but the victory of the resonance principle over the reality principle, the substitution of an electronic commons for the world we actually have in common—the world where bridges decay, people suffer, economies collapse, and ozones evaporate. . . . Our hope must be that people will get tired of the endless playback in culture, in politics, and in academic life. Although the resonance principle works by the law of desire— it assumes that you'll want now what you've wanted before— the one desire the law can't cover is the urge to be free of recycled desires. (Rosen 1992, 15)

This kind of response wouldn't call upon educators to resist Channel One, nor to modify it to fit into the customary curriculum. Instead, it would suggest careful use of the controversy itself as an occasion to critically examine both contemporary media and contemporary curriculum. As with a latter-day Diogenes, advice such as Rosen's bespeaks distrust of all conventional wisdom, urging us to make the most of the moment to criticize it. Perhaps, in citing various laws and principles, Rosen wears an encyclopaedist's robe of authority. However, his advice is, nonetheless, realistic.

Channel One and its resonances—as does the rest of popular culture—raise questions that schools must be prepared to debate. In this section—and in reference to the three idioms proposed by MacIntyre—I have framed them as varieties of moral deliberation. I contend that educators must begin their deliberations by, first, examining their own assumptions about mass public schooling accrued over centuries of ascetic predilections, state governance, and professionalized preparation. These habits of mind prevent many who are responsible for schools from more extensively reconsidering specific choices made in designing, implementing, and evaluating curricula. In their self-critiques, educators must analyze how schools have been deliberately fashioned as enclaves set apart from marketplaces, in accordance with idealistic tendencies and progressive ideologies that are manifestly unsuited to the highly technologized society—and endangered environment—in which we all now live.

In summary, Channel One is a challenge to educators to rethink their moral deliberations. Instead of resistance, schools and their communities need to reconsider what knowledge is of most worth. Teachers need reconstructed educational matter, media, and methods, not recycled ones. Citizens of a fragile world also need refreshing honesty, not repeated bromides. If debated over Channel One—or any other initiative from the marketplace, such as school choice—hasten these changes, then controversies are welcome and worthwhile.

It is a cliche that the onset of the twenty-first century marks a time of great difficulties and equally great opportunities. However, there are urgent reasons to repeat it. The dangers loosed in the destructive twentieth century are still growing. As the thief said to the joker, the hour is getting late.

CONCLUSIONS

Debates over curriculum are permanent parts of schooling. Controversies over Channel One's extension of the marketplace are but a part of a long inconclusive story in which ideas go through cycles of wax and wane, but never go away. Without decisive victories or losses, the debates continue. As rhetoricians and cynics asserted twenty-five centuries ago, there is no way out, no shortcut to Olympus, and maybe even no Olympus at all. Although old and obvious, it bears emphasis that schools and marketplaces are interdependent. The metaphor of the marketplace is bounded, because not all of nature or society can be managed by transactions based upon a cash-nexus. Cynics serve to recall those limitations by occupying the margins of marketplaces, in interstices where various kinds of criticism are possible. Thus, philosophers and educators—and jokers or thieves—depend upon marketplaces to live in, talk about, or act upon. Such mutual dependency involves distinctive distances as well as common conversation.

As participants in shared human endeavors, the two riders who have been used here to portray two types of cynicism can be placed in a dichotomous relation only if one, the joker, is said to be the idealist seeking a foundation for moral deliberation, action, and critique, as opposed to the other, the thief, who would then be the realist opposed to any such bases for morality. Thus twinned, in debate with each other, these cynics would continue to ride endlessly over landscapes, both old and new, while deliberating how best to know oneself, alter the currency, and speak the truth. But this dichotomy is false because it eventually forms a circle driven by paired symbols. The joker and the thief are linked as complements instead of opposites. The state that supports the joker also issues the money that is the thief's stock-in-trade.

Put another way, idealism and realism are interpenetrating categories of moral deliberation. No version of self, currency or truth can be shown to be finally stable. All can be demonstrated as interconnected, contingent upon each other as well as on their particular circumstances. According to modern ideas of social order since Hobbes wrote his works, human values—even idealistic ones—are set by a market that is governed but not entirely ruled by their commonwealth. Kenneth Burke described this synergistic relation as follows:

> The introduction of money as a new term in effect gives to the act of barter a new dimension. And the greater the development of the financial rationale, the greater is the "spirituality" in man's relations to material goods, which he sees less in terms of their actual nature as goods, and more in the "ideal" terms of the future and of monetary (symbolic) profit. (Burke 1969, 176)

Or, as Burke summarizes, "realism plus money equals idealism." The symbolic cash-value of a person, a society, or an idea are all dependent on the markets in which they circulate.

The metaphor of circulation is aptly used by both the marketplace and the philosopher who stands at its margin: goods, currencies, data, and ideas, all in circular flow. According to the second precept of cynicism, the value of money and ideas can be altered but cannot be ended. By extension, cynical morality assumes that existence is an endless cycle that can be altered but not broken. Unlike idealist moralities which are linearly directed at utopian ends, in cynical moralities there are no ultimate ends worth knowing or pursuing, thereby making immediacy a crucial value.

For educators, a cynical moral idiom for curriculum deliberation—such as a "genealogical" approach—has profound implications. No longer within havens of their own making and set aside from the marketplace to pursue higher ideals, educators must learn to foster free and open discussions involving all approaches to knowledge and action. These debates may never be resolved, but their conduct deeply concerns each individual and community. In a world which is instantaneously and completely linked by technology, a global network and a planetary environment are affected as well. There are no enclaves, no ivory towers in such a world, nor can the marketplace operate without heed. The joker and the thief must, nowadays, be aware of cameras following their every move.

For teachers, a cynical moral idiom entails examining each transaction in a classroom for its immediate worth, not only for such deferred worth as completing schooling, getting employed, or transmitting a culture. In classrooms of all types, reflection, critique, and honesty are daily requirements, not occasional luxuries.[8] There are no sanctuaries or retreats. The rapid flow of vast quantities of goods and information overwhelms political, intellectual, and environmental boundaries that might once have served to protect, but may now stand only to obstruct.

The joker and the thief interact with each other because their differences stem from the different ways in which they get and spend their money, not different positions on a fixed hierarchy of values. Because schools and businesses are both political and economic institutions, television commercials and social-studies lessons are therefore within the same sphere—albeit at different poles. The captive audiences that Whittle Communications seeks for Channel One have been granted to educators by common-school custom and law. However, for that, they are no less captive. Indeed, under the communications network's meshes, we are all captive audiences.

Proposals such as Channel One are miscast as invasions of schools by cynical thieves against whom all educators should mount crusades. Rather, such occasions are opportunities for marketers, sellers, media makers, teachers, students, families, administrators, scholars, and policymakers to continue debating moralities, philosophies, and politics of commerce, mass media, and schooling. Until opponents of Channel One can say that they have reflected upon themselves, altered their own currencies, and spoken the truth about their situations, Whittle's proposal—and others similar to it—will only gain cogency.

There is no way out of here. We must not speak falsely now. The hour is getting late.

NOTES

1. It is intriguing that medieval Dominican monks punningly referred to themselves as *Dominica canes* or "dogs of God."

2. The stylized social milieu of the two riders and their distance from it are presented in Dylan's song as the "princes, women, and barefoot servants" in the final stanza, as well as in the conclusion of the joker's expression of despair.

> Businessmen, they drink my wine. Plowmen dig my earth.
> None of them along the line know what any of it is worth.
> (Dylan 1968).

3. In the folklore and literature of Europe at the time of Hobbes and Descartes, a common figuration of the modern cynic appears as "Machiavel," an outlaw inspired by the works of Niccolo Machiavelli. (See Berlin 1991.)

4. Extremes of modern cynicism are more exactly called "nihilism," which originated in nineteenth-century Russian political writings and Nietzschean moral philosophy. Nihilism entails complete departures from metaphysical justifications for physical existence. (See Crosby 1988.)

5. In having this "negative capability," a modern cynic is akin to a pragmatist, liberal ironist, critical rationalist, or critical pragmatist. (See Cherryholmes 1988, James 1987, Popper 1985, Rorty 1989.)

6. An important aspect of cynicism that I regretably cannot treat here is the transformation of discourse about bodily functions which were celebrated by ancient Cynics but are abhorred by most ascetics and many variants of modern cynicism, such as that expressed by Mann; see Sloterdijk (1981). For a recent feminist critique of schooling that addresses this topic, see also Grumet 1988.

7. Social histories of curriculum deliberation are few and far between. For one notable recent example, see Ben-Peretz (1991).

8. The action research movement has a pertinent slogan, "What is happening here?" (Wood 1988, 135–150.) A comparable approach to curriculum is Gerald Graff's slogan, "Teach the conflicts." (Graff 1990, 51–68.)

REFERENCES

Alexander, Michael Van Cleave. 1990. *The Growth of English Education 1348–1648: A Social and Cultural History.* University Park, Pa., and London: The Pennsylvania State University Press.

Ben-Peretz, Miriam. 1991. *The Teacher-Curriculum Encounter.* Albany: State University of New York Press.

Berlin, Isaiah. 1991. *The Crooked Timber of Humanity: Chapters in the History of Ideas,* ed. H. Hardy. New York: Knopf.

Bikerts, Sven. 1991. "Into the Electronic Millenium." *Boston Review.* Sept.

Burke, Kenneth. 1969 (1945). *A Grammar of Motives.* Berkeley: University of California Press.

Cherryholmes, Cleo. 1988. *Power and Criticism.* New Haven, Conn.: Yale University Press.

Crosby, Donald. 1988. *The Specter of the Absurd: Sources and Criticisms of Modern Nihilism.* Albany: State University of New York Press.

Cuban, Larry. 1989. "The persistence of reform in American Schools." In *American Teachers.* ed. D. Warren. New York: Macmillan.

Curti, Merle. 1980. *Human Nature in American Thought: A History.* Madison: University of Wisconsin Press.

Dewey, John. 1980 (1917). "The need for social psychology." In *John Dewey: The Middle Works,* ed. J. Boydston. Vol. 10. Carbondale and Edwardsville: Southern Illinois University Press.

———. 1984 (1930). "Individualism, old and new." In *John Dewey: The Later Works,* ed. J. Boydston. Vol. 5. Carbondale and Edwardsville: Southern Illinois University Press.

Dudley, Donald. 1967 (1937). *A History of Cynicism.* Hildesheim, Germany: George Olms.

Dylan, Bob. 1968. "All Along the Watchtower." New York: Dwarf Music. (Permission applied for.)

Ewen, Stuart. 1989. *All Consuming Images: The Politics of Style.* New York: Basic Books.

Fish, Stanley, 1990. "Rhetoric." In *Critical Terms for Literary Study,* eds. F. Lentricchia and T. McLaughlin. Chicago: University of Chicago Press.

Foucault, Michel. 1970. *The Order of Things.* New York: Vintage.

Friedman, John. 1992. "Big business goes to school: The Whittle-Alexander nexus." *The Nation.* Feb. 17.

Gallagher, John. 1989. "Wooing a captive audience." *Time.* Feb. 20.

Goodson, Ivor. 1988. *The Making of Curriculum.* London and Philadelphia: Falmer Press.

Graff, Gerald. 1990. "Teach the conflicts." *South Atlantic Quarterly.* 89:1.

Green, Andy. 1990. *Education and State Formation: The Rise of Education Systems in England, France, and the U.S.A.* New York: St. Martin's Press.

Grumet, Madeleine. 1988. *Bitter Milk: Women and Teaching.* Amherst: University of Massachusetts Press.

Hammer, Joshua. 1990. "A golden boy's toughest sell." *Newsweek.* Feb. 19.

Hartey, Sheila. 1979. *Hucksters in the Classroom: A Review of Industry Propaganda in Schools.* Washington: Center for the Study of Responsive Law.

Hobbes, Thomas. 1985 (1651). *Leviathan,* ed. C. B. MacPherson. London and New York: Penguin.

Hoffman, Lawrence. 1991. "The meanings of Channel One: Curriculum, instruction and ethics; history, control and rhetoric." Paper presented at the annual meeting of the American Educational Research Association. Chicago.

James, William. 1987 (1907). "Pragmatism." In *William James: Writings 1902–1910*, ed. B. Kuklick. New York: Library of America.

Keizer, Garrett. 1988. *No Place But Here: A Teacher's Vocation in a Rural Community.* New York: Viking Penguin.

Kleinfield, N. R. 1991. "What is Chris Whittle teaching our children?" *New York Times Magazine.* May 19.

Kliebard, Herbert. 1986. *The Struggle for the American Curriculum, 1893–1958.* New York: Routledge.

MacIntyre, Alasdair. 1990. *Three Rival Versions of Moral Enquiry.* Notre Dame, Ind.: Notre Dame University Press.

Mann, Horace. 1839. *Second Annual Report to the Massachusetts Board of Education.* Boston: Dutton and Wentworth.

———. 1848. *Twelfth Annual Report to the Massachusetts Board of Education.* Boston: Dutton and Wentworth.

Mattingly, Paul. 1975. *The Classless Profession: American Schoolmen in the Nineteenth Century.* New York: New York University Press.

Michaels, Walter Benn. 1986. *The Gold Standard and the Logic of Naturalism.* Berkeley: University of California Press.

Nietzsche, Frederich. 1954 (1873). In *The Portable Nietzsche,* ed. trs. W. Kaufmann. New York: Viking.

Olson, John. 1989/1990. "Do not use as directed: Corporate materials in the schools." *Educational Leadership.* 47:4. Dec./Jan.

Oxford English Dictionary. 1st ed. 1971. *Compact Edition.* Oxford, England: Oxford University Press.

Popkewitz, Thomas. 1991. *A Political Sociology of Educational Reform.* New York: Teachers College Press.

Popper, Karl. 1985 (1958). "The Beginnings of Rationalism." In *Proper Selections,* ed. D. Miller. Princeton, N.J.: Princeton University Press.

Rist, Marilee. 1991. "Here comes McSchool." *American School Board Journal.* Sept.

Rorty, Richard. 1989. *Contingency, Irony and Solidarity.* New York: Cambridge University Press.

Rosen, Jay. 1992. "The return of the expressed." *Boston Review.* 17:1. Feb.

Ross, Andrew. 1991. *Strange Weather: Culture, Science and Technology in an Age of Limits.* New York: Verso.

Rowell, C. Glennon. 1990. Ed. "Why condemn advertising in news videos for school?" *Educational Digest.* 56:Nov.

Rudinow, Joel. 1989/1990. "Channel One Whittles away at education." *Educational Leadership.* 47:4. Dec./Jan.

Rukeyser, William. 1989/1990. "No hidden agenda." *Educational Leadership.* 47:4. Dec./Jan.

Sayre, Ferrand. 1938. *Diogenes of Sinope: A Study of Greek Cynicism.* Baltimore: J. H. Furst.

Schwartz, Tony. 1973. *The Responsive Chord.* Garden City, N.Y.: Anchor Press.

Shakespeare, William. *King Lear.* I:4. Act I Scene IV Lines 195–196 1961 Ed. H. Craig Chicago: Scott Foreman p. 989.

Shweder, Richard, N.d. "Confusionism and the varieties of the moral." *Human Development.* (Forthcoming)

Sloterdijk. 1987 (1981). *Critique of Cynical Reason,* trs. M. Eldred. Minneapolis: University of Minnesota Press.

Taylor, Charles. 1989. *Sources of the Self: The Making of Modern Identity.* Cambridge, Mass.: Harvard University Press.

Tichi, Cecilia. 1991. *Electronic Hearth: Creating an American Television Culture.* New York: Oxford University Press.

Tyack, David, and Elizabeth Hansot. 1982. *Managers of Virtue: Public School Leadership in America, 1820–1980.* New York: Basic Books.

Vickers, Brian. 1988. *In Defence of Rhetoric.* London and New York: Oxford University Press.

Walsh, M. 1990. "Whittle to unveil new programming for teachers." *Education Week.* Oct. 30.

Wood, Patricia. 1988. "Action research: A field perspective." *Journal of Education for Teaching.* 14:2.

Contributors

Michael W. Apple is John Bascom Professor of Curriculum and Instruction and Educational Policy Studies at the University of Wisconsin, Madison. His most recent book is *Official Knowledge: Democratic Education in a Conservative Age*. He started his professional career as an elementary public school teacher.

Ann Marie Barry is Associate Professor of Communication at Boston College. Author of *The Advertising Portfolio*, a selection of the Graphic Artists' Book Club (NTC, 1990) *El Portafolio Creativo del Publicista* (McGraw Hill, 1992), and a variety of articles on visual communication. She has also been a Visiting Professor at DDB Needham Worldwide Advertising in New York, a communication consultant to the Advertising Educational Foundation, and a recipient of the NBC/Carnegie National Teacher's Award for Excellence in Teaching.

John C. Belland is a professor in the Department of Educational Policy and Leadership at the Ohio State University. He recently has been developing materials to teach scientists to use Supercomputing better, editing the *Journal of Visual Literacy*, and teaching graduate students in the Instructional Design and Technology Program. His most recent publication is Paradigms Regained: The Uses of Illuminative, Semiotic and Post Modern Criticism as Modes of Inquiry in Educational Technology which he edited with Denis Hlynka. Professor Belland started his professional career as a high school mathematics teacher.

Ann De Vaney is professor and head of the program, Educational Communications and Technology, at the University of Wisconsin-Madison. She explores issues of representation in educational and commercial media. She began her career as a high school English teacher.

Barbara Erdman is an Assistant Professor in the Department of Educational Policy and Leadership at the Ohio State University, teaching courses in educational telecommunications and school library and media. Her research interests include the impact of mediated lessons on teaching and learning. She started her career as an art teacher in the public schools.

Peter Hayes is an assistant principal at Arcadia High School in Phoenix, Arizona. Graduate Studies include a doctorate in Educational Administration from Arizona State University and a masters from Boston University. Previously, he taught high school mathematics for sixteen years.

Nancy Nelson Knupfer is Director of Multimedia Design and Production for the Kansas Rural Child Welfare Project and Assistant Professor of Educational Communications and Technology in the Department of Foundations and Adult Education at Kansas State University. Dr. Knupfer has been involved with teaching all levels of students, from early childhood through adults, for over twenty years. In addition, her own four children keep her actively involved with the public schools. Dr. Knupfer's research interests have focussed on the design, utilization, and effectiveness of interactive multimedia and distance education. Dr. Knupfer has taught 7 years at the elementary level, 2 years at the high school level and was a supervisor of student teachers at the UW-Madison for 3 years.

Robert Muffoletto is an Associate Professor of Education at the University of Northern Iowa. His research interest centers on the sociology of knowledge, the social implications of technology in education, and questions over power, education, and benefit. His most recent work is Social Foundations of Computers in Education, a book edited with Nancy Knupfer. He has taught 5 years at the K-12 level, 10 years in higher education in Ed Tech, and was Coordinator of Graduate Programs in Ed Tech for 6 years at Cal Poly, Pomona.

Dr. Rhonda Robinson is professor of Instructional Technology, Department of Leadership and Educational Policy Studies, Northern Illinois University, DeKalb, Illinois, where she coordinates the master's degree program and teaches courses in visual literacy and qualitative research. She has worked with several educational settings on distance learning issues and researches affective areas of technology utilization. She started her career as a high school English teacher.

Henry St. Maurice is Director of Field Experience and an assistant professor of education at the University of Wisconsin-Stevens Point, Stevens Point, WI. He has taught in a variety of settings, including elementary, secondary, and rehabilitation programs. His research interests center on rhetorical, philosophical, and historical studies of teacher education.

Index

A

"A Nation at Risk," 43, 172, 176, 184
"A&E" Classroom, 128
Action for Children's Television,
    107, 190
Adolescent, 90, 99, 143, 162
Advancement of Learning Through
    Broadcasting, 128
Advertisement, 102–32, 130, 138, 162
    coercive, 138
    Channel One, 2, 13, 15, 42–46,
        49, 58, 73, 76, 120, 191, 199,
    in school, 193–95
    modern and postmodern, 139–40
Advertising Research Foundation,
    124
Aesthetics, 153, 154, 165
African-American, 150
Alexander, Lamar, 6, 7
"America 2000," 112, 113
American Association of School
    Administrators, 107, 127, 128
American Federation of Teachers,
    107, 124
Analysis:
    content, 140, 144, 145
    policy, 190
    textual, 138, 147
Anchors, 158, 161, 165
Annenberg, 12
Apple, Michael, 191, 202, 204
Art and Entertainment Channel, 127
Associated Newspapers of Britain, 7

Attention, 55, 57, 73, 84, 137,
    158, 163,
Audience, 197, 198, 201
    captive, 2, 7, 117, 124, 125, 129,

B

Bacchanalian, 137, 146, 149
Bennett, William J., 3
Bierdeman, Daniel, 3
Billerica High School, 122, 123
Bodies, objectified and commodi-
    fied, 140, 146, 148, 149
Bordwell, David, 154
Brookings Institute, 3
Browning, Dominique, 3
"Business Desk," 159
Business-education partnerships,
    43, 112, 113, 118, 120, 171, 189,
    193, 198, 201, 202

C

"C-Span in the Classroom," 128
Calabrese, Robert, 106, 114
California, 2, 103, 104, 106, 138, 189,
    194–97, 201–3
Campus Voice, 116
Capital:
    flight, 172
    human, 175
Case study, 21, 22

Caucausian, 150
Center for the Study of Commercialism, 119, 123,
Central Park East Schools, 185
Chicagoland, 21
Chicago Schoolwatch, 185
Choice of school, 3, 113, 174
Chubb, John E., 3, 6
Cincinatti, 104, 119
Classrooms, 4, 54, 64, 102, 105, 109–13, 138, 189, 191, 194, 197, 204
CNN Newsroom, 14, 44, 104, 112, 127, 154, 157, 162, 164, 165
Coalitions, 185
Codes, visual and verbal, 12, 143
Commercial messages, 2, 27, 29, 87, 88, 97, 98, 122, 123, 124, 132, 149, 161–64, 194–96, 202, 204
Competition, 103, 113, 117, 169, 180, 189
Computers, 5, 6, 113
"Connections," 116
Consumer, 118, 119, 124
Consumerism, 62, 73, 76, 141, 149
Consumption, 17, 191, 203
Contracts with Whittle Communications, 8, 61, 65, 103, 111–13, 170, 193–95
Control of curriculum, 16, 104, 138, 164, 185, 189–91, 194–200, 203, 205
    lack of, 35, 37
Controversy, 2, 44, 87, 102, 114, 205
Critical thinking, 175
Cultural literacy, 71
Culture:
    common, 167
    mass, 202
    popular, 99, 141, 148, 149, 153
    teen, 140
Current events, 2, 42–49, 58, 59, 68, 106, 159, 160, 162, 189, 191
Curriculum control. *See* control of curriculum
Curriculum, 16, 24, 56, 59, 62, 115
    industrialized, 176

planning, 137
rationalized, 176
theory, 190
Cuts:
    jump, 147
    match, 147
Cynic, 209–11, 215, 217, 219, 220, 222, 227

D

Decisions to adopt Channel One, 62, 84, 107,190, 198, 204
Democracy, 88, 98, 100, 167, 181, 185
Denver, 113
Descartes, Rene, 211
Deskilling, 172, 176
Detroit, 104, 106, 114
Dewey, John, 16, 218–22, 224
Diogenes of Sinope, 209, 211, 218
Discourse, 9, 15, 16, 141
    popular culture, 98
    public, 87, 89, 189, 194, 200, 201
Discussion of Channel One program, 55, 68, 73
Disney's Discovery Channel, 44
DJ's, 13
Dylan, Bob, 211–13, 215

E

"Earth Clock," 163
Economic utility, 175
Economics, 168, 181, 196, 200–203, 205
Edison Project, 3, 5 , 121, 131
Editing, 90, 94
Education as industry, 88
Educational reform. *See* Reform
Educational media, 117, 153–55, 165
Educational value. *See* value
Effectiveness, 16, 42–44, 46, 85, 124, 203
Efficiency, 200, 203

Egalitarianism, 168
Eisenberg, Lee, 3
Elitism, 7
Enlightenment, 211
Equipment for Channel One, 2, 22,
    58, 61, 104, 109–13, 120, 138,
    170, 193, 201, 202
Equity, 189, 202
Ethics, 189, 200, 201, 205

F

Feature Story, 92–94, 96, 97, 109
Federal Communications Commis-
    sion, 107
Female, 140, 157, 158
Field trip "Around the World," 92
Finances, 25, 41, 59
Finn, Chester E., 3, 6
Fiscal concerns, 116, 169, 194
Florida, 169
"Focus," 161
Fogel, Jeremy, 138, 139
Ford Foundation, 4
Formalist methodology, 14, 122,
    154–56, 161, 164, 165
Foucault, Michel, 214
Free market, 175
Friedman, Milton and Rose, 16
"Future Desk," 159, 160

G

Gallup Poll, 107, 109, 111
Gender, 97, 151
Genre, 14, 155–58, 164
Geography, 71
    of the televised space, 143
Georgia, 192

H

Hardware for Channel One. *See*
    equipment for Channel One

Harty, Sheila, 114
Headline, 89, 90
Hechinger, Nancy, 3
High school:
    senior, 48, 49, 51, 62, 63, 71, 81,
        85, 189
    junior, 22, 48, 49, 52, 56–58, 62,
        63, 71, 81, 85
Hispanic, 150
Hobbes, Thomas, 211, 213, 214
Home Library, 130
Honig, Bill, 138, 194–96

I

Idaho, 192
Ideology, 178, 181, 183, 185
Image, fragmented, 129, 143, 144
Impact, 108
Implementation, 55, 58, 61, 67, 68,
    84, 85
Inequity, 171, 173, 185
Influence, 197
Information, 108
    access, 202
    capitalism, 91
Installation and problems, 46, 48,
    61, 65, 66, 84, 202
Instructional materials. *See*
    materials
Interviews, 62, 63, 85, 109

J

Journalism, 15, 156
Julian the Apostate, 210

K

Kansas City, 104, 119
Kervin, Denise, 142, 144, 150
Kliebard, Herbert, 189, 191, 204, 219

Knowledge:
   legitimate, 190, 197, 200, 201
   student, 42–46, 58, 84, 167,
      177, 219
Knoxville, 6, 102

L

Lasch, Christopher, 141, 142
Lead-in, 89, 90
Learning, 9, 42, 194, 200
Lesson plan, 121
Lessons, 124, 164, 165, 176
Lifetime Learning Systems, 115
Literacy, 38, 108, 114, 167

M

MacIntyre, Alasdair, 215, 221
Magazine on the wall, 129
Males on Channel One, 93, 96, 140,
      149, 158, 159
Mann, Horace, 216, 217, 219, 220
Maps, 94, 95, 160, 161
Marketplace, 9, 13, 15, 202, 227
Market:
   free, 175
   student, 163
Marketing, 117, 118, 120, 130, 132
Massachusetts, 104, 106, 109, 114,
      116, 121, 170
Materials:
   commercial, 176
   educational, 115
   instructional, 198, 199, 203, 204
Material base, 138, 148
McLuhan, Marshall, 143
Media or Learning Center Director,
      21, 22, 24, 25, 35, 37, 38, 40, 57,
      59, 67, 68
Messages. *See* commercial messages
Michigan, 104, 192
Mind set, 2

Modern, 138
Moe, Terry, 6
MTV, 12, 13 143, 144, 148
Mueller, B., 145, 150

N

Narrative:
   technique, 149
   fractured, 143, 144
National Association for Secondary
      School Principals, 107, 127
National Defense Education Act, 4
National Education Association,
      128
National Parents and Teachers As-
      sociation, 107, 128
National School Board Association,
      127, 128
National Teacher's Association
      (NEA), 44
National launch, Channel One,
      102, 122
"New American Schools," 6, 7
New York, 2, 103, 106, 138, 192, 193,
      201–3
News, 46, 52, 61, 106, 108,
      analysis, 87, 89–91, 94–6
   on Channel One, 17, 121, 137,
      154, 156, 160, 163, 164, 178, 179
Nietzsche, Frederich, 214, 215, 220
North Carolina, 103, 123, 170, 189,
      194, 197–203

O

Observations, 22, 54, 62, 68
Ohio, 124
"On This Date," 159
Opinions. *See* students; parents;
      teachers
Opportunism, 62, 84
"Our World," 159

P

Parental choice. *See* choice of school
Parents' opinions, 17, 62, 64, 66, 71,
    85, 165, 196, 205
Parrhesia, 209, 212, 215
Partnerships. *See* business-
    education partnerships
Perception theory, 144
Persian Gulf War, (Desert Storm), 1,
    2, 28, 33, 54, 90
Peters, Sylvia, 3
Phillips Electronics N. V., 7
Pilot program, Channel One, 102
"Planet Patrol," 163
Plato, 208, 219
Point -of -view, 93
Pop quiz, 49, 50, 52, 58
"Pop Ouiz," 30, 34, 97, 162, 163
Popkewitz, Thomas, 190, 191, 200,
    204, 219
Popular culture. *See* culture
Post Structural, 14, 144
Postmodern, 138, 143, 145
Power, 190, 191, 194, 197, 200,
    204, 205
Principals, 37, 41, 48, 57, 65,
    113, 195
Private sector, 5, 8, 14, 91, 202
Products, consumer, 61, 98, 99, 141
Producers, 123
Production techniques, 97, 98, 116,
    143, 147, 153, 154, 157
Programming, 4, 87, 89, 158, 160,
    190, 202
Progressive education, 200
Public Broadcasting System, 12
Public service announcement
    (PSA), 123

Q

"Quote of the Day," 159

R

Rabelais, 138, 149
Race, 151
Reader theories, 138
Readers, 14, 15, 142, 149
"Ready Set Learn," 128
Reform, 4, 16, 113, 168, 184
Remember, 53
Representation, 149
Retention, 42, 49
Rethinking Schools, Milwaukee, 185
Rhetoric, 9, 15, 16, 140, 141, 148, 183
Rhode Island, 2, 103
Right, the new, 174
Rindge School of Technical Arts,
    Boston, 185
Rukeyser, William, 120

S

Salomon, Gavriel, 11, 13, 95, 139
Satellite dish, 66
Schmidt, Benno, 3, 125
School board, 103, 113, 191, 194,
    197–99, 204, 205
School district, 62, 138
Schools for profit, 113, 119, 131, 184
Schwartz, Tony, 224
"Science Desk, " 160
Sesame Street , 11, 12
Shots, 147
Signs and symbols, 140, 142. *See also*
    symbolic function
Social:
    alliance, 174
    critique, 11
Sound devices, 157
South Carolina, 192
Southern Coalition for Educational
    Equity, 185
*Special Reports,*130
Square One TV, 143

Students, 62, 64, 163, 164, 179
  opinions, 29, 31, 85
Style, 154
Superintendents, 62, 63, 65
Survey, 63, 64, 80, 85, 108–10
Symbolic function, 16, 189, 191, 200,
  203–5

T

Targeting, 126, 130, 145
Taxes, 113, 167–70, 174
Teachers, 14, 17, 99, 120, 160, 162,
  164, 165, 176, 179, 180
  opinions, 25, 26, 32, 48, 49, 55,
  56, 62–67, 71, 76
Technology, 42
  as feature story, 92–94
Teens, 30, 110, 140, 145, 146
Television Bureau of Advertising,
  128
Television:
  commercial, 5, 6, 15, 18, 128, 143
  grammar, 12, 144
  instructional and educational, 8,
  9, 12, 44, 45, 109
  public, 103
  broadcast and cablecast, 8, 9, 76,
  144, 145
Television monitors, 66, 103, 106,
  110, 113, 138
Tennessee, 192
Texas, 103, 192
Test scores, 51, 52
Texts, 9, 139, 140, 142
  electronic, 14, 147, 148
Thompson, Kristin, 154
Time-Warner, 7
TLC Elementary School, 128
"Top Story," 159, 160
Turner, Ted, 44, 156

U

U.S. News and World Report, 31,
  47, 48
Understanding, 42
"Up Front," 161

V

Value, educational, 44, 65
Values, 10, 92, 132, 167, 175, 179
Visual language, 9, 12
Viewer, 138, 140, 142, 149 154, 155,
  163
Vocabulary, 90, 160
Voucher plan, 7, 174, 181

W

Washington, 103, 113, 114, 169
  D.C., 102, 119
Whittle Communications, 2, 8,
  13, 28, 48, 66, 71, 87, 102–6,
  108, 110–13, 115, 116, 138,
  139, 154, 160, 168, 170, 180,
  183, 189, 190, 192, 208, 222,
  223, 229
Whittle, Chris, 2, 5, 7, 44, 103, 104,
  107, 113, 114, 115, 118, 119
Wiring, 2, 8, 13, 65, 110, 111
Wisconsin, 192
Wittgenstein, Ludwig, 171
Wulfmeyer, K. 145, 150

Z

Zooming, 95, 162